CLARENDON LIBRARY OF LOGIC AND PHILOSOPHY
General Editor: L. Jonathan Cohen

EQUALITY, LIBERTY,
AND PERFECTIONISM

EQUALITY, LIBERTY, AND PERFECTIONISM

VINIT HAKSAR

OXFORD UNIVERSITY PRESS
1979

Oxford University Press, Walton Street, Oxford OX2 6DP

OXFORD LONDON GLASGOW
NEW YORK TORONTO MELBOURNE WELLINGTON
KUALA LUMPUR SINGAPORE JAKARTA HONG KONG TOKYO
DELHI BOMBAY CALCUTTA MADRAS KARACHI
NAIROBI DAR ES SALAAM CAPE TOWN

© *Vinit Haksar 1979*

Published in the United States
by Oxford University Press
New York

British Library Cataloguing in Publication Data

Haksar, Vinit
  Equality, liberty and perfectionism.
  – (Clarendon library of logic and philosophy).
  1. Civil rights
  I. Title
  323.4'01   JC571   79-40339
  ISBN 0-19-824418-5

*Composed by
Graphic Services, Oxford
Printed and bound by
Billing & Sons Ltd.
Guildford, Worcester,
London, Oxford*

Acknowledgements

I am very grateful to Brian Barry, Jonathan Cohen, and Herbert Hart for valuable suggestions and encouragement.

I am indebted to those whose views are referred to in this book. In particular, I owe much to the stimulus provided by John Rawls's *Theory of Justice*. An earlier version of chapter 10 originally appeared in the *British Journal of Political Science* (1973), pp. 487-509 as a review article of Rawls's book. It was there that I first stressed, as against Rawls, the need for perfectionism as a political principle.

I would like to thank Joan Stevens for typing some of the chapters of this book.

Contents

I

Introduction

1. Introduction to perfectionism

The book is about equality, its foundations, and its implications. It is also about liberty. It examines some of the presuppositions and problems of the liberal–egalitarian philosophy; it is not primarily concerned with non-egalitarian versions of liberalism. One of the main themes of the book is the importance of perfectionist considerations; perfectionism is needed both to provide the foundations of egalitarianism and to work out its liberal implications. Since this is so and since perfectionism, unlike equality and liberty, is not a term that most people are familiar with, it is worth saying something at the outset about perfectionism.

Perfectionism has sometimes been used to refer to beliefs such as the following:

(1) Some human beings are intrinsically inferior to other human beings.

(2) Some forms of human life are intrinsically (or inherently) inferior to other forms of human life.

I shall extend the term perfectionism to include the following views as well:

(3) Human beings, with the possible exception of some such as congenital idiots, have more intrinsic worth than animals.

(4) Human ways of life, at any rate those that are not anti-social such as Nazism, have more intrinsic worth than animal forms of life.

Rawls thinks that perfectionism can and should be bypassed as a political principle. He thinks this partly because judgements of intrinsic value are controversial and controversial judgements should, he thinks, be bypassed. He seems committed to bypassing all the above four views, for all these views involve judgements of intrinsic value.

It is argued in this book that egalitarianism (that is to say the doctrine that all human beings have the right to equal respect and consideration) cannot satisfactorily bypass perfectionism. I do not however mean that each of the four views mentioned above must be presupposed by egalitarianism, but rather that some of the above views must be presupposed by egalitarianism. In particular 2 and 3 and probably 4 are presupposed. It is important to distinguish 2 from 1. Egalitarianism cannot accept the view found in some thinkers such as Nietzsche and Rashdall that some human beings are intrinsically superior to other human beings and that political principles should take such differences of intrinsic worth into account: '. . . the lower well being—it may be the very existence—of countless Chinamen or negroes must be sacrificed that a higher life may be possible for a much smaller number of white men.'[1] But one can quite consistently believe that some forms of human life are intrinsically superior to other forms of human life without believing that some human beings are intrinsically superior to other human beings: 2 does not entail 1. In chapter 14 the significance of the distinction between 1 and 2 is discussed.

Rawls, though he is an anti-perfectionist, admits that he appeals to a certain ideal of a person.[2] He would say that his own ideal of the person is neutral and can be justified from a rational impartial standpoint. So when he is against perfectionism as a political principle, he is presumably against admitting those ideals into political theory, or into a theory of justice, that cannot be justified from a neutral, impartial standpoint. He, in effect, uses perfectionism as a pejorative term to refer to the ideals of his opponents, such as Nietzsche and Rashdall. But these opponents would deny that their ideals and views about some human beings being intrinsically superior to others are less rational than the Kantian ideal of the person that Rawls appeals to.

Rawls is against the admission of considerations of intrinsic value into a theory of justice. This, as we have seen, is closely linked with his rejection of perfectionism. He contrasts his views with those of people like Moore who appeal to judge-

[1] Hastings Rashdall, *The Theory of Good and Evil* (London, 1907), i. 238–9.
[2] J. Rawls, *A Theory of Justice* (Oxford, 1971).

ments of intrinsic value and who implicitly appeal to a perfectionist standard. He thinks that his own views are more like those of Mill, for Mill, too, according to Rawls, uses the choice criterion of value.

Rawls resorts to the choice criterion of value to distinguish rational values and ideals from non-rational ones. The values and ideals that he resorts to are, he would claim, the ones that people would choose, under conditions of liberty. And so he would claim that his values and ideals are rational in a way in which those of his opponents are not. In chapter 11 I will point out the limitations of the choice criterion of value. At best, this criterion works if we presuppose a background of values and ideals that cannot itself be justified by appealing to the choice criterion of value. If this is so, it would follow that the choice criterion of value does not enable Rawls to bypass perfectionist considerations.

When we say that some forms of human life, such as the life of contemplation, are inherently superior to other forms of human life, such as the life devoted to bestiality and the eating of one's excrement, we sometimes mean that given human nature, the former are more suited to human beings than the latter are. This is consistent with the admission that if human nature had been different then perhaps different forms of life, such as bestiality, would have been suited to human beings. Perhaps what we take to be human nature does vary to some extent from society to society. And to that extent the answer to the question which forms of life are superior (in the sense of being suited to human beings) may vary from society to society. And if in some future Brave New World we could alter sufficiently the genetic endowment of human babies, we might be able to alter radically the basic nature of the New Men, that is to say of the men who would be produced under the Brave New World; and forms of life that we now rightly regard as inferior, such as slavery and bestiality, may well be suited to the New Man.

But sometimes when we say that a form of life x is inherently or intrinsically superior to another form of life y, we mean something stronger; we imply that whatever human nature turns out to be, whatever form of life satisfies people more, it would still be the case that x would be intrinsically

superior to y. For instance, we may believe that the autonomous form of life is intrinsically superior to slavery, even if
the New Man were to replace us and even if slavery is more
suited to the New Man than the autonomous form of life is.
Let us call this kind of perfectionist view the strong sense of
perfectionism, and let us call the perfectionism described in
the last paragraph the weak sense of perfectionism.

If in the future we ban the production (for instance by
genetic engineering) of the New Man, we may have to justify
our ban by appealing to perfectionism in the second sense;
we may have to maintain that the New Man (and his way of
life) is intrinsically inferior to the present Man (and his way
of life). Again, the view that human beings are more wonderful
or sacred creatures than animals involves perfectionist judgements in the strong sense. If my arguments in the first two
parts of the book are correct, then the view that egalitarianism
does not extend to animals would involve an appeal to perfectionism in the strong sense.

Some philosophers distinguish instrumental rationality
from expressive rationality. Instrumental rationality is concerned with what means it is rational to use for the attainment
of our ends. Assuming that you want to become a millioniare
your choice of certain means, such as joining the academic
profession, becomes less rational than your choice of some
other means, such as joining big buisiness. But instrumental
rationality cannot evaluate ultimate ends. In order to do that,
so the argument runs, we have to appeal to the notion of
expressive rationality. Some ends such as the life of contemplation are more expressive of human nature, of what men
really are, than certain other ends, such as a life devoted to
bestiality and the eating of one's excrement.

In my view the notion of expressive rationality can at most
be helpful in enabling us to make perfectionist judgements in
the weak sense, but it cannot, any more than instrumental
rationality, enable us to make perfectionist judgements in the
strong sense. It cannot, for instance, enable us to discover
whether or not the doctrine of equal right to respect extends
to animals. In the case of perfectionism in the strong sense
we shall have to make judgements of intrinsic value in some
strong sense that cannot be bypassed by appeals to what

human beings would choose for themselves under conditions of liberty, or by other such appeals to the Nature of Man. Perhaps this point could be illustrated by considering some of Moore's and Ross's ideas with those of Rawls and Mill (as interpreted by Rawls).

Moore and Ross used to make judgements of intrinsic value by conducting an imaginary experment. Imagine two worlds where everything else is the same, except that one has more x in than the other has. If we judge the world with more x to be better, then in our opinion x has intrinsic value. However not everyone who believes in judgements of intrinsic value is committed to using Moore's and Ross's method. They may exercise their judgement without the aid of such an imaginary experiment. But all people who go in for such perfectionist judgements in the strong sense assume that there are objective values, that some things have objectively greater value than other things, and that the job of human beings is to discover these values, not to invent them or bring them into existence by an act of will or of choice.

Now Rawls and Mill (as interpreted by Rawls) take a radically different line. Rawls commends the choice criterion of value, which he claims bypasses talk of intrinsic value. According to this criterion, in the way it is used by Rawls, we do not need to assume that there is a world of values existing independently of us. The Good is what human beings would choose for themselves, under conditions of liberty. Do Mill (as interpreted by Rawls) and Rawls succeed in bypassing talk of intrinsic value? I think not. If the criticisms in chapter 11 of the choice criterion of value are valid, then this criterion cannot be used to bypass perfectionism in the strong sense. For the view that animals have less intrinsic worth than human beings cannot be bypassed by appealing to the choice criterion of value. Even if it is true that, under conditions of liberty, human beings would choose for themselves autonomous forms of life in preference to non-autonomous forms of life, the most that would follow is that autonomous forms of life are more suited to human beings. It would not show why we should not extend egalitarianism to include animals; the fact that certain forms of life are not suited to human beings provides no reason at all for the view that non-human beings

who practise such forms of life are worthy of less consideration than human beings.

As long as animals including the lower animals, and insects
are excluded from the egalitarian club, egalitarianism does
involve an appeal to perfectionist considerations (for instance,
that ants and bees are less wonderful creatures than human
beings and so they can be excluded). A heroic solution would
be to extend egalitarianism to include all sentient creatures,
including insects; a consequence of this would be that we
must not only be vegans, but also live a Jain-like life that involves the minimization of the destruction of all sentient life,
including the tiniest insects. If egalitarians do not want to
extend their doctrine in this way, then they must be willing
to appeal to perfectionist considerations.

Perfectionist judgements in the strong sense are of course
controversial judgements. There is no mechanical method of
establishing the truth of such judgements. Perfectionist judgements in the weak sense are also controversial. Even if some
forms of life are more expressive of human nature and more
suited to human beings, there is no mechanical and non-controversial method of recognizing such forms of life. Yet an adequate liberal–egalitarian political theory has to resort to such
perfectionist judgements. Rawls, like quite a few liberals,
attempts to build a liberal theory without appealing to controversial knowledge; he wants to build his theory only by appealing to common sense and to evidence and ways of reasoning
acceptable to all. So he rules out all appeals to perfectionist
and metaphysical judgements, for such appeals are controversial. Rawls does, however, appeal to a theory of human nature
in order to bolster his theory of justice. He appeals to the
Aristotelian principle according to which human beings prefer
more complex and intricate ways of life to simple forms of
life. And he appeals to the Kantian idea that an autonomous
life expresses human nature in a way in which a heteronomous
or non-autonomous life does not. Presumably Rawls thinks
that such views of human nature (or the method of establishing them) are non-controversial, for otherwise he would not
use them to support his theory. I do not necessarily disagree
with his substantial views about human nature, but his views
and the method he uses to establish them (such as by appeal-

ling to the choice criterion of value) are controversial and not value-free.

Liberal political theory cannot and should not bypass controversial problems, such as whether human beings flourish more under liberal institutions or under non-liberal institutions. Even though there is no mechanical method of making such judgements (for instance, by appealing to the choice criterion of value) it does not follow that we should not make such judgements.

Ronald Dworkin has asked us to beware of basing liberal political principles on controversial views of human nature.[3] For he fears that such controversial views may turn out to be false and we might find that our liberalism had been built on shaky foundations. Dworkin refers to the views of Ronald Laing, according to whom human nature is such that human beings are more satisfied and fulfilled without civil liberties. Dworkin says that we cannot be sure that such psychological views will not turn out to be right. So he thinks the best thing is to build the case for liberalism without appealing to theories of human nature. What are we to make of Dworkin's argument? It seems to me that if psychological views, such as those Dworkin attributes to Laing turn out to be true, if empirical evidence shows that liberalism is not well suited to human beings and that some other form of life is better suited, then we should be willing to admit that the case for liberalism is weakened, other things being equal. No doubt we may still believe in liberalism for other related reasons; for instance, we may think that although an alternative non-liberal society, such as Plato's Republic, is more suited to human beings, we may be sceptical about the possibility of realizing that ideal in practice, we may worry that an attempt to realize that ideal in practice may lead to tyranny. Or we may use the strong form of perfectionism to bolster our liberal beliefs, we may maintain that other things being equal some forms of life are intrinsically better than others, whatever human nature turns out to be. But we need not deny that whether or not human needs are better satisfied in a liberal set-up is one important consideration to be taken into account in evaluating the liberal set-up *vis-à-vis* the alternative set-ups.

[3] R. Dworkin, *Taking Rights Seriously* (London, 1977), p. 272.

Dworkin distinguishes right-based approaches, which stress that the doctrine of human rights sets constraints which we must not violate while pursuing our goals, from goal-based approaches, such as utilitarianism which justify actions, institutions, and policies by their consequences. Like Dworkin, Nozick, and Rawls, I am in the right-based tradition. But unlike them I adopt a perfectionist approach. A perfectionist approach can either be consequentialist or non-consequentialist (see chapter 4, section 3). In this book a non-consequentialist perfectionist approach is adopted; an attempt is made to combine a right-based egalitarian approach with a perfectionist approach. Often egalitarians and liberals tend to be suspicious of perfectionism as a political principle; many egalitarians fear (wrongly) that perfectionism necessarily commits one to the anti-egalitarian belief that some human beings are superior to others, while many liberals think (wrongly) that liberalism is incompatible with perfectionism as a political principle, for they want the liberal state to be neutral between different forms of life (except for obviously anti-social ones such as Nazism). They admit of course that at the private and non-political level individuals should be allowed to pursue their own perfectionist ideals; for instance, some people may choose to pursue a religious ideal, while others may choose to pursue more materialistic goals. Indeed, it is considered one of the charms of a liberal society that, unlike totalitarian societies, it allows and encourages people to choose and pursue their own ideals or life styles. But they (wrongly) insist that at the political level perfectionism must be bypassed, the state must not come out in favour of any of the several perfectionist ideals. It is argued in this book that at several points a liberal–egalitarian theory needs to appeal to perfectionism as a political principle; if this is so it is one of the tasks of a liberal–egalitarian philosophy to reconcile itself with the admission of perfectionism as a political principle.

2. Outlines of the book

Of the famous trilogy, Liberty, Equality, and Fraternity, this book deals explicitly with Liberty and Equality; the term Fraternity does not occur except in this paragraph, but much the same idea is covered by the family argument (discussed in chapter 3) according to which all human beings are members of the same family. In my view, to provide a proper foundation of a liberal–egalitarian set-up we have to appeal to perfectionist considerations, and the idea of fraternity will not suffice (see the limitations of the family argument discussed in chapter 3). Hence the title of the book is partly different from the famous trilogy.

The book is in three parts. The first part (that is to say, the second and third chapters) examines some attempts to provide the foundations of the doctrine of equal respect and considera-tion without appealing to perfectionist considerations. The contractarian argument, the family argument (which appeals to the idea that we are all members of the human family), the argument from sympathy, and some other arguments that try to bypass perfectionist considerations are examined. I argue that such non-perfectionist considerations cannot provide an adequate foundation of the doctrine of equal respect; rather, such non-perfectionist considerations need to work within the constraints set by the doctrine of equal right to respect.

In chapter 2 the problem about the grounds of equality is raised and there is a discussion of Rawls's contractarian attempt to provide the foundations of egalitarianism. Before reading this discussion readers who are not familiar with Rawls's ideas could read my exposition of Rawls's theory in chapter 10, section 1. The reason why the exposition of his ideas is post-poned until Part III of my book is that the bulk of his ideas are concerned with the implications of egalitarianism rather than with the foundations of egalitarianism.

The second part (that is to say, chapters 4–9) is more con-structive. An attempt is made to unearth the perfectionist and metaphysical presuppositions of the right-based egalitarian approach (which stresses that the doctrine of rights set moral constraints within which our policies must operate). In chap-ters 6 and 7 I contrast what I call the dynamic version of the right-based approach, which allows an individual to have the right to equal respect in virtue of his relevant potential, with the static approach, which does not allow an individual the right to equal respect in virtue of his potential. I argue that the dynamic view harmonizes better with the egalitarian intui-tions than does the static view.

The simple view of personal identity, which is criticized by Parfit and according to which the person is a persistent substance, is distinguished from the complex view advocated by Parfit, which, rather like the Buddhist and Humean theories of personal identity, denies the existence of any persistent substance or permanent self. In chapters 5, 6, and 7 it is argued that much of our egalitarian intuitions and moral system presuppose the simple view rather than the complex view.

Also in Part II, I construct and commend the doctrine of transitivity of ends in themselves. There used to be a popular song which went something like this: 'A guy is a guy wherever he may be.' Caricaturing the doctrine of transitivity of ends in themselves one might say 'an end in itself is an end in itself whatever it may be.' A less facetious introduction to this doctrine is provided in chapter 6.

Many people think that the doctrine of equal respect applies to all human beings including human infants, psychopaths, idiots, and future generations of human beings, but not to animals, nor to sperms nor to the unfertilized ovum; and they are perplexed about whether it applies to the foetus and if so at what stage of its development. An attempt is made to show that the theory which I construct harmonizes with our egalitarian intuitions and practices and can be used to give a ruling on controversial cases such as whether the foetus is a member of the egalitarian club; in order to deal with this last example the problem of when human life begins is discussed (see chapter 5). To put it portentously, the second part of the book tries to present the deep structure of our egalitarian beliefs and practices. Also, in the second part, there is an examination of how the egalitarian principle can be related to other moral considerations which have claims on our allegiance, such as the claims of our family, of our ideals and commitments, of utility (see chapters 8 and 9).

The third part of the book is concerned with working out some of the implications of egalitarianism, with the way egalitarianism is related to other values such as liberty and autonomy, and with some of the problems facing liberalism, such as the limits of paternalism and the place of tolerance. Many liberal–egalitarians such as Rawls and Ronald Dworkin think that we can derive a liberal set up from egalitarian premises.

I have argued as against them that this derivation will only work if we supplement egalitarianism with perfectionism.

In chapter 10 an outline of and critical discussion of Rawls's theory is provided, and some of the spheres where a liberal–egalitarian theory has to appeal to perfectionism are pointed out. It is argued that the Brave New World (where people are brought up in a world where they do not grow up into autonomous adults but are conditioned to be content with the form of life that they have been brought up to believe in) cannot be rejected without appealing to perfectionism. And in the last section of chapter 10 there is a discussion of the problem of paternalism with regard to the young and it is shown why an appeal to perfectionist ideals is necessary in that area too.

Rawls attempts to bypass perfectionist considerations by resort to the Aristotelian principle (according to which human beings prefer complex and intricate activities to simple ones) and the choice criterion of value. He admits that liberalism needs to appeal to ideals, but he thinks that such ideals can be justified by appealing to the fact that they would in fact be chosen by rational human beings. In chapter 11 I argue that such attempts at bypassing perfectionism do not work. Chapter 11 also contains a comparison of some of the views of Mill and Rawls on liberty.

Chapter 12 consists of a discussion of the problem of paternalism towards sane adults. Here also the need for perfectionism is stressed.

Even if we accept a liberal set-up, there is the problem of why some liberties are more important than others. In chapter 13 there is a discussion of this problem of ranking different liberties in some rough order of importance. I contrast my answer with Dworkin's and argue that this problem too cannot be answered without an appeal to perfectionist considerations. Also in chapter 13 it is contended that once we supplement egalitarianism with perfectionism, we can defend egalitarianism against certain arguments used by Nozick.

In the final chapter an attempt is made to clear some misunderstadings of perfectionism; in particular, the charge that the perfectionist doctrine is inherently tyrannical, anti-egalitarian, undemocratic, and intolerant is refuted. While the use of perfectionism as a political principle is probably incompatible with Rawls's doctrine of equal liberties, it is quite compatible with the toleration of inferior forms of life. Chapter 11, section 4 suggests that Mill, the great champion of liberty, was committed to something like toleration without equal liberty. In the final chapter I myself commend toleration without equal liberties.

The outline provided in this section is not intended to be comprehensive. Potential readers who want some idea of what the book is about could also glance at the list of contents and at the index.

3. Reflective equilibrium

I have in this book used the reflective equilibrium model, according to which we match and mutually adjust our moral and other principles with our moral beliefs and intuitions until we get a harmonious fit. Now those of us who go in for this approach have to face the problem that moral beliefs and intuitions vary from society to society, and even within a given society, from individual to individual. For instance, in this book I have shown sympathy for the view that infants are members of the egalitarian club. But there are societies where infanticide has been widely practised and condoned and where infants are not given anything like the respect and consideration that is given to the adults. Again, there are societies where slavery has been practised and condoned. So which of the conflicting beliefs and intuitions should an impartial person go by when he used the reflective equilibrium approach?

What are we to make of such objections? Now if one is interested in unearthing the foundations of egalitarian moral beliefs and practices, then we should go by egalitarian moral beliefs and intuitions rather than by non-egalitarian ones, such as those found among slave-owners or among those who believe that the Brahmin is more worthy of respect and consideration than the untouchable is. But there is still the residual problem that even among those who belong to the egalitarian tradition, people's moral beliefs vary; thus some people think that the doctrine of equal respect applies to foetuses and newly-born infants while others think that it does not. How then do we adjudicate between such views? I have tried to construct an egalitarian theory which harmonizes better with our egalitarian intuitions *in general,* than alternative egalitarian theories do. My criticism of alternative egalitarian theories is not just that they cannot deal with the controversial egalitarian beliefs, such as whether foetuses are members of the egalitarian club. Thus, in the case of the contractarian theory, I also argue that it cannot deal with the problem of those in a weak bargaining position. Again my preference for the dynamic view over the static view is not just based on the argument that the former, unlike the latter, can extend the doctrine of equal respect to foetuses and to the newly-born infant. I try to show that the dynamic approach has quite a few advantages over the static view, and that it harmonizes better with egalitarian intuitions in general than the static view does; moreover, I provide a theory which tries to make sense of the egalitarian intuitions by showing that these are not just an arbitrary collection of isolated intuitions, but form part of a coherent system.

There are several reasons why it is important to find out the principles and the metaphysics that underlie our egalitarian beliefs and practices. First, such principles can be useful in operating the egalitarian code, they can be used to give a ruling on controversial cases. Secondly, even if one wants to do something more ambitious and compare the pros and cons of the egalitarian moral code with those of non-egalitarian moral codes, one needs to discuss how sound the foundations of egalitarianism are compared to the foundations of other moral codes. If a Brahmin attempts to defend his view that the Brahmin's life is more worthy of respect than is the untouchable's, he has to defend the relevant metaphysics, for instance that a Brahmin, unlike the untouchable, did good deeds in his previous lives and so is more deserving of respect than the untouchable. An egalitarian too has to face the problem about how sound the foundations of egalitarianism are, he has, for instance, to justify why people are worthy of equal respect and consideration, in spite of differences in qualities such as rationality, intelligence, moral sense, and autonomy.

If we are to rationally and knowledgeably decide whether a particular moral code is better than another we should not blindly make a choice just on the basis of which one we happen to like and commend for general acceptance. We must also examine how sound the relevant foundations are.

PART I

THE FOUNDATIONS OF EQUALITY: SOME NON-PERFECTIONIST APPROACHES

Equality and Contractarianism

1. The problem about the grounds of equality

Talk of egalitarianism occurs at various levels. For instance, there are egalitarians with regard to things like wealth, income, and education, who want to abolish privileges and inequalities in economic and social matters; thus, such egalitarians want to abolish private schools which confer privileges and advantages on the children of the well-off. Now there are many other people who are willing to allow inequalities in such areas as education and income distribution, so at one level such people are not egalitarians, but at the deepest level some of these people may well be egalitarians in so far as they take the line that every human being has an equal right to respect and consideration; they may take the view that in justifying moral and political institutions and policies everyone's interests should be given equal consideration. They may allow social and economic inequalities when they are convinced that such inequalities work out to everyone's advantage or for the common good.

John Rawls (whose views are explained in more detail in chapter 10, section 1) for instance, allows some economic and social inequalities, so at one level he is not an egalitarian; but at the deepest level he is an egalitarian, for he allows only those inequalities that he thinks are sanctioned by egalitarianism at the deepest level, for his original position is meant to be a position of equality between human beings.[1] Similarly there are some people who allow private schools to confer advantages on the children of the well-off, if and when this results in the promotion of the common good; such people too could be egalitarians at the deepest level. Even those who are politically conservative may be egalitarians at the deepest level; they

[1] See R. Dworkin, *Taking Rights Seriously*, pp. 180-1.

may think that the conservative policies that they support are likely to be in harmony with the common good and with the principle of equal respect and consideration for everyone. Of course there is much scope for self-deception here; people may promote selfish and anti-social causes by convincing themselves that their causes are for the common good; but I am not here concerned with such problems. In the first two parts of this book I shall hardly touch on the important problem of the implications of egalitarianism at the deepest level. Instead, I shall be primarily concerned with the problem of the *grounds* of egalitarianism at the deepest level. What are the grounds of the view that all human beings have a right to equal respect and consideration? Why does not egalitarianism extend to animals? Animal interests are given consideration but not equal consideration to human interests. What is the rationale of this? I shall in the first two parts of this book examine some of the answers that have been given and might be given to such problems. Before this is done, however, it should be made clear that references to egalitarianism or to the doctrine of equality, are, unless otherwise stated, to egalitarianism at the deepest level. The foregoing discussion should have helped the reader to understand what is meant here by egalitarianism at the deepest level. If not, I can only hope that this point will become clearer as I discuss the answers to the problems that arise with regard to such egalitarianism.

It is sometimes said that all human beings should be given equal respect and consideration because they have equal intrinsic worth, but this shifts the problem. What are the grounds of equal human worth? If we consider some of the alleged grounds we are left dissatisfied. For instance, it is sometimes thought that human beings, unlike animals, have rationality. But some idiots are less rational than some animals, so why should we give more weight to the interests of idiots than to the interests of animals? Moreover, even among some adult human beings some are more rational than others, so why should we not give greater intrinsic weight to the more rational ones? Similar problems arise with other suggested grounds for human equality, such as capacity to form life-plans or ideals and follow them through with zest (William James), capacity for moral sentiments and for a sense of justice, self-consciousness, ability to use language, autonomy, and so forth. We could have a cut-off point which is high enough to exclude all non-human animals, but then there are problems about congenital idiots, and also other problems such as why those above the cut-off point should all get equal consideration. Even if there is nothing logically inconsistent about maintaining both that (*a*) those below the cut-off point (for instance, animals) should get lower status than those at or above the cut-off point, and that (*b*) those at or above the cut-off point should get equal weight in our moral calculations, one wants to know what is so sacred about the cut-off point? If the reason for giving creatures below that cut-off point lower worth is that they score less well on some test, then why not use similar tests to discriminate between those who are above the cut-off point. There may well be a reason why one should not discriminate between people above the cut-off point, but only between those who are below the cut-off point and those who are not; but one is at least entitled to ask for that reason. The onus is on the egalitarian who does not want his egalitarianism to include animals, to provide the justification for such a view. The mere fact that no logical inconsistency has been shown is not a sufficient justification for this view! Compare: suppose someone asks why doctors should be paid more than teachers, it is hardly a sufficient answer to be told that no logical inconsistency has been shown to exist. One is entitled to ask for the justification of paying doctors more, though one must not of course assume in advance that no such justification will be forthcoming.

Faced with such problems, some egalitarians simply deny the need for a justification by appealing to the view that egalitarianism at the deepest level, which involves equal respect and consideration for all human beings, is one of those ultimate principles that is used as a standard for justifying other principles, institutions, and policies, but which is not itself in need of any justification. Non-ultimate principles can be proved by appealing to other more fundamental principles, but when one comes to the ultimate principles one has to accept them or reject them, one cannot appeal to any more ultimate principles, since *ex hypothesi* there is nothing more ultimate than an ultimate principle. Such a move does not commit one to a denial of an objectivist or cognitivist account. A fundamental principle such as egalitarianism could be clear and obvious once we reflect upon it, in an unbiased way.

What are we to make of this position? It will not give the egalitarians all they need. It is true that beyond a certain point, argument becomes pointless, at least at the practical level. That there are tables and chairs in front of us is obvious, and no one other than a philosopher or a madman seriously asks us to justify such obvious facts. Although there is considerable disagreement regarding the metaphysical proofs of the existence of tables, at the practical common-sense level all reasonable people accept such facts as obvious. But the egalitarian claim is not so obvious. One feels, even at the practical level, the need for asking the egalitarian certain questions, such as why only human beings belong to this class where talk of equal considerations and respect is relevant, and not also animals? The principles 'like cases should be treated alike' is sometimes used to bolster the egalitarian position. But this principle is a formal one, and by itself it cannot give us substantial results; we still need to know what similarities are relevant. For instance, the principle by itself cannot tell us whether animals should be given less weight in our moral calculations at the deepest level. Even if it is true that animals in general lack certain capacities that human beings possess, we need to know if these capacities are morally relevant. Compare: even if it is the case that women in general differ from men in some respects, it would not follow that the egalitarian should give less weight to the interests of women. What, then, is the justification for the principle of applying egalitarianism between all human beings, but not between human beings and animals?

Since it will not do to simply deny the need for justification of the egalitarian principle, the egalitarian can try to justify his principle in one of two main ways. First, he may try to give a metaphysical and/or perfectionist justification of the egalitarian principle. Secondly (and alternatively), he may try to give a justification that appeals neither to metaphysical nor to perfectionist considerations.

The metaphysical-cum-perfectionist justification, if it is to work, has to do two things. First, it has to maintain that human beings, unlike animals and other inferior beings, have some common property (or set of properties), and secondly, it has to maintain that this property constitutes a ground for giving greater weight to those who possess it. That all human beings possess a common property that members of other species do not share, is not impossible to show. For instance, the property of belonging to the human species is perhaps a genuine property that human beings have in common; but one still has to answer the problem of why such a property should constitute a ground for giving superior status to human beings over other sentient creatures.

Those who resort to the metaphysical defence of egalitarianism could maintain that though at the empirical level human beings seem to differ in important respects (for instance, some are more autonomous than others, or more rational than others), yet at the metaphysical level they have some relevant thing in common. On certain metaphysical assumptions, all human beings have one thing in common and this thing then can be used as the basis for equality among human beings. We would still have problems. For instance, even if all human beings do have some distinguishing property or essence, such as a soul or a common humanity, in common, why does this give them human rights? Suppose someone says that though all human beings have a soul, this fact leaves him cold, and he does not see why we should respect people because they have souls; or again, why should we respect people because they have freedom at some metaphysical or noumenal level? Or again, suppose the sceptic admits that all human beings belong to the same natural kind, and have in common some essence (or property), such as a common humanity, and that such a property distinguishes human beings from animals; yet he does not see why such considerations should be used to apply egalitarianism among all human beings, but not between human beings and animals. The really important thing from the moral point of view, he may argue, is not what natural kind one belongs to, but what all one is capable of doing either now or in the future. Suppose a dolphin could talk, laugh, argue, and respond to moral considerations, surely we would be strongly inclined to give it equal consideration. And do such considerations not show that what is really important is not what metaphysical essences an individual has, but what empirical properties he possesses?

To meet such a challenge the metaphysician has not only to show that human beings possess some common essence, or property. He must also try to show why the possession of such a common essence or property, should be a ground for superior status being accorded to human interests. Kantians and Hegelians do attempt to do this; thus they try to show that a creature without freedom (such as an animal) has no intrinsic value, he is not an end in himself, he can be treated as a means or an instrument.

One point to observe about many such claims is that they are conducted at a non-empirical level; which is not to say that they are false, but it does show how difficult it is to agree with them. And this does create problems for liberal-egalitarians such as Rawls, who want to keep metaphysical and perfectionist considerations out of bounds because they want to construct a system of political principles that command general acceptance and that are neutral between points of view that are controversial.[2] Although metaphysical considerations are different from considerations of perfectionism, what they both have in common is that they are controversial, which is why Rawls wants to exclude them both when he constructs his political principles. However this position of Rawls's is not tenable, and I argue in this book that it is not possible to construct an adequate political theory without appealing to controversial matters. Rawls himself without realizing it appeals to a metaphysical theory of the nature of the person.[3] He assumes that a person is a persistent entity and his criticism of utilitarianism is based on that assumption. Thus he complains that utilitarianism does not treat seriously the difference between persons. As Parfit rightly points out, this would only work as a criticism of utilitarianism if Rawls were right about the nature of the person.[4] I agree with Rawls, as against Parfit, that the person is a persistent entity, but one must admit that this involves a metaphysical view

---

[2] Rawls, *A Theory of Justice*, pp. 213-14.
[3] Ibid., p. 423.
[4] D. Parfitt, 'Later Selves and Moral Principles', in *Philosophy and Personal Relations*, ed. A. Montefiore (London, 1973), p. 160.

which is controversial. Perhaps Rawls thinks that his conception of the person is the common sense conception of the person rather than a metaphysical conception. But it seems to me wrong to think that our alleged common-sense ideas, especially regarding philosophical issues, are free from controversy and from metaphysical influences.

Metaphysical and perfectionist considerations should not be excluded from a defence of egalitarianism, but anti-empirical views should be excluded. What I mean is this. Some philosophers, such as Kant and Sartre, seem to argue that man is Rational with a capital R, or Free with a capital F, and they seem to imply that all human beings are, in spite of empirical appearances to the contrary, in some deep sense rational or free and that this forms the basis of their being worthy of respect and dignity. Now against such views it can be pointed out that there is good empirical evidence that some human beings (such as idiots) are lacking in freedom or in rationality and it is dogmatic to insist that at some deep, noumenal level they must be free and rational. I am against the use of metaphysical arguments that involves going against empirical evidence, but I am not against appealing to metaphysical and perfectionist considerations in constructing a political theory; indeed it is argued in this book that egalitarianism (between human beings but not between human beings and animals) presupposes metaphysical and perfectionist considerations.

2. The contractarian solution

In this section and in the next chapter I shall critically examine some of the chief attempts to justify egalitarianism without appealing to perfectionism.

First, there is the contractarian model that tries to give a justification of equality (between human beings) without appealing to perfectionist considerations. We saw that one difficulty that egalitarianism faces is that at the empirical level qualities such as rationality, autonomy, and freedom vary, and the sceptic can ask how any such quality can reasonably form the basis of equality. The person who defends egalitarianism by appealing to the contractarian model may defend egalitarianism by making an analogy with a club.

Suppose, to be a member of a certain sports club, you have to attain a certain minimum proficiency in the sport. It does not follow that among those who have joined the club, there must be discrimination in favour of the better players. It is quite consistent for such a club to treat its members equally, even though it excludes people below a certain standard. Now in the case of political institutions we sometimes have something similar. Thus in order to vote a person has to reach a certain minimum maturity (a person aged 10 cannot vote in the general elections), yet among those who are entitled to vote, there is one man, one vote. Now animals can be excluded from many human practices on the grounds that they are not qualified to play the relevant game. Thus, there is no point in giving an animal the right to vote, or freedom of speech.

Sometimes it is argued that animals cannot have rights, because only those who can perform duties can have rights. A variant of this argument is found in Rawls: 'Those who can give justice are owed justice.'[5] Rawls thinks that the game of justice applies to all those who can play the game of giving justice. So we can see the similarity with the club idea. Rawls thinks that his approach bypasses perfectionist consideration. He claims that he does not need to assume any notion of intrinsic worth. It is just true as a matter of fact that human beings, unlike animals, can take part in the game of justice, they can make rational contracts. We need not postulate that they are more wonderful creatures than animals are. Does Rawls succeed in bypassing perfectionist considerations? I think not (see chapter 10). Even leaving aside the problem that arises from the fact that babies and idiots cannot play the game of justice, Rawls's approach does not successfuly bypass perfectionist considerations. Any adequate doctrine of equal respect of all human beings will need to be supplemented or qualified by perfectionism.

Now it is true that there are at least certain moral practices that can only be practised by those who possess the relevant minimum capacity. Thus with all those above a certain minimum rationality, you can make deals such as 'I will not kill you if you do not kill me', or 'I shall help you in need if you help me in need.' You cannot make such deals with beings, such

[5] *A Theory of Justice*, p.510.

as animals, who are below the minimum level of rationality. Now as a result of these deals you may enter into certain obligations with regard to those with whom you have made them. Rational contractors can have special obligations towards non-rational contractors. Let us call these contractarian obligations. Now rational human beings can have two kinds of duties: contractarian obligations and non-contractarian obligations (or duties). Some people reserve the term 'obligations' for contractarian obligations, so that it makes no sense to talk of non-contractarian obligations. Thus obligations, according to Rawls, must be voluntarily undertaken. But this is a verbal point, and does not affect the substantial point under discussion. We could still divide duties into contractarian duties (or obligations) and non-contractarian duties. In Rawlsian language the division would be between obligations and natural duties; for Rawls refers to non-contractarian duties as natural duties.

Now if we use rights in such a way that an individual cannot have rights unless he can play the game of justice, of making reciprocal agreements, so that only those who can give justice can be eligible to be subjects of rights, then it follows that animals, for instance, do not have rights. But such verbal devices cannot show why animal interests should be given less weight than human ones. There is a sense in which we can talk of animal rights, we can make demands on behalf of animals at several levels; it is arguable that even at the deepest moral level we should demand that animal interests be taken into account. Whether we use the term 'rights' when championing animal interests is not so important provided we are clear about the facts and about the moral demands being made.

A dog cannot vote, and it is absurd we give him the right to vote. Nor can he play the game of justice, of recognizing other people's rights, and so forth. But none of this shows why we are justified in sacrificing animal interests when they clash with human interests. Such a justification, if it works at all, will probably need an appeal to perfectionist considerations. We may have to assume that human being have more worth than animals. They are wonderful creatures, compared with animals. And so we shall be back with the problem, what is it in virtue of which human beings get superior status to animals; and if there is some such quality that distinguishes humans from animals, is this quality not found in different degrees among human beings? If so, should not some human beings be regarded as superior to others?

The contractarian (or the club) model presupposes the existence of morality, especially moral duties, in at least two ways. First, as Hume pointed out, it presupposes the duty of promise-keeping. That we ought to keep our agreements is something presupposed by the contractarian model. Some contractarians try to bypass such presuppositions by appealing to the prudential interests of rational beings to explain why we should keep our agreements. But I will not discuss here how far such a move works. For there is a second and more important way in which morality must be presupposed by the contractarian model. Suppose rational contractors agree to split the world's resources in certain ways. Is such an agreement binding? Now, if such an agreement violates certain moral requirements, it is void. Suppose the strong agree to enslave the weak, such that each strong man has a weak man as his slave. This agreement between the strong is morally void, because it is grossly immoral. And it remains morally void, even though all the strong freely consent to such an agreement. Now similar points apply regarding deals that all rational contractors (the strong and the weak ones) make, even if every rational contractor is a voluntary party to such a deal. For what about the interests of non-rational contractors, such as animals and babies? The claims of animals, babies, and God (if he exists) may only have been taken into account by the rational contractors to the extent that they have repercussions on the interests of the rational contractors.[6] Can the rational contractors explain, for instance, why we should respect the rights of babies? Why not go in for a policy of selective infanticide as means of controlling the population?

It could be argued that we should be kind to babies, because otherwise their parents and relations, who are rational contractors, will suffer. But this surely does not do justice to the feeling that if we kick a baby we are primarily doing wrong to the baby, and any wrong to the baby's mother is relatively unimportant. Also, what about the case of unwanted orphans,

---

[6] V. Haksar, 'Autonomy, Justice and Contractarianism', *British Journal of Political Science,* iii (1973), 487–509.

and other unwanted babies? They too acquire rights even when harming them does not necessarily involve harming rational contractors. Is there not something wrong with a system that allows infanticide provided the parents of the infant consent to it?

Rawls may take the line that rational contractors will take into account the interests of babies because rational contractors do not know whether, once the veil of ignorance[7] is removed, they are babies or not. But then are rational contractors allowed to know that, once the veil of ignorance is removed, they will at least be born? Could they not be just foetuses? Or just potential foetuses? Or animals who might in some future reincarnation become human?

Are babies owed justice? We saw earlier that according to Rawls only those who can play the game of justice are owed justice. But Rawls weakens this argument by including not only those who have the relevant actual abilities to play the game, but also those such as babies who have the potential to play such a game (and would he include foetuses here?). Now it is interesting to see Rawls's justification for doing this. He gives two reasons.

First, he says that 'since infants and children are thought to have basic rights (normally exercised on their behalf by parents and guardians), this interpretation of the requisite conditions seems necessary to match our considered judgements'.[8] This is one illustration of the fact that Rawls's hypothetical contractarian model can be constructed in different ways, with different initial conditions. Thus you can allow the people in the original position to know that they are born and so could be foetuses, or you may deny them even this knowledge; or again, you may construct the original position in such a way that the parties know that they have

---

[7] Those who are not familiar with Rawls's idea of the veil of ignorance may find the following quotation useful: '. . . if a man knew that he was wealthy, he might find it rational to advance the principle that various taxes for welfare measures be counted unjust; if he knew that he was poor, he would most likely propose the contrary principle. To represent the desired restrictions one imagines a situation [the original position] in which everyone is deprived of this sort of information. One excludes the knowledge of those contingencies which sets man at odds and allows them to be guided by their prejudices. In this way the veil of ignorance is arrived at in a natural way.' *A Theory of Justice*, pp. 18–19.

[8] Ibid., p. 509.

reached the age of reason, in which case they would know
not only that they have got beyond the foetal stage, but also
that they have got beyond babyhood. Rawls believe that we
ought to construct the model in such a way that its results
best match our considered judgements. Thus he would think
that we ought not to allow the parties in the original position
to know whether they are babies or not, on the grounds that
this way of constructing the model best matches our considered
judgements that babies have basic rights and are owed justice.
But now it would seem that the best way of constructing the
model would depend, at least partly, on our considered judgements; and does this not show that in a way his contractarian
model presupposes moral constraints? For if it give morally
unacceptable results, we alter the model in a suitable way.
And so we are still left with the problem of justifying such
moral constraints or considered judgements. It seems to me
that if we have to justify our considered judgement that
babies have basic rights we shall have to appeal to perfectionist
considerations, such as that babies are rather wonderful beings
and so their interests and needs ought to be catered for in
a suitable theory of justice. Some Rawlsians would say that
our considered judgements are justified by appealing to the
contractarian model, and the model itself is constructed to
meet our considered judgements, and that there is nothing
circular in this; the two are revised until you get the best
harmonious fit. But what appears the best fit to some will
not appear so to others. How do we argue against these who
believe in the infanticide of unwanted babies? Suppose such
a person just does not grant that babies have rights, he is not
likely to grant that the best fit comes if you construct the
contractarian model in such a way that harmonizes with the
view that babies have rights. What is the best and most coherent fit will depend to some extent upon our judgements and
our judgements may partly vary with our metaphysical and
perfectionist ideas. Thus those who think that animals are
rather wonderful creatures, whose interests should not be
subordinated to human interests, will not be very impressed
by Rawls's model where animals' interests are taken into
account only to the extent that they have repercussions on
human interests. Of course, one could construct the model

by neglecting certain other moral and perfectionist considerations, but in that case the contractarian model will not give a decisive answer about what we ought to do, how we ought to distribute resources, and so forth.[9] The way out of such difficulties is not to abandon the reflective equilibrium model but to abandon Rawls's special version of it which rejects metaphysical and perfectionist considerations.

Rawls gives a second reason for the view that all those (such as babies) who have the potential to take part in the game of justice are owed justice, whether or not they have the actual ability to take part in the game of justice. He says that 'regarding the potentiality as sufficient accords with the hypothetical nature of the original position, and with the idea that as far as possible the choice of principles should not be influenced by arbitrary contingencies. Therefore it is reasonable to say that those who take part in the initial agreement, were it not for fortuitous circumstances, are assured equal justice.'[10]

Now is it arbitrary to leave babies out of the contractarian experiment? Whether something is arbitrary or not depends upon our purposes. If the idea is to play the contractarian game, and make deals such as 'I will not ill-treat you if you do not ill-treat me', then there is nothing obviously arbitrary about leaving babies outside the club. True, they can join the club when they attain the age of reason, but that is not a reason for given them membership while babies. It can at best be a reason for taking their future interests as adults into account. Benn says that the reason why we should not ill-treat infants is that 'some infants do grow up into persons . . . because the person he (the infant) *will* be (provided he grows up) emotionally stunted or impaired if he is deprived of love and tender care as an infant, it is for the sake of those that will grow into persons that we take care of all babies now.'[11] But how can Benn explain what is wrong if we were to painlessly kill half the infants so that the other half can live fuller and less congested lives in the future? The reason Benn gives for not maltreating infants is that such maltreatment will lead

---

[9] See Haksar, 'Autonomy, Justice and Contractarianism'.

[10] *A Theory of Justice*, p. 509.

[11] S. Benn, 'Abortion, Infanticide, and Respect for Persons', in *The Problem of Abortion*, ed. J. Feinberg (Belmont, 1973), p. 102.

us into an attitude of callous unconcern for other infants who will grow up into persons. But this view cannot explain that maltreatment of an individual baby, who dies while still a baby, involves primarily an injustice to this particular baby, and any other resulting injustice to other future adults is a separate wrong.

To give an adequate account of what is wrong with infanticide we shall have to contend that babies (perhaps partly in virute of possessing the relevant potential) are wonderful creatures even as babies. And that is a kind of perfectionism. Again some people would argue that justice is only a part of morality, and that killing a baby is not unjust, though it is immoral. But we would still need to explain why it is immoral, and can we do so without appealing to perfectionist considerations?

In the last quotation from Rawls one of the reasons he seems to give for treating infants as belonging to the club is this. If we talk of an actual contract, then the parties to the contract can only be those who can now play the contractarian game, in other words they must have enough sense to make a contract. But if we talk as he does of a *hypothetical* contract, then it is no longer necessary that the only parties should be those who have the relevant actual abilities; it will suffice if they have the potential. But this raises several problems; for instance, since there is not an actual contract why not have animals represented in the original position? True, they cannot sign an actual contract, but some human beings could speak on their behalf in the original position. Moreover, this argument of Rawls's is rather like the argument that since the contract is an imaginary device, therefore we should allow imaginary beings such as ghosts and centaurs to be parties to the contract. Rawls says that animals are excluded from the sphere of justice because they cannot make claims.[12] True, babies cannot make claims, but their guardians can make claims on their behalf, they decide in view of what the infants are presumed to want when they attain the sense of justice. But animals, says Rawls, will never attain this sense. But is this difference decisive for not giving animals rights? Why cannot

---

[12] 'The Sense of Justice', in *Moral Concepts,* ed. J. Feinberg (Oxford, 1969), pp. 120-40.

others just complain on behalf of animals? Rawls replies rather dogmatically that in that event the relevant duties will be owed to the men who speak on behalf of the animals, rather than to the animals.[13] I do not see why we cannot owe animals duties, even though only someone other than the animal would complain on its behalf.

Moreover, Rawls's hypothetical experiment raises the problem about whether it has any relevance to showing how we can bypass perfectionist considerations. Rawls seems to think that his contractarian model bypasses perfectionist considerations because those who 'can give justice are owed justice'.[14] What are we to make of such an argument? Now a non-perfectionist cannot assume that those who can give justice are intrinsically superior to those who cannot. So we can ask such a person why it is the case that those and only those who 'can give justice are owed justice'? Is it not because we make deals with such people and so owe them justice? But if so, a hypothetical contract is not enough, there must be an actual contract, not necessarily an explicit contract, but at least a tacit contract. But with babies and with members of future generations you cannot even make a tacit contract. In any case, for reasons given in this chapter, even an actual contract has to work within moral constraints and so Rawls has now shown how the contractarian model can bypass all perfectionist considerations.

Suppose a body of white men go to a remote part of the world where there are some native inhabitants. And suppose the white men, who are equipped with superior weapons, start shooting the natives for sport, somewhat as people in Britain go grouse-shooting. Now even if it is the case that the aborigines can give justice, why does it follow that the whites owe them justice? True, if the whites make a deal, even a tacit deal, with them that the whites will not kill them if they do not kill the whites, then the whites will owe the natives justice in virtue of such a deal. But let us suppose the whites are strong and can look after each other well, and, unlike men in Hobbes's state of nature, they do not need to make peace with the natives. It seems that it would still be unjust of the whites

[13] Ibid.
[14] *A Theory of Justice*, section 77.

to kill the natives for sport. And this is because the natives are human beings and human beings are wonderful beings who have certain rights in virtue of being human, not merely in virtue of being able to make reciprocal deals with each other. If you and I make a deal with each other 'I will not kill you as long as you do not kill me', and then if I kill you without your attempting any harm to me, it would follow that what I have done is a double injustice. First, I should not have killed you because you are a human being and not a mere animal. Secondly, I should not have killed you because I promised not to kill you. The fact that the second reason is present in some cases should not blind us to the presence of the first reason for not killing. And this first reason does involve an appeal to perfectionist considerations. For if we believe that it is wrong and unjust to kill a human being, but not an animal, then this view is best defended, if it can be defended at all, by the view that human beings have superior status to animals.

Again, many of us believe that human needs are more important than animal needs. If animals are starving, this is bad, but not quite as bad as if human beings were starving. A Benthamite utilitarian would go just by who is suffering more; but to many of us it would seem that human starvation is more worrying, not merely because human beings suffer more, but because human beings have superior claims to animals, other things being equal. And is this not because we believe that human beings are in some important sense more wonderful creatures and have more intrinsic worth than animals? And so would we not be committed to a kind of perfectionism?

Murphy says:

we treat rational beings as ends because of their freedom of Willker, because they are responsible persons and not things. This freedom to choose for good or evil is what gives morality a point. For if a man were not capable of choosing to better himself, then it would be pointless to address imperatives of rational morality to him. One might as well talk morality to stones or dogs. Similarly, if men could only do good, such imperatives would also be pointless . . . The essence of morality for Kant, is simply action that honours the absolute worth, of all rational beings by respecting their freedom.[15]

---

[15] J. Murphy, *Kant: The Philosophy of Right* (London, 1970), p. 85.

Now there are two issues here. First, is it the case that moral imperatives are only to be addressed to rational beings? Secondly, is it the case that rational beings are ends in themselves, have a kind of absolute worth, whereas non-rational beings have only instrumental worth or that even if they have some intrinsic worth that worth is less than that of rational beings? Now even if the answer to the first question is yes, and even if that answer can be given (as Murphy does in the above quotation) without an appeal to perfectionist considerations, it does not follow that the answer to the second question is also yes. Moreover, it seems to me that if one were to answer the second question in the affirmative, the justification given would involve a kind of perfectionism. For without assuming that forms of life that exhibit rationality are superior to non-rational forms of life we could not properly answer the second question in the affirmative.

If moral imperatives cannot be addressed to dogs, it follows that dogs do not have moral duties; it does not follow that they do not have moral rights, nor that they have less intrinsic worth than those to whom such imperatives can be addressed. Of course some philosophers would define rights in such a way that only a creature who has duties can have rights. This definition would be unobjectionable provided rights are not always used to trump (that is to say override) non-rights. However, if one uses rights to trump non-rights then this definition would be used to beg a substantial issue. The substantial issue is: are the interests of creatures, such as animals and idiots, who do not have moral duties always subordinate to the interests of those who do have moral duties?

If we value rational creatures, or moral creatures, or creatures with a sense of justice more highly than creatures without such qualities does this not commit us to a kind of perfectionism, for instance to the view that rationality is an intrinsically good thing, or that a rational way of life is superior to a sub-rational way of life?

Contractarian models are of two kinds. First, there are those such as Locke's that work within certain moral constraints which they presuppose. Let us call this kind the restricted contractarian approach. Secondly, there are those such as Mackie's which try to construct morality, or an important part of it such as justice, without presupposing moral constraints. Let us call this second kind of approach the extreme contractarian approach. As for the restricted contractarian approach I have no objection in principle; the important problem that remains, however, is to spell out the moral constraints that are presupposed. My contention is that we cannot adequately justify these constraints without appealing to perfectionist considerations. We may appeal to the doctrine of natural rights that sets the relevant constraints, but can such a doctrine be justified without appealing to perfectionist considerations? As for the extreme contractarian approach, it has serious limitations; similar limitations apply to what is sometimes known as the conventionalist approach to our morality. John Mackie tries to explain our moral constraints in contractarian terms. He sees morality as concerned primarily with the well-being of rational beings, who are engaged in a partly competitive life. Moral rules are introduced in order to allow these rational adults to get the benefits of co-operation and to provide the necessary constraints on their competition for the benefit of all the competitors. Now a major problem with such an extreme contractarian approach is that it cannot adequately deal with the problem of those who do not have proper bargaining power, such as babies, idiots, senile people, future generations, and so forth. Mackie points out that we constantly move in and out of some of these groups, such as children and the sick. Now I admit that it is in the interests of the contractarian parties to provide for the sick, the infirm, and the senile, for they may one day become sick or senile. But this does not explain our obligations to other groups in a weak bargaining position, such as members of future generations, or even our obligations to children. It is true that we have sympathy towards children (we were once children ourselves!), but as I have argued elsewhere in this book such considerations are not sufficient to protect the interests of children; at best they explain why we have certain duties of charity towards children, and they cannot explain that we have certain duties of justice towards children. The fact that we were once children ourselves does not ensure that we respect their interests sufficiently. Compare: a politician may originally have come from the weaker section of the population, but it does not follow that the interests of the weak are safe in his hands! It is true that on the contractarian approach it could be in our interest to make an agreement not to kill each other's children. I want you to refrain from killing my child, so I had better refrain from killing your child. And so we could all reach an agreement forbidding people to kill other people's children. But this approach does not explain what is really wrong with a system which allows parents to kill their own infants. I would have thought that a system which banned the killing of other people's children, but which allowed parents to kill their own child, is more in harmony with a contractarian approach that is not subject to non-contractarian moral constraints.

Some contractarians would argue that even when we kill our own babies, we are indulging in an undesirable practice, since such conduct would weaken our humane dispositions and loosen our inhibitions against killing fellow members of the contractarian club. But such utilitarian-looking arguments from side-effects are not forceful (see chapter 8, section 1). There is the added complication that contractarians who are also liberals (as most of the modern ones are) must not use such arguments from side-effects as a basis for criminal punishment, unless the dangers are fairly 'clear and present'. As Mill pointed out, on the liberal view one must not punish people merely because they neglect the cultivation of their humane dispositions; there must be a *definite* risk of damage.[16] So how can an extreme contractarian who is also a liberal justify having criminal sanctions against those who kill their own babies?

A striking way of showing the limitations of the extreme contractarian approach of the kind that Mackie adopts (that is to say, one according to which the moral rules and constraints are invented by the contractarian parties, and not presupposed by them) is by considering the case of our obligations to future generations. Mackie is committed to the view that the claims of future generations lie outside what he regards as the core of morality. It is only gratuitous extension of morality that covers them. A humane disposition that is necessary for the contractarian parties in their dealings with each other,

[16] J. S. Mill, *On Liberty* (London, 1859), chapter IV, para. 10.

overflows in such a way as to ensure that we have some respect for members of the future generations as well as members of other non-contractarian parties such as babies.

My objection is that such factors may ensure that we show some respect for such individuals, but they do not cater sufficiently for the interests of such individuals. Our sympathies for the future generations get weaker and weaker as we look more and more into the future. For similar reasons, other considerations, such as family considerations, are not sufficient to ensure that we care sufficiently for those who will live in the distant future; our family ties get weaker and weaker. Nor are such considerations jointly sufficient, for they all suffer from similar defects, they get weaker and weaker as we consider generations that are more and more remote from us in time. And it will not do to argue that the contractarian parties must not neglect the interests of their remote descendents because such neglect will weaken the humane dispositions of the contractarian parties towards each other. It is possible that such weakening could be more than compensated by the advantages that accrue to the contractarian parties, for instance as a result of having increased use of the world's scarce resources.

So what is necessary is to insist that members of the future generations (assuming that they will exist) have certain rights that we must respect. For instance, they have certain rights to the share of the world's scarce resources and they have a right not to have the environment polluted. It is perfectly consistent to assume that though future generations do not have a right to be conceived and born they have certain rights on the assumption that they will be born (or conceived). Their rights are what Feinberg calls contingent rights,[17] they have rights on the assumption that they will exist, but since it is fairly certain that future generations will exist, we must act on the assumption that they have rights.

It seems to me that an extreme contractarian approach cannot explain why morality should extend to all human beings. Geoffrey Warnock tries to answer the problem of why

[17] J. Feinberg, Introduction to *The Problem of Abortion*, and 'The Rights of Animals and Future Generations', in *Philosophy and Environmental Crisis*, ed. W. Blackstone (Georgia, 1974), pp. 43-68.

morality should extend to all persons.[18] He thinks that things are likely to go badly for us because of the indifference or even hostility of other people; and the point of morality is to counteract this tendency. And he claims that a system of moral principles will not achieve this end fully unless the scope of these principles is extended to include all persons. He advances two reasons for not confining the scope of our principles only to a sub-class of all persons. First, he thinks that if we confine our principles only to our group, then a member of our group is liable to suffer if he strays into another group with whom we do not share common principles. This argument of Warnock's is not a conclusive one. It does not really show why, for instance, the British when they colonized Australia should have extended the scope of their moral principles to include the aborigines. When they went into aborigine territory they may have felt safe enough with a gun. Moreover, even if one does become more secure as a result of morality being extended to all human beings, one may (from a prudential point of view) lose out in other ways by losing the chance to exploit weak foreigners. Many of us prefer to have a system that allows the driving of cars, even though there is a slight risk that under such a system we may get run over. Similarly, many people may prefer to exploit foreigners even though this involves some risk that if and when they were to be at the mercy of these foreigners, they would be ill-treated. They may try to minimize such risks by carrying a gun—such precautions may be fairly adequate in the case of weak foreigners who only have primitive weapons.

Warnock's second reason is that 'if conduct is to be seen as regulated only within groups, we still have the possibility of unrestricted hostility and conflict between groups.'[19] Such considerations do not show why a strong group should extend its principles to include weak groups; they do not show what would be wrong if the strong groups reached an agreement with each other to exploit the weak groups. Warnock's approach cannot deal adequately with the problem of why justice should extend to children, the senile, future generations, and other groups who are in a weak bargaining position.

[18] *Object of Morality* (London, 1971).
[19] Ibid, p. 150.

3

Some More Non-perfectionist Approaches

In this chapter some more attempts at justifying egalitarianism without appealing to perfectionist considerations are examined and rejected.

1. The family argument

Some Christians have argued that we should treat human beings with equal respect because human beings are all equally children of God. There is a secular analogy of this argument. According to this argument—which I shall call the family argument—human beings all belong to a common family. Even if there is no God, the common father of all human beings, we are all related by being members of the human species, and so we have obligations to each other that we do not have to members of other species. This view bypasses perfectionist considerations; it is not asserted that human beings are intrinsically superior to animals, it is just that human beings have special obligations and loyalties to people who are members of the human family (Bernard Williams seems to subscribe to some such view).[1] This explains why even idiots have a right to be respected in a way that animals do not—we eat animals but we do not eat idiots. Now there is some force in this argument, and the problem is to find out how much force. Can it really bypass perfectionist considerations?

It is true that you have special obligations to your children which you do not have to my children; other things being

[1] 'Persons, Character, and Morality', in *Identities of Persons*, ed. A. Rorty (London, 1976), pp. 197–216.

equal you have greater duty towards your child than towards mine. And to justify this view one need not appeal to perfectionist considerations and make the absurd assumption that your child has greater intrinsic worth than mine. It is just that you have certain special relations with your child. Now what is wrong with extending this family argument from your individual family to the family of all human beings? We all belong to the human family and so have special relations with members of the human species which we do not have with members of other species, and this explains why animals are outside the egalitarian club, whereas children and idiots are members of it. In this way egalitarianism between human beings but not between human beings and animals can be defended without appealing to perfectionism.

What are we to make of this argument? One problem with this argument is that different people may have different ideas of what constitutes the relevant family. Some people may agree that they have special relations with some individuals, but they may claim that they have closer ties with animals in their vicinity than with human beings in remote lands. A Briton may say he has closer ties with a British dog than with a foreigner living abroad. Why not divide the family geographically rather than biologically, so that a British dog is part of the British family but the Japanese human is not? To say that family is by definition a biological rather than a geographical concept does not solve the problem but only shifts it. In estimating our special obligations why should more importance be attached to biological considerations than to considerations of geographical nearness? Some people do enjoy closer relationships with animals in their neighbourhood than with human beings in distant lands. Even if the above difficulty is solved there are other problems facing the egalitarian who uses the family argument. The egalitarian who does not extend his egalitarianism to include animals has to show not only why animals should be given lower status than human beings; he has also to show why there should be egalitarianism between human beings. Now even if the family argument can show why animals should get less consideration from us than human beings (later we shall see that the family argument, when supplemented by the argument from sympathy, may be able to show this), can the family argument show why we should give equal consideration to all human beings? Even within the class of human beings, the family argument can be narrowed down to apply with greater force to only a sub-class of human beings. Racists may argue that they have special obligations to members of their own race. Racism of the kind that Hitler and Mussolini believed in rests on false empirical assumptions about difference in race, and so it could be rejected; but we could, without appealing to falsehoods, narrow the family argument by appealing to special ties that we have with members of our own nation, province, or tribe. So instead of supporting egalitarianism, may the family argument not be used to support nationalism, provincialism, or tribalism? Thus a British chauvinist may say that as a result of a common culture and common history he has special relations with fellow Britons which he does not have with foreigners, and so his obligations to his fellow-Britons, who belong to the British family, are much stronger than his obligations to foreigners. So he may argue that he wants to apply the doctrine of egalitarianism not between all human beings but only within a narrower class of human beings. And he would do this without an appeal to perfectionism; he would not postulate that his own countrymen are intrinsically superior to foreigners, indeed he could grant that some of his best friends are foreigners, even coloured foreigners, it is just that he has special obligations to his fellow countrymen in virtue of having special ties with his fellow countrymen. So how does the egalitarian who resorts to the family argument deal with such problems?

What are we to make of such difficulties? It might be thought that this is not a *reductio ad absurdum* of the family argument, but rather it shows the limitations of egalitarianism. It is perfectly acceptable to take the line that we have special obligations to fellow countrymen. But now what becomes of egalitarianism between all human beings? Do we just abandon it? Now it seems to me that this will not do. There are some positive obligations such as giving food to the poor and it makes sense to argue that other things being equal one's positive obligations to one's own countrymen are greater, just as your obligations to give food to your child is much greater than any obligation that you may have to give food to my child other things being equal. But there are certain duties that you have even to my child, and the most striking cases of such duties are the negative duties such as the duty not to kill my child. Similarly even if Britons have special obligations to members of the British family (to all Britons) they still have negative duties to all foreigners—for instance, they should not kill a peaceful foreigner even when the foreigner is outside British soil. Suppose a Briton goes abroad and kills a foreigner, he has taken a human life which is very wrong. Moreover, the wrong he has done is a wrong to the foreigner; it is the foreigner's right to life which is the ground of our duty not to kill him. And now we are back with the problem of why it is morally wrong to kill a peaceful (human) foreigner, but it is not wrong to kill a peaceful lamb or cow. Do we not have to appeal to perfectionist considerations, such as that human life has greater intrinsic worth than animal life, that human beings are more wonderful creatures than animals?

It might be replied that the family argument can explain why it is wrong to kill a foreigner in a foreign land but not wrong to kill an animal. A foreigner is part of the human family, a Briton has closer family links with fellow Britons than he has with the foreigner, but he still has family links with the latter that are closer than his links with animals, and this explains why it is wrong to kill the foreigner but not wrong to kill the animal. But in that case should it not be more wrong for him to kill a fellow-Briton than it is for him to kill a foreigner? For a fellow Briton is more closely related to him than the foreigner is. The family argument does have this consequence but perhaps this consequence is not so absurd as it looks. Or is it? To go back to the individual family, if you kill your innocent child you would (according to the family argument) do a wrong because your child is a member of the human family, and this reason will be there even if you were to kill someone else's innocent child. But in the case of your killing your own child, there is an added wrong that you would have done, namely having killed your own child. Similarly, in the case of killing an innocent compatriot you (a Briton) would have done a special wrong over and above the wrong of killing a member of the human species, for you have killed someone with whom you had a special relationship, the relationship of belonging to the British family. And so (according to the family argument) what you have done is, other things being equal, worse than if you had killed an innocent foreginer living in a remote land, which is not to deny that it is very wrong to kill such a foreigner.

To many of us the family argument is more powerful in the case of positive obligations, such as giving food to the poor. Other things being equal, people have greater obligation to feed the poor in their own country than in some remote country. In the case of negative duties or prohibitions, such as 'do not kill', the family argument may be less powerful. Even if it is an added wrong to kill a fellow countryman it could be argued that the major or primary wrong is to kill a human being and this primary wrong is just as much present when you kill a foreigner in a remote country as when you kill a fellow countryman. Some people would disagree with this and argue that there is something especially terrible about killing a fellow countryman, and that the evil involved in killing a human being is *relatively* unimportant, compared to the special evil involved in killing one's fellow countryman. But there would be fairly general agreement that there is one important evil in common to the killings in these two instances, namely that in both cases you have killed a human being and this is very wrong. In both cases you have violated your duty not to kill, a duty which you owe to all human beings, except to those who have forfeited their right to life.

But we must not digress. The important point is that the family argument cannot solve all the problems facing the egalitarian. For the family argument could be used to give greater consideration to the interests of those human beings with whom our family links are closer. And even if this is not obviously inconsistent with egalitarianism it cannot provide the grounds of the doctrine of equal considerations and respect between all human beings. Perhaps the view that there are certain rights held equally by all human beings has to be defended, if it can be defended at all, in a different way. For in the case of the family argument our duties to a human being seem to depend upon certain relations we happen to have with him, whereas the doctrine of rights would require that at least some of our duties are owed to him in virtue of something objective about the person himself. For instance, we must not kill a foreigner, not simply because the foreigner has certain relations with us, but because he has certain rights, such as the right to life; these rights set moral constraints within which the family argument operates, so these constraints themselves cannot be derived from family considerations. The idea of rights setting constraints for the operation of family considerations can be illustrated by an example. The British Government has special relations with the British people and it is quite in order for it to care more for the interests of the British people than for the interests of foreigners; indeed, its primary task is to care for its people. But this does not mean that it should pursue these interests whatever the costs to foreigners; in particular, it must not violate the legitimate rights of foreigners living in other countries. And so we are still left with problems such as what justifies the doctrine that all human beings have a right to respect and consideration and why animals should get less consideration than human beings. The doctrine of egalitarianism, if valid, sets certain constraints within which the family argument operates; so the family argument cannot provide the grounds for such egalitarianism.

Another limitation of the family argument is this. Suppose you come across a member of another species, such as a dolphin or a Martian, who has rationality, self-consciousness, ability to plan its life, and autonomy, as much as human beings have. It would be quite wrong to kill such a creature (assuming that it is peaceful and not attacking us) even if it did not belong to the human species, to the human family. And how can the family argument justify the view that it is wrong to kill such a creature but it is not wrong to kill an animal such as a lamb or a cow, who lacks self-consciousness, autonomy, and so forth? Our family ties are not closer with the Martian; indeed our family ties may be closer with the cow with whom we at least share a common ancestor in the remote past. The view that the rational Martian has greater rights than a lamb or cow will have to be defended, if it can be defended at all, by appealing to other considerations; and will not these considerations involve an appeal to perfectionist considerations, for instance that a creature with certain traits or potential traits such as autonomy, self-consciousness, ability to plan its life, is a superior creature to one who lacks such capacities?

To acknowledge the limitations of the family argument is not to deny that family considerations are important. They do generate some important special duties; for instance, we have special duties to members of our family and this could apply even if the family is extended to include the whole species. Thus if some human beings are starving in Ethiopia and some rational Martians (or rational dolphins) are starving, it is plausible to argue that, other things being equal, our duty to fellow humans is greater, for they are linked by family ties to us, closer than the family ties that we may have with members of other species, however rational and autonomous the latter may be. But for reasons given earlier the family argument does not succeed in solving all the relevant problems. The family argument will have to be combined with other considerations, such as considerations of rights, if it is to do justice to our egalitarian intuitions. Later we shall see in outline the relations between family considerations and certain other considerations, such as considerations of sympathy and considerations of human rights.

I have as yet not discussed the Christian version of the family argument, which is really a metaphysical-cum-perfectionist arguement. On this view every human being has equal right to respect and consideration because every human being is equally the child of God; and the egalitarian doctrine does not extend to animals because animals are not children of God. This doctrine is metaphysical for it presupposes talk of God and of children of God. It is also, at least in one important version of it, a perfectionist doctrine. The reason why you must not kill another human being is not that he is related to you but that he is a child of God and there is something wonderful or sacred about being a child of God. No doubt since you are also a child of God, you are related to other human beings, but that is not the real justification of your obligation to other human beings; the real justification is that the other human being is a close relation of God and of Christ. Thus Christ says 'In as much as you have done it unto one of my brethren you have done it unto me' (Matthew 25: 40).

Here Christ is stressing that what is important is that human beings are related to Him; the fact that they are also related to you (who have duties towards His brethren) is relatively unimportant. Now this view escapes certain pitfalls of the secular version of the family argument. For instance, on the secular version we saw that you have duties to foreigners, because you belong to the same family. And it was pointed out that on this view it is not clear why you should not give much greater respect and consideration to those who are more closely related to you, even to the point of sacrificing the interests of those who are more distant relations of yours. The Christian version of the family argument can deal with such problems because according to it the important thing, from the point of view of your obligations, is not how closely a given human being is related to you, but how he is related to God; and if all human beings are equally children of God, it makes sense to argue that they are equally worthy of respect and consideration.

The major problem that many of us find with the Christian version of the family argument is that we find it difficult to accept the metaphysics that is presupposed by it. The secular version of the family argument is free of the metaphysics that is presupposed by the Christian version; in Part II of this book we shall see how it can be combined with and constrained by the doctrine of rights, which itself presupposes perfectionist and metaphysical considerations. So though the secular version of the family argument does not itself presuppose perfectionist and metaphysical considerations, it is constrained by a doctrine that presupposes such considerations and so it cannot enable us to bypass such considerations.

During the rest of this book references to the family argument are, unless otherwise stated, to the secular version of this argument.

2. Sympathy and equality

Let us turn to another related attempt to justify the principle of equal respect and consideration, without resort to perfectionist considerations. This is the argument from sympathy and sentiments. It is said that human beings are so made that they can sympathise with other human beings, they can put themselves into the shoes of other human beings, and see the world from their point of view. We can sympathize with fellow human beings in a way that we cannot with animals and this helps to explain (does it also justify?) why we extend the principles of equal respect and consideration to human beings but not to animals.

Now many people do sympathize with animals and so it is not clear why we should leave animals out of the egalitarian club. Or is it that sympathy for animals when it is as strong as sympathy for fellow human beings, is unnatural, it is against human nature? But in that case we seem to be bringing in perfectionist considerations though the back door. For this view of human nature cannot be justified simply by appealing to empirical considerations. The counter-examples to this view have to be explained away by appealing to perfectionist considerations, for instance that though some human beings feel just as much sympathy for animals as they do for some human beings, such sympathy is a degenerate sort of sympathy.

It may be said that since other human beings resemble us much more than animals do, it is only natural that we sympathize more with them than with, say, dogs. Some such view is implicit in Hume: 'All human creatures are related to us by resemblance. Their persons . . . must strike us in a lively manner and produce an emotion similar to the original one.'[2] Some such view can explain why we feel sympathy even with the idiot, more than with the animal. For the idiot shares with us human form, he is born of human parents, even though he does not have the relevant capacities. Again, some such view could explain why we feel more sympathy for the rational Martian than for animals for the former resembles us in possessing capacities such as rationality, self-consciousness, and autonomy even though he does not share with us human form. Animals such as lambs and cows neither resemble us (as much as the idiot does) in their external appearance, nor resemble us in possessing the relevant capacities such as autonomy (as the rational Martian does), and hence they are given lower status than idiots and the rational Martian. Some such

[2] *Treatise of Human Nature,* ed. L. A. Selby-Brigge (Oxford, 1888), Bk. 2, Part 2, section 7.

view can also explain why the bees and ants are given even lower status than dolphins and monkeys, for the latter resemble us more than the former do. Such considerations can also explain (if not justify) why we regard infanticide with greater horror than abortion; we have more sympathy for the infant with whom we are acquainted than with the unseen foetus. So there is considerable force in this argument from sympathy (especially as a device to explain many of our views), but the argument is in need of supplementation. It does not by itself solve all the relevant problems that face the doctrine of equal respect for all human beings.

The view that it is only natural for us to sympathize with our fellow human beings is rather like the family argument—it is only natural that I should sympathize more with members of the human family since I myself am a member of it. And the difficulties that were pointed out in the way of using the family argument to support the doctrine of equal respect apply *mutatis mutandis* to this argument from sympathy. For instance, we sympathize more with some human beings than with others, and so it is not clear why considerations of sympathy should support the doctrine of equal respect and consideration.

Hume, though not concerned to justify the doctrine of equal respect, was aware of similar problems with his view that our sympathy was connected with our judgements of moral praise and blame. If we make judgements of praise and blame just from our own point of view, reflecting the sympathy we feel, then we shall not be able to communicate effectively with others. Thus, since I feel less sympathy for the victims of a tyrant in a distant nation, if I say that therefore such a tyrant is not so blameworthy as the tyrant nearer home, with whose victims I feel greater sympathy, then I cannot expect to communicate effectively with people who are situated near the victims of the tyrant who is very distant from me. So, according to Hume, the need to communicate effectively with others causes us to correct our judgements of moral praise and blame, so that we do not make such judgements from our own private points of view, but from a public impartial point of view.

Now could not similar considerations explain why considerations of sympathy, corrected by our need to communicate with fellow human beings, should lead us to believe in the doctrine of equal respect and considerations for all human beings? For if we insisted that human beings are more deserving of respect when they are closer to us then we would not be able to make ourselves understood to those human beings who are situated further away from us and who sympathize much more with a different set of individuals. A similar argument may be used to try to save the family argument from the charge that it leads to greater respect being given to some human beings than to others.

But this does not solve all the problems for the principle of equal respect. If we believe that our obligation to respect a person arises from his right to be respected, then there is the problem of the justification of such a right. If we say that a human being has a right to *equal* respect but an animal does not, then there is the problem of what justifies such a view. If we appeal to the argument from sympathy, then the existence of the right to equal respect becomes dependent upon the existence of certain human sentiments. And even if these human sentiments are very deeply rooted in human nature, they are still a contingent fact about human nature. Can the right to equal respect be a fundamental right and yet depend upon something outside itself? On a right-based theory rights are the ground of our duties. Compare: if our duty not to kill others is based solely on a command of God not to kill others, then the rights that human beings acquire not to be killed are in a sense not fundamental, they are not the ground of our duty not to kill them. Similarly, if our duty to respect human beings equally arises from human sentiments, then the right of people to equal respect is not fundamental but derivative, and such rights are not the ground of our duty to respect them equally. This point by itself only shows that the fundamental right to equal respect could not be defended by the argument from sympathy. It does not necessarily invalidate the doctrine of equal respect for all human beings. One might believe in equal respect for all human beings, without grounding this on the right of people to equal respect; one might simply 'ground' it in human sentiments. So even if the argument from sympathy cannot support the fundamental right of all human beings to equal respect, may it not still support the doctrine of equal respect? The view that human beings should be respected equally does not entail that equal respect is owed to every human being. The latter view entails that people have a right to equal respect, but the former view does not.

But there are difficulties facing the argument from sympathy, even if it is used only to defend the doctrine of equal respect of human beings, without being used to defend the doctrine of the fundamental right of human beings to equal respect. For instance, there are weaknesses in the Hume-like defence of the argument from sympathy that I discussed earlier. It is true that we need to look at things from a public point of view, but we could do this, for instance, by confining equal respect to a narrow class of human beings, such as members of one's own tribe, or country or élite. Now it may be objected, but in that case how would we communicate with people outside our narrow group? This objection is not difficult to answer. If we appeal to perfectionist considerations and claim that members of our group are intrinsically superior to those outsiders, then that is a view we can hardly expect other people to understand unless we point out some relevant respects in which members of our group are superior to outsiders. But if we just appeal to the fact that members of our group are a kind of family, tied together by ties of mutual sentiment and sympathy, and that such sympathy is much weaker between members of this group and outsiders, then there is nothing unintelligible in the view that members of this group respect each other in a way that they do not respect outsiders. No doubt outsiders may ask us to come out of our shell, but there is nothing unintelligible in the view that we want to stick to our group. It may be objected that there are moral constraints that we must not violate in pursuit of the interests of the members of our group; for instance, we must respect the rights of outsiders. But now we are back to problems such as, why must we extend the doctrine of right to equal respect to all human beings, but not to animals? How can such a view be defended without appealing to perfectionist considerations, such as that human beings are more wonderful creatures and have more intrinsic worth than animals? If we reject an appeal to such perfectionist considerations it is not clear why the egalitarian club must include all the members of the human race; why could it not just include only a sub-class of all human beings?

There are two related problems here: first, why the doctrine of equal respect should apply to all human beings; secondly, what justifies the view that we have a duty not to kill a peaceful human being, whether or not he is a member of our group, but we do not have a similar duty not to kill an animal. The argument from sympathy, as well as the family argument, may succeed in answering this second problem by appealing to the fact that human beings are tied to each other by closer ties of family and sympathy than they are tied to animals. But now the first problem is not easy to solve. For human beings have closer ties within groups than across groups, and so why should they not sacrifice interests of other groups of human beings for the interests of their own group, somewhat as they are willing to sacrifice animal interests for human interests? If we take the line that the pursuit of the interests of our group have to take place within certain moral constraints (such as that we must not trample on the legitimate rights of our group) then there is the problem of whether we can spell out those moral constraints without appealing to perfectionist considerations.

The argument from sympathy can supplement the family argument and the two together can form a powerful argument. Some of the defects of the family argument could be partially remedied if it were supplemented by the argument from sympathy. For instance, we saw that the family argument could not explain what was wrong about killing a peaceful rational Martian. The argument from sympathy, however, can explain why we feel revulsion at killing the rational Martian; for the latter resembles us in important respects and so elicits our sympathy, in a way that ordinary animals do not.

But the argument from sympathy has one important limitation, whether it is used separately or in conjunction with the family argument. The argument from sympathy at best helps to explain why something is regarded as immoral, but it does not explain why it should be regarded as unjust. In Hume's moral system, sympathy played a large part, but Hume believed that the sphere of justice was different from the sphere where humanity or kindness predominates. He

SYMPATHY AND EQUALITY   51

believed that justice only applies if there is rough equality of power between the parties. In our dealings with animals he thought that our compassion and kindness provide the sole checks on our behaviour towards them for they have very little power compared to us; so Hume believed that cruelty to animals, and other wrongs with regard to animals, may constitute immoralities but not injustices. Our sympathy for the victim cannot explain that an injustice is done to the victim. Hume believed that it is only among people who are roughly equal that justice obtains. His doctrines clearly cannot explain what is unjust about killing some rational Martians or some rational members of a weaker species, who have substantially fewer powers than us. And Hume was wrong in thinking that justice presupposes the existence of rough equality between the relevant parties–his view would imply that where slaves are in a weak position *vis-à-vis* the masters, slavery is not unjust. But he was right in his view that where our relations are governed by sympathy and humanity, such sympathy and humanity cannot explain how we can act unjustly towards each other. The fact that we feel sympathy for the rational Martians or for a peaceful foreigner (because they resemble us in the relevant respects) can at best explain why it would be regarded as immoral or unkind to kill them; it cannot explain why such killing should be regarded as unjust. So we are still left with problems such as why is it unjust to kill the weak rational Martians or peaceful foreigners living in remote lands, but not unjust to kill animals? And why is it unjust to kill the rational Martian even though we have no family ties with him? Is it not because he has certain rights, such as the right to life? And what are the features in virtue of which he has rights, such as the right to life?

3. Equality with animals

Let us now turn to a more radical solution of the problem confronting the doctrine of equal respect and consideration. One of the chief problems facing this doctrine is how, without appealing to perfectionist considerations, we can justify the view that the doctrine of equal respect and consideration should be extended to all human beings but not to all sentient beings, including ants and bees. One radical way of dissolving this problem would be to say that the doctrine should indeed be extended to include all sentient creatures. As Bentham said, the important thing is not whether animals can reason and talk but whether they can suffer. Now it is certainly plausible to contend that suffering is an evil wherever it is found, whether among human beings or among animals. But if one is worried primarily about suffering and the like, it is difficult to account fully for our duty not to kill. Bentham thought that it is all right to kill animals when they are killed suddenly and painlessly, for animals do not have pains of apprehension from the fear of being killed in the future and because they are likely to have a more painful death if they die a natural death than if they are killed by human beings. But if suffering is what primarily worries us, then why not go in for a policy of selective (human) infanticide? Human infants do not suffer from the pains of anticipation. So why not kill some infants, who are going to suffer because of over-population and poverty? By killing them painlessly we can put an end to their future suffering, as well as making life more comfortable for others who survive in this overcrowded planet. True, the parents of many of the infants will suffer a lot if we killed their infants, but this does not explain what is really wrong with a system of killing infants only when the parents of the infant consent. In any case, is not what is really wrong with infanticide the fact that a wrong has been done to the infant? Any suffering caused to the parents is only an additional wrong. And how can a Benthamite utilitarian explain the fact that a wrong is done to the infant who is killed? (Elsewhere in this book other related arguments concerning the rights of infants are examined.)

True, utilitarians believe not only in reducing evil, but also in promoting the good, which includes things like pleasure. But even so, it is difficult to adequately explain why we should not take life (see chapter 8).

If we take a thoroughgoing utilitarian line, then an individual, whether a human being or an animal, is a mere means to the production of utility. Though it is true that the individual's own good will be taken into account in making the final moral calculations, the individual's interests and his life can be sacrificed when such sacrifices lead to a net gain in utility.

Critics of utilitarianism such as Nozick and Ronald Dworkin rightly point out that in our dealings with human beings the pursuit of utilitarian goals is subject to certain moral constraints. That is part of what is implied by the Kantian view that human beings should be treated as ends and not merely as a means; for if there are no moral checks to the pursuit of the utilitarian goal, then human beings are treated merely as a means to the promotion of the utilitarian goal. The doctrine that human beings have a right to equal respect, can if appropriately interpreted, help to provide the relevant moral constraints on the pursuit of utilitarian goals. Now if the principle of equal respect and consideration is to be extended to animals, are animals also to be treated as ends in themselves and not merely as a means to the promotion of utilitarian goals? But if so, we are entitled to ask what are the grounds of the principle of equal respect. If the answer is given in terms of the capacity for suffering and the capacity for enjoying the good (such as pleasure), then we are faced with problems such as why should not those with greater capacity for the good not get greater consideration? Could this not lead to inequalities among human beings.

Also, the idea that the doctrine of equal respect and consideration should be extended to include all sentient beings involves strange results. The view that the interests of sentient beings other than human beings should be given some weight does not seem strange, but the view that the interests of ants and bees should be given equal consideration to the interests of human beings seems very radical indeed. On the other hand, if we do not extend the doctrine of equal respect and consideration to all sentient creatures, we are still left with problems such as what are the grounds of excluding some sentient creatures such as ants and bees from the egalitarian club? And is it possible to avoid answering such a question without appealing to perfectionist considerations, for instance that human beings in virtue of certain capacities and potential are more wonderful creatures, have more intrinsic worth, than ants and bees. Some philosophers want to extend egalitarianism to include animals, at any rate the higher animals, because they are impressed by the fact that the higher animals have at least as good claims for equality of consideration as human babies and idiots. For instance, many higher animals are not less rational than idiots and babies. Later we shall see that there are special considerations that can explain why idiots get a better deal from us than animals do. As for (human) babies, there is the argument that though they are not as yet any more rational than animals, they have potential for leading a significant life that animals lack. We shall examine this idea later.

There are at least two kinds of egalitarianism worth distin-guishing. There is one kind of egalitarianism which is com-patible even with a full-blooded utilitarian theory. Thus if you believe, as Bentham did, that pleasure is the only intrinsic good and pain the only intrinsic evil, and that actions are justified by their consequence, you could be an egalitarian in the sense that you attach the same moral weight to pain and pleasure, irrespective of the status of the individual who has them. The intrinsic evil of a pain does not vary whether the individual who has the pain is a prince or a pauper. Indeed on this view pain is just as much of an intrinsic evil even when it is found among animals. *If* in a particular case a dog suffers as much as a human being does, then for a Benthamite utili-tarian, the intrinsic evil involved in the two cases is the same. So such utilitarianism involves a kind of equality between human beings and animals. But there is another kind of egali-tarianism which is more connected with right-based theories. On this view all human beings have an equal right to respect and consideration. On an extreme version of this theory, no person's rights should be sacrificed for utilitarian considera-tion; on less moderate versions of this theory, such right-based considerations have to be balanced against utilitarian consi-derations; sometimes the utilitarian considerations may out-weigh the right-based considerations, at other times right-based considerations may outweigh utilitarian ones. The moderate version is implicit in some of H. L. A. Hart's writings.[3] Thus Hart believes that an individual has a right not to be punished unless he commits a crime and so gives society a licence to punish him; such rights are not derived from utilitarian con-siderations, but Hart admits that sometimes when a lot of utility is at stake, an innocent individual's right not to be

---

[3] See *Punishment and Responsibility* (Oxford, 1968).

punished may be overridden by utilitarian considerations. The extreme version is found in the writings of philosophers such as Kant and Rawls. Unlike Hart, Kant does not allow us to punish an innocent man even when that is necessary to prevent a social catastrophe. Rawls too takes this extreme view when he says 'Each person possesses an inviolability founded on justice that even the welfare of society as a whole cannot override'.[4] The reason why such views are egalitarian in an important sense is that the right not to be sacrificed for utilitarian goals is supposed to be possessed by 'each person'. Now such egalitarianism, at any rate in its more extreme version, is difficult to extend to animals; most people would allow a dog to be sacrificed if such a sacrifice were the only way of averting a social catastrophe. Of course, extreme positions such as those of Kant are difficult to accept even with regard to human beings! Would many people agree with Kant in rejecting the Pharisaic maxim according to which it is better that one (innocent) man should die than that the whole people should perish? But what about the more moderate thesis which allows rights to be overridden in some cases by utilitarian considerations? Could not animals, at least the higher animals, possess rights that have to be balanced against utilitarian considerations?

Many people would admit that animals do have a right to consideration. What is much more doubtful is that they have an *equal* right to consideration compared to human beings. At any rate, as I said earlier, even if egalitarianism is extended to include the higher animals, it is difficult to avoid an appeal to perfectionist considerations; how else can we exclude ants and bees from the egalitarian club?

4. Rights and some conceptual requirements

I shall in this section (and in chapter 6, section 3) examine some arguments which claim that there is a conceptual connection between the grounds of rights and the possession of rights. If such arguments are correct, then we could bypass an appeal to perfectionism. But I shall contend that such arguments do not work.

[4] *A Theory of Justice*, p. 3.

Philosophers who argue that there is a conceptual connection between the grounds of rights and the existence of rights, imply that they can give the grounds of rights without appealing to perfectionist considerations. Michael Tooley, for example, has argued that there is a conceptual connection between the possession of a right and the capacity to have the corresponding desire.[5] He illustrates his point by considering the right to life. The right to life he thinks can only be possessed by those who satisfy certain conceptual requirements. He does not assert that those who satisfy such requirements (such as adult human beings and perhaps some grown-up animals) are intrinsically superior to those (such as infants, including human infants) who do not satisfy them; so he does not appeal to perfectionist considerations. It is just that some individuals satisfy the relevant requirements, while others do not. In the case of the right to life he points out that an individual cannot possess the right to life unless it is the case, or was at some point in the past, that the individual is capable of envisaging a future for itself and of having desires about that future, is capable of possessing the concept of a continuing subject of experiences and other mental states, is itself such an entity, and possesses self-consciousness, or at least the capacity for self-consciousness. Human infants do not satisfy the above requirements, while human adults do, and so Tooley allows infanticide. Tooley has to face the problem as to why we should accept the above requirements. His answer is that there is a connection between the above requirements and the capacity to have the desire to live. Those who do not satisfy one or more of the above requirements do not have the capacity to have the deisre to live. And he believes that there is a conceptual connection between having the right to life and having the corresponding desire. But what is there to be said in favour of the view that there is this conceptual connection? Tooley answers in a utilitarian vein that his

basic intuition is that a right is something that can be violated and that, in general, violation of an individual's right to something involves frustrating the corresponding desire. Suppose for example that you own a car. The I am under a *prima facie* obligation not to take it from you.

[5] 'A Defence of Abortion and Infanticide', in *The Problem of Abortion*, ed. J. Feinberg (Belmont, 1973), pp. 51–91.

However, the obligation is not unconditional; it depends in part upon the existence of a corresponding desire in you. If you do not care whether I take your car then I generally do not violate your right by doing so.[6]

Now Tooley's argument does not succeed. There are two claims worrth distinguishing. Firstly, there is the view that a person who has a right to x can release others from their correlative obligations to him by saying 'I do not want x' or 'I do not care about x.' Secondly, there is the view that an individual's right to x would not exist unless he had a corresponding desire for x or the capacity for such desire. Even if the first claim is true, the second is not, and the second claim does not follow from the first. It seems to me that the reason why my professed indifference about x can be taken as releasing you from your obligation to me with regard to x, is that I may be taken as tacitly consenting to releasing you from your obligation to me. Somewhat as a nod from me can in certain contexts be taken as releasing you from your obligation to me, so also my professed indifference can be taken as releasing you from your obligation to me. In order to release you from your obligation to me, I do not have to explicitly say 'I release you from my obligation to me.'

Some philosophers such as Locke have argued that there are certain rights that a person has, which he does not have the moral power to waive. Thus Locke thought that a person's right to life was such that he could not release others from their correlative duty not to kill him; if he gave others his consent to their killing him, such consent would be morally void.

But even if it is the case that an individual's consent can release others from their obligation towards him, it does not follow that an individual could not have rights unless he had the corresponding desires, or that others would not have correlative obligations towards him unless he had the corresponding desires.

If I am indifferent to whether you take my car, but do not tell you that I am indifferent, you still have a duty that you owe me not to take my car. I shall not exercise my right to exclude you from the use of my car, for if I did that would tend to show that I did care after all and was not

[6] Ibid., p. 60.

indifferent. But my right to exclude you from the use of my car does not disappear merely because I do not exercise that right; unless my silence or my indifference on the matter is taken to show consent for your using the car, in which case it is really my consent that has extinguished your obligations, not my indifference or my silence. My indifference or silence is relevant only if it is taken as evidence of my consent.[7]

Now in the case of infants, though it is true that they do not have the requisite desire to live, it is not the case that they are indifferent to whether or not they live. Even the state of being indifferent to whether or not they live is something quite beyond infants; since they do not know anything about what life is, they cannot be indifferent to it. Their lack of desire to live is neither evidence of their indifference to live, nor of their desire not to live. All such desires are too sophisticated for them. Anyway, the important point is that they do not consent to waive their right to life. And Tooley's analogy with the car case is quite inadequate. In my view, in the car case, my indifference should only be considered relevant because it is taken to imply consent. The infant, however, cannot consent to be killed. The fact that the infant does not have the desire to live is not evidence for the view that the infant consents to release others from their obligation not to kill him.

Tooley's theory of rights is really a utilitarian theory of rights. For according to it the basic reason why it is wrong to violate a person's rights is that this involves frustration of the right-holder's desires. Now one trouble with such a theory is that it does not do justice to the idea that rights set constraints within which utilitarian and other teleological policies may be pursued. According to right-based theories, rights set constraints on the pursuit of utility and so rights must not be derived from utilitarian considerations, for if they were so derived they would not be able to perform their function of setting moral limits within which utilitarian policies may be pursued.

Nor does Tooley's theory offer any adequate solution to the problem of what we should do when different rights con-

[7] See V. Haksar, 'The Nature of Rights', *Archiv für Rechts- und Sozialphilosophie*, lxiv (1978), 183-204.

flict, for instance when an animal's right to life conflicts with a human being's right to life. I suspect that at least in the case of some of these conflict situations we shall have to appeal to perfectionist considerations, for instance that human beings are more wonderful creatures than animals are, and this would serve as the rationale for our giving our limited food to human beings who are starving abroad rather than to dogs who are starving abroad; again, if there were limited space on a crowded raft, it would be morally preferable to sacrifice grown-up dogs rather than sacrifice human infants. Tooley's theory however would imply the opposite for he thinks that adult animals such as dogs have the requisite desire to live and so have the right to life, whereas human infants do not have the capacity to desire to live and so they do not have the right to life. The doctrine that all human beings have the right to equal respect and consideration is inconsistent with Tooley's theory. For since infants do not have the corresponding desire to be respected and to have their interests considered, on Tooley's theory it would follow that they do not have the right to equal respect and consideration.

It is worth making some cautionary remarks about the use of conceptual analysis in connection with talk of equal rights. Conceptual analysis of the kind that Tooley and others go in for has a clarificatory role to play; without it issues may remain even more obscure. But there is a danger that conceptual points may be regarded as more important than they are, more particularly there is a danger of begging certain substantial issues. Thus we might say that unless an individual satisfies condition x, it does not have rights. Now this might not matter, if rights did not matter. But to say that some individuals have rights while others do not, usually implies that where there is a conflict of interests those who have rights should get priority. What we must discuss is whether the presence or absence of x is really a relevant ground for giving such moral priority. Hegel believed that rights were conceptually connected with the possession (at least in potential form) of a will. He inferred that animals have no right to life, since they have no will to live.[8] This last conclusion is a

[8] Hegel, *Philosophy of Right,* transl. T. H. Knox (Oxford, 1967), Addition to para. 44.

substantial one. It allows us, for instance, to eat animals. Such substantial issues must not be decided merely by a discussion of the concept of right. Hegel, like Kant, thought that individuals who lacked will also lacked dignity and worth, and he thought of them somewhat in the way that we think of machines. But why must creatures with a will have a superior claim over creatures who do not have a will? Such substantial issues require unbiased discussion. Hegel does make some substantial points but his language of rights, with its conceptual connection with possession of will, is heavily biased. The substantial point that Hegel makes (or that is implicit in his work) is that animals do not have will, they are creatures of desires or instincts, without self-consciousness and autonomy; nor, unlike children do they have the potential for such characteristics. They do not and never will follow ends that they have set up themselves. He seems to regard them as we regard machines. Machines have no intrinsic worth but only serve the purposes of human beings. So, too, for Hegel animals have no intrinsic worth or dignity, but are instruments of their owners. Now one might object that animals, unlike machines, are sentient creatures, and does this not give them some claim to consideration? Such objections deserve to be treated seriously, but they are hardly likely to be seriously treated if we make conceptual connection between rights and the possession of a will, and then dismiss the claims of those who do not have a will.

Another philosopher who insists on certain conceptual requirements before an individual can be said to have rights, is Joel Feinberg.[9] Though he does not insist that only a creature with a will can have rights, he insists on certain other conceptual requirements that must be met. He asks, 'What kinds of beings can have rights?' and he seems to think that this question, boils down to the question, 'What sorts of beings then are conceptually appropriate subjects of rights?' He replies that it is a conceptual truth that only a creature with an interest can have rights. He then explains that 'interest' presupposes a rudimentary cognitive equipment, for interests are compounded of desires and aims.

[9] Introduction to *The Problem of Abortion*, and 'The Rights of Animals and Future Generations', in *Philosophy and the Environmental Crisis*, ed. W. Blackstone.

Feinberg's view is that newly-born infants and foetuses do not possess rights proper but only contingent rights. A contingent right is a right that will come into existence if and when the required conditions are fulfilled. Feinberg thinks that foetuses 'lacking actual wants and beliefs, have no actual interest in being born, and it is difficult to think of any other reason for ascribing any rights to them other than on the assumption that they will in fact be born'.[10] The rights of the foetus, according to Feinberg, are contingent upon the assumption that it will in fact develop into a creature that has interests. For similar reasons, Feinberg grants that newly-born infants have no non-contingent rights; for they lack the 'rudimentary intellectual equipment necessary for the possession of interests'.[11] It follows from Feinberg's views that if you kill a foetus or a newly-born infant, you have not violated anyone's right to life. On the other hand if you do not kill it but only maim it, then you may well have violated its right—for it will develop into a creature that has rights (once it acquires the necessary intellectual equipment and possesses an 'interest')— and by maiming it now, you are violating its future right to consideration. But of course if you kill it before it has acquired non-contingent rights, then it will not acquire any non-contingent rights, and so you can safely kill it without violating its rights.

Some legal systems do imply that foetuses have a non-contingent right to be born. Feinberg would say that such systems are involved in a conceptual muddle. He gives the example of the hospital patient who refused to take blood transfusion even though she was warned that she and her unborn child might die without the transfusion. The Supreme Court of New Jersey ordered in this case that the patient must receive the transfusion on the grounds that the 'unborn child is entitled to the law's protection'.[12] Feinberg expresses surprise that in such cases no one seems ever to have found that idea (of an unconditional right to be born) conceptually absurd.

In fact such ideas are not absurd. We should beware of

---

[10] 'The Rights of Animals and Future Generations', p. 64.
[11] Ibid., p. 62.
[12] Quoted ibid., p. 65.

bringing in talk of conceptual absurdity, for such talk tends to block the discussion of substantial issues. If a foetus is not the sort of being that can have a right to be born, and since rights trump non-rights, it would follow that the mother's right to life or health should get preference over the foetus's life, in cases on conflict. Such substantial and controversial conclusions may sometimes be correct but we should beware of defining our terms (intentionally or unintentionally) in a way that is loaded in favour of certain substantial views.

Talk of conceptual absurdity also gives us the illusion of bypassing perfectionist considerations. Thus Feinberg does not assert that the foetus or the newly-born infant is an inferior creature compared to creatures who have rights; it is just that it is not the sort of creature that has any interests.

The substantial issues that need discussion are issues such as why individuals who have an already functioning cognitive apparatus (such as adult human beings and adult animals) should get priority over sentient creatures, such as foetuses or newly-born infants, who do not. Why should the life of the foetus be sacrificed when that is necessary for the health of the mother? There is a danger that talk of conceptual absurdity would beg such substantial issues. There is a genuine problem of how much weight should be given to the claims of sentient creatures who do not have even the rudimentary cognitive apparatus and so do not possess 'interests' in Feinberg's sense. Feinberg's stipulation would tend to disenfranchise such creatures, and it may make us relatively cavalier about pain caused to such creatures, expecially when such pain is necessary to promote the interests of some individuals. For do not creatures with an interest get moral priority over those without an interest?

Later in the book we shall see that there are other philosophers, such as Hart and Benn, who also insist on certain conceptual requirements that must be satisfied before an individual can be said to possess rights. I want to contrast their views with my own, so the discussion of their views will be postponed until my own positive views have been explained.

PART II

THE FOUNDATIONS OF EQUALITY:
A PERFECTIONIST APPROACH

4

Some Perfectionist Presuppositions, and Idiots

1. Some perfectionist presuppositions of egalitarianism

The second part of this book attempts to unearth some of the presuppositions of some of our egalitarian moral beliefs. Of course what the presuppositions are may vary with what the moral beliefs are whose presuppositions we are trying to find out. So before attempting to discover the presuppositions let us outline at least roughly the moral beliefs whose presuppositions we are looking for.

Many people believe that there are certain rights held equally by all human beings. A prime example of such a right is the right to life. We have a duty not to kill a human being even when he is not related to us in virtue of some contractual tie, or in virtue of belonging to a common tribe or nation. Moreover many of us believe that this duty not to kill a foreigner is owed to the foreigner, it is the foreigner's right to life which is the ground of our duty not to kill him. This view can be contrasted with the view some people may hold, according to which we have a duty not to kill others simply because God has commanded us; if God commands us to kill others, it shall be our duty to kill others, however peaceful these others are. Many of us also believe that we can sacrifice animal interests for the sake of furthering our national interests, but that we must not sacrifice the rights of individual human beings (and of their groups) living abroad (such as their right to life) in order to further our national interests. Even though we believe that animal interests do count for something, many of us think that, other things being equal, they count for less than human beings even when the human beings are infants or foreigners living in remote lands. Many of us would allow political principle to give less weight to the interests of animals than to those of human infants or to those of foreigners. And many of us believe that if there are beings in other planets who are not members of the human species but who have rationality, autonomy, self-consciousness, and so forth, in the way that human beings have, then such creatures have a right to life. Now let us examine some of the presuppositions of such views. It will be argued that such views make sense against a perfectionist background. I shall not prove that such perfectionist views are true; it is not possible to do that. Rather, an attempt will be made to show that the above-mentioned moral views presuppose perfectionism. An attempt will also be made in this second part of the book to indicate the kind of metaphysics that is presupposed by such moral views.

There are at least two problems here. First, in virtue of what features do human beings (including foreigners and babies) get priority over animals? Secondly, why do these features not constitute an argument for unequal consideration between human beings, for giving greater consideration to those human beings who possess these features to a higher degree? Both these problems must be answered by the person who believes that there are certain rights held equally by all human beings, and that this doctrine of equality does not extend to animals.

Bentham pointed out that grown-up animals such as horses are more rational than human infants, but he wrongly concluded that rationality and other related properties were morally irrelevant. It could be replied to Bentham that though human infants exercise less reason than horses they do have a greater potential for exercising such powers than horses do. So in order to include human infants in the egalitarian club we must take the line that what suffices is the possession of the relevant potential, and the actualization of the potential is not necessary.

Now, leaving aside congenital idiots and their like, all human beings unlike animals have the potential to acquire certain capacities such as the ability to use language, self-consciousness, autonomy, the ability to form life-plans and to carry them out with zest, capacity for moral sentiments, capacity for sense of justice. Even if it is the case that some animals possess some of these capacities at a very rudimentary level, we could make the cut-off point sufficiently high so that all human beings, except for congenital idiots, possess the relevant potential, whereas all non-human animals fall below the cut-off point.

Alen Gewirth defends egalitarianism by appealing to the fact that human beings have purposes.[1] Though they differ in their ability to achieve their purposes, this is irrelevant, according to Gewirth. The important thing is that they all have purposes. Now Gewirth is presumably using 'purpose' in a strong sense so as to exclude animals from having purposes (otherwise his egalitarianism would have to extend to animals, which he does not want it to do). This view would also exclude some human beings, such as congenital idiots, from the egalitarian club. Even leaving aside this complication, there seems something missing in the view that the having of purposes is the only relevant thing from the point of view of worth, the ability to achieve the purpose being irrelevant. The missing element is supplied by William James's theory, which is more persuasive than Gewirth's. William James argued that what gives significance to human life is that human beings form or have ideals of life which they carry out with zest. James points out that the mere possession of an ideal is not sufficient to give significance to life. Ideals by themselves are barren. If ideals alone were all that mattered, then, says James, the life of your stuffy college professor would be the most significant of all! In order to have depth or significance we must have, in addition to ideals, 'pluck or active will, we must back our ideal visions with what the labourers have, the sterner stuff of manly virtue'.[2] In short, we must not only have ideals we must also pursue them with zest. To say that ideals need to be accompanied by pluck and will, in order to give significance to human life, is not of course to say that will and pluck by themselves are sufficient to give significance to human life.

[1] A. Gewirth, 'The Justification of Egalitarian Justice', *American Philosophical Quarterly*, viii (1971), 331–41.
[2] William James, *Talks to Teachers on Psychology and to Students on Some of Life's Ideals* (New York, 1899), p. 294.

Now James's theory has many attractions. For instance, it can explain why animal life is not significant in the way that human life is. And it could harmonize with our intuition that we should regard as significant the life of the rational beings from another species or from another planet. If a Martian has ideals which he pursues with zest, then his life has a significance, and we must respect his life, we must not, for instance, kill him for sport. But James's views do pose a problem for the egalitarian. Are not some people better at forming ideals than others, and do not some human beings carry out their life-plans with greater zest than others? Should we then say that the lives of those who are better at such things have greater worth than those who are less good at such things? Some people autonomously form their plan of life, others adopt without reflection the ideals that are prevalent and fashionable, while still others seem to drift from day to day without any ideals to guide them. Do such differences reflect differences in the worth of different lives? If so, what becomes of the doctrine of equal consideration and respect? Should we follow Rashdall and turn the doctrine of equal respect and consideration into the doctrine 'everyone's good to be considered as of equal value with the like good of every other individual'? According to Rashdall it is not really individuals considered simply as individuals but individuals considered 'as capable of certain kinds of good that are intrinsically valuable, and entitled to consideration equal in so far as their capacities are equal, unequal in proportion as their capacities are unequal'.[3] Rashdall's view is unfashionable now, at any rate among those who believe in the doctrine of equal respect. People nowadays tend to interpret that doctrine to mean that human beings, simply as human beings, should be regarded as having equal worth, whether or not their capacities for the good life are equal. Now we can give a partly pragmatic defence of this modern view. Even if human beings have unequal worth because of their differences in the relevant capacities, when framing political principles and policies, it is pragmatically justifiable to neglect such differences of worth.

Voltaire said that if God did not exist, he would have to be invented. We could similarly argue that if human beings

[3] *The Theory of Good and Evil*, p. 263.

did not have equal worth, the doctrine that they have equal worth would have to be invented, in the sense that it would be worth treating it as if it were true. Of couse Voltaire's view does not entail that God does not exist, it simply says that *if* he did not exist, he would have to be invented; so his doctrine is compatible with the existence of God. Similarly, the doctrine that equality of worth between human beings would need to be invented if it did not exist, does not entail the denial of the view that such equality really exists. Even if there are differences in intrinsic worth between different human beings, such differences are worth neglecting when framing political principles and policies; and this view is consistent with the view that such differences do not exist.

What is the pragmatic case for inventing the doctrine of equality between human beings, so that they are taken to have equal intrinsic worth? If there are differences in intrinsic worth, is it not our duty to recognize them and perhaps opt for a political system such as some form of *laissez-faire* or free-for-all, where there is competition between individuals so that those with the greatest capacities come out on top? Why not opt for a political system where the supermen are encouraged to come to the top?

One answer to this is that there is no guarantee that those with the greatest intrinsic worth would come to the top. In a free-for-all those with the greatest aggressiveness, deviousness, and guile may well succeed, but these are not the qualities that give greater worth to the individual.

It is worth treating people equally even if they have unequal worth, because if we said that people with greater worth should get greater facilities, this will lead to considerable quarrels among individuals as to who are the superior ones— for instance, Nazis will claim that they are the superior ones. So it is worth postulating the doctrine of equal worth between human beings. If differences of intrinsic worth between human beings were well marked, then it would be feasible for political principles and policies to take such differences into account. But in fact the differences are not well-marked—except perhaps in the case of idiots and their like. There are at least two major sources of scepticism here. First, there is considerable difference of opinion about what the relevant features are in virtue of which human beings have worth. So even if it is the case that one individual has greater capacity for, say, rationality than another, it is not clear whether rationality is all that important; there are perhaps other relevant considerations, such as the capacity for moral sentiments. Secondly, even assuming agreement about what the tests of human worth are, there is enormous difference about who scores better in these tests. Suppose we grant that those who have greater potential for a significant life have greater worth. We may still quarrel a lot about who has (or had) greater potential. True, many people seem to drift from day to day, and their lives seem less significant (in William James's sense) than the lives of those who are guided by a well-ordered conception of the good life and who follow this conception with zest, yet even the former may have had just as good a potential for such a significant life. It may be that their potential was gradually 'destroyed' by bad social conditions and they should not be penalized for that; if the test is how much potential they had, then you cannot go just by how much of the potential has been realised. Similar arguments apply *mutatis mutandis* to other criteria of human worth such as freedom and autonomy, and the capacity for moral sentiments.

Even if some adult individuals lead less autonomous and free lives than others, it does not follow that they had less potential for the autonomous life, and so we cannot infer that they have less worth than others who lead a more autonomous life. Again, even if psychopaths have little or no moral sentiments and sense of justice, we cannot infer that they did not in the past have the potential to acquire moral sentiments; perhaps their potential was destroyed by adverse social conditions.

Of the two sources of scepticism just mentioned, the second may become less powerful with advances in human knowledge, but the first source of scepticism, that is to say disagreement about what the relevant criteria or worth are and the weight to be given to the different criteria, is likely to remain powerful.

The argument here advanced in favour of equality of respect between human beings is partly an argument from ignorance. But of course it is not wholly so. If we are completely ignorant of the criteria of intrinsic worth then it is not at all clear why we should not extend the egalitarian doctrine to the higher animals, and even to the 'lower' animals such as ants and bees. If we are to give a lower status to animals than we do to human beings, including human infants, then we must postulate some kind of perfectionist norm, for instance, that there is something rather wonderful about human beings who possess certain capacities (such as the capacity to lead a significant form of life) or the potential for them. So perhaps we can advance a perfectionist-cum-pragmatic presupposition of the doctrine of equality of respect and consideration between all human beings, but not between human beings and animals. Animals are given inferior status because they fail to meet certain perfectionist requirements; for instance they do not have life-plans, or the potential for such life-plans. And among human beings we can advance the pragmatic argument mentioned earlier for neglecting any differences of intrinsic worth. So the two arguments together can be called perfectionist-cum-pragmatic.

2. Perfectionism and idiots

In this section I shall examine whether egalitarianism should extend to idiots. There is the complication about congenital idiots who never had even the relevant potential They are not born with a potential that is any greater in the relevant respects than the potential that animals are born with. How, then, can we justify the inclusion of such people in the egalitarian club while animals are excluded? Benn tries to solve this problem by suggesting that even the imbecile shares a common human nature with human beings; it is just that he is deprived of the possibility of realizing his nature.[4] He falls short of what he ought to have been, given the species to which he belongs; whereas the dog who is lacking in rationality of the kind that human beings possess, is not falling short of the standard of his species. That is why there is something tragic and appalling about the limitations of the imbeciles, whereas the average dog's limitations are only natural and amusing. Such considerations show, according to Benn, that imbeciles should be

---

[4] S. Benn, 'Egalitarianism and the Equal Consideration of Interests', in *Equality: Nomos,* ix, ed. J. R. Chapman and J. R. Pennock (New York, 1967), 61–78.

given special compensatory consideration rather than be given less moral weight compared to that given to the ordinary human being.

What are we to make of this argument? If the interests of human beings are given greater weight than the interests of animals, and if this presupposes that there is something especially wonderful about human beings, as a result of which they are entitled to greater consideration than animals are, then we can ask whether the congenital idiot really shares with human beings the relevant wonderful qualities. The congenital idiot lacks even the potential for such qualities as being able to have significant life-plans and autonomy, so how can he be on a par with normal human beings and above animals? Now some people would say that it is not just that individual human beings are more wonderful than individual animals, but the human species as a whole is more wonderful than animal species are. Since the congenital idiot too is a member of the human species, so, *qua* member of the human species, he too is a wonderful being. The aura of the species rubs off on him too. But should it? If one talks of rights in the way that individualism does, then it is individuals, rather than the species, who possess rights. If one takes the individualistic line, the congenital idiot may appear as a parasite. As an individual he is a very miserable specimen. If all others were like him, the human species as a whole would not be any better than some of the animal species. The congenital idiot is a parasite; for people claim for him privileges because he is a member of the human species, yet he does not (unlike normal people) contribute to the true grandeur of the human species, neither now nor (as normal babies will) in the future. He is a degenerate specimen, so why should this not be reflected in his status *vis-à-vis* the normal specimens? Why should the doctrine of equal respect apply to him?

Some people would reject individualism, they would adopt instead some form of collectivism; it is society as a whole, or even the species as a whole, that is really important, and individuals get their importance from being members of the larger group. But on this view too it is difficult to see why egalitarianism should extend to including congenital idiots; why not value people in proportion to their contribution to the social good? Indeed on this view it is difficult to see why there should be egalitarianism of the kind that asserts that human beings have equal *intrinsic* worth; for on this view human beings do not seem to have *intrinsic* worth, but rather instrumental worth in proportion to their contribution to the social good. The view that there are certain rights that all human beings have simply *qua* human beings, presupposes an individualistic approach. Of course such an approach need not deny that individuals develop only in society, but it would assert that the social organism is not an end in itself but a means to the good of individual human beings. And the problem remains, if individuals are ends in themselves, why should idiots be considered ends in themselves when animals are not so considered? To abandon individualism would involve abandoning the view that human beings are ends in themselves; and so how can we defend the view that idiots too are ends in themselves by abandoning individualism? And yet we have seen that if we adhere to individualism, it is again difficult to see why egalitarianism should extend to include congenital idiots. So the view that egalitarianism should extend to include congenital idiots seems difficult to defend; it cannot be defended by abandoning individualism, nor is it easy to defend it if we adopt an individualistic approach.

The argument that the idiot deserves some special compensatory treatment would be persuasive if it were the case that some injustice had been done to him in the past. But if he were a *congenital* idiot, no injustice need have been done to him by society or by any individual. Perhaps it is true that it was his bad luck that he was born an idiot and not a normal human being. But then is it not a dog's bad luck that he was not born a human being? Perhaps it makes no sense to say of a particular dog that he could have been born as a human being, but then does it make much more sense to say of a particular congenital idiot that *he* could have been born a normal human being? Is not being an idiot essential to the congenital idiot's identity in the sense that he would not have been the same human being if 'he' had not been born an idiot? Moreover, from the fact that the idiot would have had right to equal consideration if he had been born normal, it does not follow that he has such a right even though he is a congenital idiot.

It is true that the congenital idiot falls short of the standard of his species. But it does not follow that any injustice was involved, and so it does not follow that compensatory treatment is due to him. But I admit that in the case of many mental defectives, they have been victims of neglect or of injustice; had they been brought up properly their human potential would not have been destroyed. And in *these* cases compensatory treatment may be fitting.

To be sure, there can be a case for giving special consideration even when no prior injustice has taken place. Thus if a normal human being falls ill, even when the illness was due to natural causes and not due to any injustice or neglect by others, he may be entitled to special consideration, such as extra money to buy medicine. Such special consideration is quite consistent with the doctrine of equality of respect.

Similarly in the case of some mental defectives, they may have been born (or conceived) with the relevant potential, and yet their potential may have been destroyed because of natural causes, and not as a result of any injustice or neglect by others In such cases one may again make out a case for giving them special consideration; for since they once had the relevant potential they were members of the egalitarian club and entitled to special consideration when they suffer natural calamities or when they suffer calamaties due to injustice. The egalitarian club does not expel members when they lose the relevant potential—once a member, always a member. As Vlastos implies, even murderers are not expelled from the egalitarian club; they may lose their right to liberty or right to life, but they retain their right to respect.[5] I contend similarly that people are not expelled merely because they become senile or mentally defective.

But the problem with *congenital* idiots is that they never had the relevant potential, they were such degenerate specimens that one doubts if they ever qualified for membership of the egalitarian club. Though the egalitarian club does not expel members for becoming idiots or for becoming senile, it can refuse to admit members who do not have the relevant potential. So the problem remains, since congenital idiots

[5] G. Vlastos, 'Justice and Equality', in *Social Justice*, ed. R. Brandt (Englewood Cliffs, 1962), p. 48.

throughout their lives have been such degenerate specimens, why admit them to membership of the egalitarian club?

Suppose we grant that congenital idiots have less intrinsic worth than ordinary human beings. For practical purposes we may still neglect such differences, at any rate as long as the differences between congenital idiots who started at conception without the relevant potential, and those defectives who had the potential but whose potential has been destroyed, is not well-marked. If the latter are members of the egalitarian club, and if it is difficult to distinguish them in practice from the congenital idiots, then there is a pragmatic case for treating congenital idiots as if they were members of the egalitarian club. There is the danger that if you give inferior status to the congenital idiot, some ordinary human beings as well as some non-congenital idiots may be given inferior status by mistake or by malicious design. So, at any rate until human knowledge (including knowledge of moral matters) advances sufficiently, it is worth treating the congential idiot as if he had the same worth as other human beings; so there is a pragmatic case for extending the doctrine of equal respect to include congenital idiots.

The pragmatic argument for extending the doctrine of equality of consideration to include congenital idiots may not satisfy all egalitarians. Some egalitarians would not be content with the view that it is useful to treat congenital idiots as if they are entitled to equal consideration. They may contend that all such idiots are really entitled to equal consideration, quite apart from pragmatic considerations.

Now we do treat the interests of idiots as having greater weight than the interests of animals. We use animals for medical experiments, but we would be appalled if idiots were used in a similar manner as guinea-pigs. But this does not show that we believe that idiots have greater intrinsic worth than animals. Idiots are part of the human family (see the secular version of the family argument discussed in chapter 3, section 1) and this, along with considerations of sympathy (see the argument from sympathy discussed in chapter 3, section 2) can explain why we are reluctant to use idiots in the way that we treat animals. So there is no need to appeal to the view that (congenital) idiots have greater intrinsic worth than animals. Indeed this view is very difficult to defend. For what could be the grounds for thinking that they have greater intrinsic worth? Neither their potential nor their actual capacities are greater than those of animals. Now if congenital idiots do not have greater intrinsic worth than animals and if the doctrine of equal right to respect and consideration does not apply to animals, why should it apply to congenital idiots? The family argument (in its secular version) as well as the argument from sympathy can at best show why we do (or even should) show greater consideration and respect to congenital idiots than to animals; but such arguments do not show that congenital idiots have a right to respect and consideration that is equal to that given to other human beings. Nor do such considerations show that congenital idiots have greater intrinsic worth than animals. Compare: I have greater family obligations to my child than to yours, but this does not imply the view that my child has greater intrinsic worth than yours. So we still have the problem, if the doctrine of equal right to respect and consideration does not apply to animals, why should it apply to idiots?

The pragmatic argument for extending the doctrine to cover all idiots can answer this question. Congenital idiots are more difficult to distinguish from non-congenital idiots and other human beings, whereas animals can easily be distinguished from human beings. So the practice of giving inferior status to animals is not likely to be abused in the way that the practice of giving inferior status to congenital idiots is. With the advance in human knowledge (including moral knowledge) such pragmatic arguments may become weaker; and when that happens, the pragmatic case for including congenital idiots in the egalitarian club will also become weaker, *other things being equal.* Of course, there may be other considerations, such as the considerations emphasized by the family argument and the argument from sympathy, that might ensure that idiots get a better deal from us than animals do.

The view that idiots have no more intrinsic worth than animals is consistent with the view that idiots do and even should get a better deal from us than animals do; it is also consistent with the view that idiots have a greater right to consideration *from us* than animals do. Somewhat as your child has a greater right to consideration from you than my child has, even though the two have the same intrinsic worth. In one sense your child and my child have equal right to respect; the doctrine of equality of respect applies to both of them. But your child has greater right against some individuals such as yourself than mine does. Similarly, even if animals and (congenital) idiots have equal right to consideration in one sense, yet the latter could have greater rights against the human family of which they are members. But now there is perhaps one important dissimilarity. In the case of your child and my child, the fact that your child has greater rights against you than my child has, appears consistent with the view that in some sense the doctrine of equality of consideration applies to both the children, for my child has greater right against me than your child has, and so he need not be getting less consideration in general than your child who has greater rights against you. In the case of animals and the idiots, if the idiots have a greater right against the human family, there is something hollow in the assertion that in some important sense the animals and idiots have equal right to consideration and respect. For since as a matter of fact the human family is the only family that consists of moral agents, the fact that animals get less consideration from us human beings, implies that they get less consideration in general than idiots do. What is the point of asserting that they deserve equal respect with the idiot, if the family argument shows that we should show greater consideration to idiots? Perhaps it is implied that if there were moral agents other than human beings, then such non-human moral agents should show equal consideration to the interests of animals as they do to the interests of (human) idiots. But as long as such non-human moral agents do not come into contact with our planet, there is something hollow about the assertion that idiots and animals are deserving of equal respect and consideration, unless one is prepared to add that animals are equally deserving of consideration from human beings. In a sense, animals too belong to a family. For instance, dogs belong to the dog species, in the way that the idiot belongs to the human species. But since dogs are not moral agents, it makes no sense to say that a dog deserves consideration from fellow dogs in the way that an idiot deserves consideration from fellow human beings.

Earlier we saw that the family argument does have its limits; it has to operate within certain moral constraints. The fact that animals are not members of the human family does not entitle us to violate their rights, such as their right not to be tortured. But the existence of these constraints is consistent with the view that in many ways idiots should get a better deal from us, than animals should; for after all they are members of the human family. Thus, if idiots are starving and dogs are starving, it seems plausible to take the line that we have greater obligations to feed the idiots (since they belong to the same family as we do) than we do to feed the dogs.

I have argued that idiots should get a better deal from us than animals do, other things being equal. But this does not imply that congenital idiots are full members of the egalitarian club. At most they are associate members of the egalitarian club. Even though they lack the relevant potential, they can be given the associate membership of the club for pragmatic reasons of the kind mentioned earlier, and also perhaps for belonging to the human family.

The view that congenital idiots are not full members of the egalitarian club would seem counter-intuitive to some people; just as the view of Benn and others that babies are not full members of the egalitarian club seems counter-intuitive to me. If one believes in the Christian version of the family argument, then idiots could be full members of the egalitarian club, for idiots would just as much children of God as normal men are, and it is in virtue of being children of God that human beings are due equal respect and consideration. But those of us who do not believe in the Christian version of the family argument would say that the 'intuition' that congenital idiots and normal men have equal right to consideration and respect is a hangover from the Christian family argument. Somewhat as many Jews who have given up their religion still find something abhorrent about eating port, for old habits and beliefs die hard, so also people who have given up being Christians still think that congenital idiots really have equal rights to consideration.

And even if you give idiots full membership of the egalitarian club because you believe in the Christian version of the family argument or because you believe, as many Christians do, that they have souls, it is worth stressing that you are appealing to metaphysical-cum-perfectionist considerations. For as we saw earlier the Christian version of the family argument does pre- suppose such considerations. And so too does the view that human beings are equal in virtue of possessing a soul; there is supposed to be something wonderful about having a soul, otherwise why be so impressed with it?

3. Two kinds of perfectionism

I have argued that the view that egalitarianism extends to include all human beings, but not animals, presupposes a kind of perfectionism. The egalitarian doctrine does not extend to animals who have an inferior status compared to human beings. Now there are two kinds of perfectionism worth distinguishing: consequentialist perfectionism and non-consequentialist per- fectionism. Consequentialist perfectionism is roughly the same as what is sometimes called ideal utilitarianism; it is a high- minded version of Benthamite utilitarianism. According to Benthamite utilitarianism things are ultimately justified by their consequences, and so Benthamite utilitarianism is a form of consequentialism. Ideal utilitarianism (and consequentialist perfectionism) too asserts that things are ultimately justified by their consequences, so it too is a form of consequentialism. The difference is that whereas for Benthamite utilitarianism the only relevant consequences are the production of pleasure and the avoidance of pain, ideal utilitarianism and consequen- tialist perfectionism also regard as relevant other consequences such as the promotion of knowledge, culture, beauty, and self-development.

Now opposed to consequentialist theories stand right-based theories. According to such theories rights are not derivative from consequentialist considerations, but rather set moral constraints within which utilitarian and other consequentialist theories can operate. An individual's rights are not something that should be sacrificed for utilitarian ends. Now the problem arises, what are the grounds of rights, what are such moral constraints based upon? And I have tried to argue that in answering such questions one has to appeal to perfectionist considerations, such as that human beings have more worth or significance than animals. So here perfectionism is bolstering a non-teleological (or non-consequentialist) view. That is why it is worth distinguishing such non-consequentialist perfectionism from teleological perfectionism.

So right-based theories can be divided into two kinds: those such as Rawls's which try to bypass perfectionism, and those such as the theory constructed in this book which are based on perfectionist considerations.

5

Some Metaphysical Presuppositions

This chapter deals with some of the metaphysical presuppositions of our egalitarian moral system; more specifically, it deals with views about personal identity and about the beginning of human life that are presupposed by our right-based egalitarian views.

1. Personal identity and its importance

It was suggested earlier that in order to defend some of our egalitarian moral intuitions we shall have to appeal to a perfectionist view which emphasizes the potential that an individual has. Now some people are suspicious of this approach. Thus it is argued that if the potential for the relevant capacities is what really matters, this would commit us not only to admitting infants and the foetus into the egalitarian club, but also the unfertilized ovum and the sperm. For the ovum and the sperm too could turn into persons. Thus Feinberg objects to the potentiality principle on the grounds that 'the zygote's human potentiality is more proximate than the spermatozoon's, actualizable in less time, with fewer combinatory processes, and more likely in fact to eventuate—big differences no doubt, but differences in degree for all that.'[1]

To answer such objections, one needs to appeal to certain metaphysical doctrines. Perfectionist-cum-metaphysical considerations are presupposed by our egalitarian moral views. An attempt is made in this part of the book at pointing out some of these presuppositions and some of the implications

[1] Introduction to *The Problem of Abortion*, p. 4.

of these presuppositions, but not at proving the truth of these presuppositions. Of course different moral views have different presuppositions; I am concerned with the presuppositions of the egalitarian moral beliefs that were referred to earlier (see chapter 4).

The view of personal identity that is presupposed by a good deal of our moral system is the view that is sometimes known as the simple or absolute view of personal identity. On this view the identity of persons is radically different from the identity of other things such as machines, nations, and cars. According to this view questions of personal identity must have a 'yes' of 'no' answer: 'Whatever happens between now and any future time, either I shall still exist or I shall not. Any future experience will either be mine or it will not.'[2] And one could add that on this simple view the same holds about the past; either an individual in the past was me or it was not, there must be a 'yes' or 'no' answer to such a question. On this view my survival cannot be a matter of degree; it is a matter of all or nothing, and survival on this view implies identity; if a future individual A is not identical with me, then I shall not survive as A. On this view the soul (or its secular analogue) is simple and unanalysable.

Parfit contrasts the simple view, with his own view which he calls the complex view. On the complex view the identity of persons is rather like the identities of other things such as cars, nations, and machines. What is involved in the survival of a nation are just certain continuities, such as continuities of peoples, cultures, and political systems. The nation's survival consists in the survival of these continuities; as these continuities weaken less and and less of the nation survives. These continuities are not evidence of any further fact about the identity of nations. Once we know how much these continuities have weakened, that is all there is to know; there is no further problem about whether or not the very same nation persists. Likewise with the identity of persons. A person's survival consists of certain continuities, psychological and bodily continuities. On the complex view, unlike the simple view, these continuities are not evidence of any further deep

[2] D. Parfit, 'Personal Identity', in *Philosophy of Mind*, ed. J. Glover (Oxford, 1976), p. 142.

fact about personal identity. Survival is a matter of degree. Each of us will survive less and less as time goes on, as the psychological connections between us and our future selves gets less and less. Similar conclusions hold for our past selves. There is, as it were, a series of successive selves and there is no 'underlying person' that persists. The contrast with the simple view is striking. For on the simple view there is a persistent individual, a substance, that lasts from the beginning of an individual human being's life to its end. John Doe the infant and John Doe the adult man are the same substance, even though John Doe the adult man has a very different character from John Doe the child, and remembers very little, if anything, about his infancy. Another related difference between the two views is that on the complex view whether or not an individual person is the same as another individual is in an important sense a matter of choice or decision. This is related to the point that on the complex view the various continutities are all the relevant facts there are, and there are no further facts about personhood; so that if we know how many psychological connections there are between me and a future self, it is up to us whether or not to say that the two are the same. If I say that the two are the same I am only giving my decision: another person 'could say "It will be you," thus deciding differently'.[3]

On the simple view, however, judgements of personal identity are not matters of choice, they are meant to correspond to the way things are. The simple view assumes that there is a permanent substance, common to the different phases in the life of a human being. David Wiggins distinguishes a substance sortal from a phase sortal.[4] If x is a phase sortal then from the fact that an individual ceases to be an x, it does not follow that the individual ceases to exist; for example, when John Doe ceases to be an infant, it does not follow that he ceases to exist. But if x is a substance sortal, then from the fact that an individual ceases to be an x, if follows that the individual ceases to exist. According to Wiggins, a person is a substance sortal, which implies that when John Doe ceases to be a person, it follows that he ceases to exist. Now there are

[3] Ibid., p. 160.
[4] *Identity and Spatio-Temporal Continuity* (Oxford, 1967).

plenty of problems with such a metaphysics, but I think that something like it is presupposed by our egalitarian moral beliefs. We believe that the person John Doe can continue to exist, even when John Doe the infant and John Doe the adult are the same substance, the same persistent individual.

We could be more specific and say that what is so wonderful about a human infant is not just that it has a wonderful potential (a sperm too has that), but that it has the relevant potential, such as the potential to lead a significant life *à là* William James, which it can develop while retaining its identity. It is the very same individual as the wonderful individual that it can develop into. That is why it must not, once it exists, be sacrificed for utilitarian ends, not even for high-minded utilitarian ends; it is an end in itself. Contrast this with the sperm or the unferfilized ovum, which also in a sense has the wonderful potential, but it cannot develop that potential while retaining its identity, it has to be destroyed in the process. It can at best have only a lot of instrumental worth, but not intrinsic worth. It is not an end in itself and it can when necessary be sacrificed for utilitarian ends.

On the complex view the infant is not in any deep sense the same individual, the same substance, as the adult that it will form into. And so the fact that it has this wonderful potential can at best be a reason for thinking that it has instrumental worth; on the complex view it is not easy to see why the newly-born human infant has any more *intrinsic* worth than an ant or a bee or a sperm.

Our individualist ethics, which regards the individual human being as sacred, presupposes the view that a lot of moral weight is borne by considerations of identity; it presupposes what Parfit calls the simple view of personal identity, for on the complex view (which Parfit believes in) judgements of identity are not ultimately important.

According to our individualist ethics an individual is sacred in the sense that he must not be sacrificed for utilitarian ends; his rights should be protected even if this means some sacrifice of utilitarian and other goals. Now *if* an entity such as an ovum or a sperm can only develop its potential by destroying itself in the process, there is something absurd about regarding that entity as sacred and yet insisting that it must be made to develop its potential by destroying itself. If you really regard the sperm as sacred the rational thing would be to let it retain its identity, and if the only way that it can retain its identity is by remaining a sperm, then let it remain a sperm. If all this sounds strange, this is because it is absurd to suppose that a sperm has a right to retain its identity. Now it might be objected that there is a world of difference between a sperm being simply destroyed or annihilated on the one hand and its being turned into a human being on the other. The latter involves the true fulfilment of the sperm's destiny, even if in some sense the sperm ceases to exist when it turns into a zygote.

It seems to me that none of this shows that a sperm has a right to develop its potential. The sperm derives its instrumental value from the fact that it could in the future turn into an individual that is an end in itself. Any 'right' that a sperm has would be derivative from the right of the future individual that it could turn into. But future individuals only have what Feinberg calls contingent rights, that is to say they have rights on the assumption that they will come into existence. If they do not come into existence, no rights of theirs would be violated. But if we now do things that will damage their interests when they come into being (assuming that they will come into being), then we could interfere with their contingent rights; thus assuming that an individual human being will be born from sperm X, we must not damage sperm X in such a way that it produces a serious deformity in the future human being that will come into existence. But of course if we destroy the sperm, then no contingent rights of the future individual would be jeopardized. For contingent rights only exist on the assumption that the relevant individual will come into being in the future, and if we destroy the sperm (or rather prevent it from 'becoming' a human being), then no future individual will come out of it.

Of course one can still say that by destroying the sperm, one has prevented something of intrinsic value from coming into existence, and so such destruction involves a disutility. But this is a utilitarian consideration, and it could be counterbalanced by other utilitarian considerations, for instance that there might be less misery in the world as a result of fewer people being born. It is not a matter of rights of the individual versus utilitarian considerations.

In the case of the newly-born infant, however, we have a being whom we believe to be identical with the being that it will develop into, it has the relevant potential which it can develop without destroying its identity. It is the very same individual as the wonderful person that it can develop into; it is as sacred as the adult person that it is identical with. This view will be defended more fully in later chapters.

2. When does human life begin?

What about the rights of the foetus? At what point does human life begin? This question is important. For if egalitarianism extends only to all human beings, then in order to find out whether it extends to foetuses (and to infants), it is necessary to know when human life begins. So we shall now turn to the discussion of this problem. Some utilitarian philosophers such as Hare imply that the problem about when an individual human being comes into existence is not important.[5] But on the view expounded in this book it is important. If an individual human being is sacred, then it is sacred as soon as it comes into existence. This view will be reinforced later by appealing to the doctrine of transitivity of ends in themselves.

A powerful case can be made for the view that an individual human being begins to exist at conception. Any other criteria, such as the moment the foetus becomes viable, or the moment the individual infant is born, seem arbitrary. The moment of conception, unlike other moments in the history of the foetus, seems radically discontinuous with what preceded it. If you believe in the simple view of personal identity, then it would be natural to assume that a person begins to exist all of a sudden, rather than gradually, and the moment of conception seems the least non-arbitrary moment for the beginning of human life.

Moreover, at conception the individual acquires the genetic code that will remain with the human being throughout its adult life. And it is at conception that we seem to find the

[5] R. Hare, 'Abortion and the Golden Rule', *Philosophy and Public Affairs*, iv (1975), 201–22.

beginning of the spatio-temporal chain that links the foetus to the adult human being.

The other suggested criteria for the beginning of human life have an arbitrary air about them. Thus, viability is supposed to be important because when a foetus becomes viable, it has the capacity to have an existence that is physically independent of the mother's existence. But why should such physical independence from the mother be any more relevant than, say, emotional independence or financial independence? Sometimes it is thought that as long as the foetus can only survive inside the mother's body it cannot have a separate identity from that of its mother, it is, as it were, a part of the mother. But this is false. When the foetus is 'inside' the mother, even before it is viable and capable of existence outside the mother's body, it has its own identity, with its own genetic code and its own nervous system. Of course, the foetus is influenced in important ways by its environment, but then so is the infant influenced by its environment after its birth. Another objection to the viability criterion is that viability depends upon extraneous factors such as the state of medical and technical knowledge. Similar arguments apply against using birth as the moment when the human being begins to exist.

The most plausible alternative to the view that human life begins at conception is the view that human life begins when the foetus acquires a brain. Baruch Brody has defended this view.[6] He argues that what is essential to a human being is the possession a human brain. This is shown in the fact that when a person's brain dies, he dies. Since the brain is so important in determining the end of a person's life, is it not equally important in determining the beginning of human life? But there is a lack of analogy here. As Callahan has argued, the death of the brain marks the death of the person because the death of the brain marks the end of all potentiality for personhood, whereas in the case of the early embryo, even before it has acquired a brain, it has the potential for personhood.[7] Brody replies to this by appealing to a science fiction example: 'imagine that medical technology has reached the stage at which, when brain death occurs, the brain is removed,

[6] B. Brody, *Abortion and the Sanctity of Human Life* (Boston, 1975).
[7] D. Callahan, *Abortion: Law, Choice, and Morality* (New York, 1970), p. 389.

'liquefied' and recast into a new functioning brain. The new brain bears no relation to the old one (it has none of its memory traces and so on).'[8] Brody rightly points out that if a new recast brain could be put back into the dead body, so that a person comes into being, the person will be a new one and not the old one. Until the recast brain is inserted in the body, the body will have the potential to become a person, but the new person will not come into existence until the body has got the brain. Brody seems to think that by parity of reasoning we must admit that in the case of the foetus, too, a person does not come into existence until the foetus acquires a brain, and mere potential to have a brain does not suffice.

There is an important difference that Brody has overlooked. In the case of the science fiction example, the dead body can acquire an alien brain (or a new brain that 'bears no relation to the old one'), whereas in the case of the early embryo, the embryo has, as it were, the potential to create its own brain. The brain which the early embryo will have in the future is a brain whose essential characteristics will be determined by the essential characteristics, the genetic code, of the early embryo; thus in an important sense the brain that it will acquire will not be an alien brain. So there is nothing inconsistent in arguing that in the case of the early embryo, the person that will develop in the future already exists before the acquisition of the brain, whereas in the science fiction example, the new person only emerges after the importation of the alien brain.

Another problem with the view that human life begins when the brain starts to function is this. Either one is impressed with the view that what is essential for the presence of human life is that the individual should actually manifest some human characteristics, and mere potential for such characteristics does not suffice; but in that case, one cannot say that human life exists when the brain begins to function, for the conscious life of the foetus at that time is not more human than the conscious life of animals, the consciousness of the foetus is too primitive to be considered *human* consciousness. Or one takes the view that what is essential for the existence of human life is not the manifestation of human characteristics,

[8] Brody, *Abortion and the Sanctity of Human Life,* p. 113.

but the possession of the potential for manifesting human characteristics in the future; but in that case, it is not clear why one should not take the line that human life exists even at conception.

It might be objected that if you are impressed by the potentiality for personhood, why stop at conception, why not go back further to the sperm and the ovum? True, nature is far too bountiful in the production of sperms and ova. But this in itself does not show why sperms and ova taken in pairs before conception should not be considered as individual persons. True, this would involve our believing in millions and millions of extra persons, but is this a decisive objection? Now on a conventionalist account of personal identity, according to which judgements of identity are ultimately matters of human decision and convention, we may for reasons of convenience decide not to allow certain claims to personhood because we do not want to admit too many individuals into the class of persons. But if you believe in the simple view of personal identity then you have to give a better reason for rejecting such claims. I suggest the better reason could be this.

A particular ovum could be fertilized by any one of millions of sperms. Different individual persons would emerge depending upon which sperm fertilized the ovum. So the individual person cannot be said to have begun before the fertilization. Now it might be objected against this that even after conception, and indeed even after birth and childhood, the individual that emerges is influenced in important ways by the environment. Thus the child is affected in important ways by its physical, cultural, and family environment. Yet we do not say that it becomes a numerically different individual as a result of exposure to such environment. Why, then, should the fact that the way the individual develops depends upon which sperm has fertilized the ovum be a reason to think that the individual person does not begin with the ovum before it has been fertilized? One answer to this is that the sperm plays about an equal role in determining the essential characteristics of the person to that of the ovum, and it seems arbitrary to pick out the unfertilized ovum as the starting-point rather than the sperm; since the two play about an equally important role it seems more reasonable to say that it is the union of the two that is the crucial event. True, there are many more sperms available compared to ova, many more sperms are redundant from the point of view of producing human beings in general. It does not follow that the individual sperm that does fertilize the ovum plays a less important role in producing the essential and distinguishing characteristics of the particular individual that emerges.

Now it might be objected that conception cannot be the point at which human life beings, because for a few days after conception it remains possible that the foetus may split into two. This could happen if there are identical twins present. In such cases segmentation takes place a few days after conception and it has been suggested by Paul Ramsey that human life begins at the time when segmentation may or may not take place. But this view has serious difficulties. In most cases no splitting takes place and nothing happens at the time when 'segmentation may or may not take place'. All that 'happens' is that segmentation does not take place. So should we then say in the ordinary cases (where there are no identical twins and so no segmentation) human life begins at conception, but in the case of identical twins human life begins at the time of segmentation?

How strange to argue that if the foetus at conception contains two potential human lives, then human life has not started at conception and we can abort the foetus without killing a human being, but if the foetus at conception contains only one potential human life, then human life has started at conception and if we aborted such a foetus at conception, we would have killed a human being! How can a double murder be no murder?

So we have the following problem. How can we say that human life begins at conception, for in the case of identical twins it looks as if we have to wait till segmentation before we have a unique individual? Nor can we say that human life begins at the time when segmentation may or may not take place, for, except in the case of identical twins, nothing positive happens at that time. And nor does it make good sense to say that in the ordinary cases human life begins at conception, but in the case of identical twins, it begins at the time of segmentation. So what is the solution? Probably the best solution is to contend that human life does in all cases begin at conception; in the case of identical twins the foetus from the time of conception contains two human beings, and at the time of segmentation the two human beings cease to be in the same body.

Some people are not so impressed by the argument that human life begins at conception, any other point being arbitrary. It is objected that such slippery slope arguments are not valid. We cannot, so the objection runs, tell at what point an acorn turns into an oak tree, but it does not follow that acorns are oak treees. Again, we cannot tell at what point middle age turns into old age, but it does not follow that middle age is old age; similarly, merely because we cannot pick out a non-arbitrary point after conception at which we can say that human life begins, it does not follow that the foetus is a human being from the moment of conception.

But I would contend that the slippery slope argument is more forceful in the case of personal identity because the identity of persons (according to the conceptual scheme that is presupposed by our egalitarian moral system) is simple and absolute and does not admit of degrees and of borderlines. There is no exact point at which middle age turns into old age, because there is a genuine borderline area where it is indeterminate whether an individual is middle-aged or old. And the same applies to the case of the acorn and the oak tree. But according to the simple view, personal identity is different, it does not admit of a borderline or of an indeterminate area, it is a matter of all or nothing; either a foetus at a certain stage of its development is the same individual as the human being that it will become, or it is not.

3. The rights of the unborn child and Mrs Foot

Mrs Phillipa Foot, however, takes a different line. She is impressed by the analogy with the acorn and the oak tree, and she thinks that in the case of human beings too there is a genuine borderline. She says: 'I am inclined to think that one must recognise a genuine subjectivity about the decision as to whether to count a foetus as a human being and accord it human rights.'[9] She believes that we have 'alternative criteria of what we shall count as a human being'[10] and that in cases where the different criteria give different results, it is up to us which of these alternative criteria we employ. According to one criterion, human life begins with conception, according to another it begins at the moment when it acquires separate existence or viability. It is up to us which of these alternative criteria we use.

Now it seems to me that the simple view of personal identity (which is presupposed by the system of human rights—see chapters 6 and 7) does not allow for the kind of subjectivity that Mrs Foot thinks is allowed. And our system of human rights does not allow for such subjectivity. Indeed one way of distinguishing the sphere of justice and human rights from some other parts of our moral system is by stressing that judgements regarding human rights and justice are objective in an important sense. You can pursue certain personal ideals (such as living the life of a monk) without thinking that others are doing wrong in not pursuing such ideals, but you cannot show similar tolerance in the sphere of human rights. If you think that your having an abortion would involve a violation of human rights, then you must, if you are consistent, believe that others who have abortions in similar conditions would also be involved in the violation of human rights. Whether or not a particular case of abortion involves a violation of human rights cannot vary with the opinion of the person having the abortion.

Of course there is one kind of tolerance and subjectivity that may well exist in the case of human rights. It can be very difficult to find out whether or not a particular case (or even certain sorts of cases, such as killing of the newly-conceived foetuses) involves a violation of human rights. You could tolerate and even respect other people's opinions on the issue, even when there opinions differ widely from yours. You may realize that the truth is so difficult to discern that there is room for honest disagreement. But of course such subjectivity is much weaker than the 'genuine subjectivity' that Mrs Foot assumes. On her account there is no objective truth to be

---

[9] P. Foot, 'Abortion', in *Morals and Medicine* (London, 1970), p. 37.
[10] Ibid.

discovered in such areas (at any rate in the borderline cases and in the puzzle cases), it is up to us which of the conflicting criteria to use.

There is something very strange about the view that whether an individual (or certain sorts of individuals) has (or have) human rights depends upon our decision or upon conceptual convenience. One of the tasks of a theory of human rights is to set limits to what is permissible; human rights set moral constraints that must be respected. Pursuit of utilitarian and other goals must take place within the limits set by the doctrine of human rights. The individual human being is sacred and has rights that must not be sacrificed for mere utilitarian considerations. But if it is a matter of conceptual convenience or decision whether certain sorts of beings, such as foetuses, have human rights, then it becomes difficult to understand why human rights must never be sacrificed for utilitarian ends (see chapter 7).

If a foetus has a right to life than its right must not be sacrificed for ordinary utilitarian ends, though perhaps it may still have to be overriden if some other stronger right trumps it. Even if a human right may be overridden by a stronger right, a human right cannot be made to disappear by appropriate conceptual decision. A foetus cannot have a right to life, if such a right can disappear with the decision, however seriously the decision is arrived at, of the person who wants the abortion, or of any other person; you cannot by suitably altering the criteria of a human being deprive an individual of human rights. If A decides that the foetus inside her body is a human being, but B decides that a similar foetus inside B's body is not a human being, are we to say that the foetus inside A's body has human rights but the foetus inside B's body has no human rights? What sort of degenerate right is this that is dependent upon the choice of other individuals, and how does such a right differ from a mere privilege?

To be sure Mrs Foot is not saying that we can always decide whether or not certain sorts of individuals are human beings. She would not allow Nazis to decide that Jews are not human beings and so have no human rights. It is only in the problem cases, such as the foetus, that she thinks that 'genuine subjectivity' exists. My objection to her views still remains.

For such genuine subjectivity about human rights makes no sense, not even in the problem cases. If you ar a real subjectivist in the borderline or puzzle cases, then the consistent thing for you is to deny that human rights exist in such cases. There is the added complication that our present system of personal identity (that is to say the simple view) does not allow of borderline areas; either A is the same individual as B, or it is not, it is a matter of all or nothing and does not admit of degrees.

The problem of the relation between human rights and the simple view is further examined in chapter 7.

6

Potentiality and the Right to Respect

1. The doctrine of transitivity of ends in themselves and the dynamic approach

The doctrine of equal respect and consideration urges us to respect persons, to treat human beings as ends in themselves and not merely as means to the attainment of some goal. Now there are two alternative possibilities here. First, one may believe that an individual is or could be an end in itself during a part of its life but not necessarily over all its life-span. Secondly, and perhaps more plausibly, one may maintain that if an individual is an end in itself during any part of its life-span, then it is an end in itself throughout its life-span. Let us call this second view the doctrine of transitivity of ends in themselves. This doctrine, if true, would explain why an individual human being is sacred even when he becomes irreversibly senile, as long as he remains the same individual, and it explains why a newly-born infant is sacred, but the sperm is not—assuming that the sperm, unlike the human infant, is not the same individual as the future human being that it becomes. This doctrine is also in harmony with the idea that once you are a member of the egalitarian club (where everyone is an end in himself) you cannot be expelled from it: 'The moral community is not a club from which members may be dropped for delinquency.'[1] Vlastos might have added that neither can they be dropped for extreme senility or extreme lunacy, as long as they remain the same individual.

The doctrine of the transitivity of ends in themselves goes naturally with the view that the doctrine of equality of respect

[1] G. Vlastos, 'Justice and Equality', p. 48.

and consideration applies to a human being as soon as he comes into existence. Thus, according to this doctrine, if the foetus is the same individual as the adult human being that it can develop into, then it is just as sacred as the adult human being that it can develop into, and it is arbitrary to exclude it from the egalitarian club. This view takes a long-term view about whether and to what extent an individual has a right to consideration, even when it is a foetus. On this view the right to respect an individual has, depends upon the nature of the individual, and the nature of the individual is understood dynamically, not just in terms of all that the individual can do and is like at a particular time (as on the static view) but also in terms of all that it can do in the future (as well as all that it did in the past).

I shall contrast the dynamic view with what I shall call the static view, which I attribute to Feinberg and others. But it is worth pointing out that terms like 'dynamic' and 'static' have different senses, and these terms are used here merely to distinguish certain approaches; it is not intended to use them as grading labels, for to do so would be to beg the question about which of these approaches is prefereable. One could make the same points by using other more neutral-looking labels, for instance by calling my approach, approach A and Feinberg's approach, approach B. In a sense the approach I call dynamic is static, for on this approach human beings retain the same intrinsic worth throughout their lives. The reason why in spite of such considerations I have called this the dynamic approach is that on this approach in order to answer the question, what sort of an entity a particular entity is, in order to understand its nature, we take into account not just the individual's present capacities, dispositions, and so forth, but also his potential which includes all that it can do throughout its life-span.

The dynamic view has two variants. The first of these takes into account the capacities and potential that an individual has or has had in the past, while the second only takes into account the capacities and potential that the individual now has. We can illustrate the difference between the two variants by an example. Suppose a person has become so senile that he has lost his relevant potential; in that case the second variant, unlike the first, would disregard the fact that the senile man once had the relevant potential. The second variant of the dynamic approach is still different from the static approach because the former, unlike the latter, takes into account the potential that an individual now has. Thus, while the first variant of the dynamic approach takes into account the potential that an individual now has, or has had in the past, the second variant only takes into account the potential that it now has; while the static approach takes into account neither the potential that an individual had in the past, nor the potential that an individual now has, but only the actual capacities, dispositions, etc. that the individual now possesses.

Something like the second variant is implicit in some of Hegel's views. He says that the man is implicit in the child, and he thinks that an individual is entitled to the union of his actual and potential being. It would follow that children are entitled to develop their potential. He thinks that, unlike things, which have no destiny of their own, children have a destiny of their own, and have a right to be educated so that they can fulfil their nature and their destiny. Since they are not things, but have a destiny of their own, they must not be regarded as slaves or as property of other human beings.[2]

The first variant (which probably harmonizes better with our egalitarian intuitions) is also forward-looking in the way that the second one is, and so it too would agree that to understand a baby's nature, we must examine all it can do and become in the future, we must examine its potential. But unlike the second variant, the first variant also attaches importance to the potential that an individual possessed in the past. Thus, take the example of a human being who was rational, but who has now become (irreversibly) very senile, so that he does not now have any more mental capacities than animals. In such a case Hegel would probably say that such a man has lost his soul and his rights. Thus, Hegel believed that a corpse whose concept or soul or potential has left it has no true existence and he implied that it has no rights.[3] He would probably say the same about the senile man in our example. The first variant of the dynamic approach would not automatically de-recognize a human being as soon as he

2 Hegel, *Philosophy of Right*, sections 44 and 174-5.
3 Ibid., Addition to section 21.

(irreversibly) lost his rationality. It would allow for the doctrine of transitivity of end in themselves to apply to such a case, and so it would not expel the individual from the egalitarian club as long as he retained his identity. Hegel would deny that in our example the old individual persists. For Hegel, the spiritual death of an individual would involve the death of the individual, so the senile old man who 'survives' would not be the same individual as the earlier human being. But for what it is worth our ordinary egoistic hopes and fears presuppose that an individual could survive his spiritual death. Thus, suppose you contemplate the possibility that you might have an accident, as a result of which you lose for ever your rational powers, but 'you' retain some feelings; you may well worry now in an egoistic way about whether the feelings that 'you' will have after the accident will be pleasant or painful.

It may be argued that in practice the difference between the two variants of the dynamic approach will not be substantial. For even if senile old men are not strictly regarded as members of the egalitarian club, normal human beings would find it in their interest to treat such senile people as if they retained their membership; for normal human beings would fear (rightly or wrongly) that one day they too might become senile.

But there are other examples where the two variants of the dynamic approach could give different results. Thus, consider an individual human being who was born with a normal human potential, but right from the start his life was ruined by adverse social conditions, being brought up to lead a life of a psychopath, never having developed his potential to lead a worthwhile life. Now let us suppose that after some years of leading such a psychopathic life, the potential to lead a meaningful life that he once had, but never developed, has been destroyed, through no fault of his own. In that case the first variant of the dynamic approach would extend the doctrine of equal respect to such an individual, but according to the second variant such a person would have lost his membership once his relevant potential was destroyed. In such a case the first variant harmonizes better with some of our egalitarian intuitions. For instance, we feel that such a psychopath has been unjustly treated by society and it would be an added injustice if he were to be deprived of his right to equal respect; if anything he needs compensation for being so unjustly treated in the past, for not being given proper social condi- tions in which to develop. I shall come back to such examples later in chapter 9 and argue that the view that such individuals are not expelled from the egalitarian club does not imply that we should be too soft on such individuals.

One way of stating the difference between the two variants is to say that while both variants attach importance to the possessing of the relevant potential, the first variant, unlike the second, attaches importance to the fact that the individual once possessed the relevant potential, even if he does not now possess it. Another way of stating this difference is to point out that the first variant, unlike the second variant, accepts the doctrine of the transitivity of ends in themselves.

During the rest of this book references to the dynamic approach are (unless otherwise stated) to the first variant of the dynamic approach.

2. The dynamic approach presupposes the simple view of personal identity

The dynamic approach and the doctrine of the transitivity of ends in themselves presuppose the simple view of personal identity. For instance, if we deny that the foetus or the infant is in any deep sense the same individual as the adult human being that it will turn into in the future, if it is just convenient to bundle the two together into one individual, as it is on the complex view, then it is not clear why the view that the adult human being is an end in itself should provide grounds for thinking that the foetus or the infant is an end in itself. Of course it may provide grounds for thinking that the foetus or the infant has instrumental worth, but that is a different matter and that will not really tell us what is wrong with infanticide with the consent of parents when the instrumen- tal good effects of infanticide (for instance, in controlling over-population) outweigh the instrumental bad effects (see chapter 8).

3. *The static approach and the will theory of rights*

Now such dynamic approaches can be contrasted with the static approach. Feinberg, who adopts this static approach, believes that only a creature with an interest can have rights, and then adopts a static view of whether an individual has interests.[4] According to Feinberg, foetuses and young infants, unlike many animals, do not possess actual interests because they do not possess the relevant (functioining) cognitive apparatus that is necessary for the possession of the desires and aims out of which interests are compounded. Feinberg raises the question what sort of beings have rights, and in answering this question he assumes the static view, for he talks of foetuses and infants as different sorts of beings from adults. On the dynamic view a human infant or foetus is the same sort of being as the adult that it can grow into, and an individual's interests should be understood not just in terms of its present aims and desires, but also in terms of its future and past aims and desires.

The static view, since it denies the relevance of potentiality, gets into difficulties, not only about how young infants and foetuses can possess rights, but even about how adult people can possess rights when they are in a coma, even when the coma is a temporary one, or when they suffer from catatonic schizophrenia, or even when they are in a state of dreamless sleep. On the static view there is a problem about how such beings can be the sorts of beings who have rights. And how can dead persons be the sorts of beings who have rights? And how can the psychopath whose humanity was destroyed, through no fault of his own, by his upbringing, be the sort of person who has right to respect?

Feinberg considers the case of human beings who have catatonic schizophrenia and who are so disoriented that they compare quite unfavourably with the brightest dogs or cats.[5] Do such persons have no more right to consideration than dogs or cats? Feinberg suggests that such a person can be thought of as a person rather than an animal because we can think of the patient as a genuine human being inside the vegetable casing struggling to get out, somewhat as in an old

---

[4] 'The Rights of Animals and Future Generations'.   [5] Ibid.

fairy story a pumpkin could be a beautiful maiden under a magic spell, waiting for the proper words to restore her to her former glory. But here Feinberg seems to be abandoning his static approach. Could one not similarly argue that the foetus or the newly-born infant can be thought of as consisting of a man? True, unlike the beautiful maiden who existed before the pumpkin did, the man did not exist before the infant; but the man is implicit in the child, as Hegel would say.

Actually Feinberg seems to grant that the newly-born infant and the foetus have emerging interests, which may need protection even now if they are to be allowed to come into existence at all. But it is clear from his writings that he is committed to the view that the foetus and the newly-born infants only have contingent rights, that is to say rights on the assumption that they will survive long enough to acquire actual interests when they get the cognitive equipment that is necessary for the possession of aims and desires. By parity of reasoning, Feinberg would have to say that the catatonic schizophrenic too only has contingent rights. Now if a being only has contingent rights, then we can destroy it without violating its rights, for its rights are conditional upon its surviving to achieve the relevant cognitive state in the future. So on Feinberg's view if we kill foetuses, newly-born infants, people in a temporary coma, or people suffering from catatonic schizophrenia, we are not violating the rights of such victims, even if such beings, had they been allowed to survive, could have become perfectly normal human beings in the future.

Perhaps defenders of the static view would say that if we killed such a being we would be doing an injury to the being who existed earlier on and possessed rights. Thus, if you kill a catatonic schizophrenic now you violate the interests and rights of the human being who existed before he became schizophrenic. It is in the interest of normal men not to be killed even when they are in a coma or asleep. This justification does not work in the case of unwanted infants. Nor does it easily work in the case of an adult who does not consent to our killing him but who even in his normal working state is indifferent to whether or not he is killed when he is in a temporary coma or asleep. On Feinberg's static view ants and bees, if they possed the necessary cognitive equipment, could well have higher intrinsic worth than normal newly-born human infants who do not as yet have the functioning cognitive equipment.

I shall discuss another version of the static view, which is found among some philosophers who believe in the will theory of rights. The limitations of such static approaches will be pointed out, but it must be admitted that something like the static approach does work in the case of many rights. There are many rights that we can only acquire when we have satisfied a particular requirement; mere potentiality does not suffice. In such cases something like the static approach works. Thus the adult has the right to vote, but the baby, while a baby, does not have the right to vote merely because it has the potential to become an adult. There are many rights that we only acquire when we exercise our will or rational powers, or, as Hegelians would say, when we put our will into things. Rights derived from contract fall into this category. Again, there are certain rights that we acquire when we assume certain offices or roles. The mere potential to assume these offices or roles does not give us the rights that an individual assumes when he attains that office or role. But it is a serious mistake to generalize and assert that potentiality can never be a ground for the possession of non-contingent rights. There are some rights, such as the right to equal respect and consideration, that human beings could have simply in virtue of their nature, where their nature is not understood statically, only in terms of what they can do now, but dynamically in the way explained earlier.

There is nothing inconsistent in the view that while many rights require the attainments of our rational powers and the exercise of our rational powers, there are others that we could get simply in virtue of possessing the relevant potential. Hegel (on my interpretation) was not inconsistent when he believed both that there are many rights that we acquire through putting our will into things, and that babies have the (non-contingent) right to fulfil their destiny, even when as babies they cannot put their will into anything.

If, however, one assumes that all rights are acquired through or presuppose the exercise of our faculties, then of course mere potential to exercise our faculties will not suffice. And some such assumption is made by some of the philosophers who think that it is conceptually absurd for babies to have rights. Herbert Hart is the most famous modern exponent of the will (or choice) theory of rights:

The idea is that of one individual being given by the law exclusive control, more or less, over another person's duty so that in the area of conduct covered by that duty, the individual who has the right is a small-scale sovereign to whom the duty is owed. The fullest measure of control comprises three distinguishable elements: (i) the right holder may waive or extinguish the duty or leave it in existence; (ii) after breach or threatened breach of duty he may leave it 'unenforced' or may enforce it by suing for compensation or, in certain cases, for an injunction or mandatory order to restrain the continued or further breach of duty; and (iii) he may waive or extinguish the obligation to pay compensation to which the breach gives rise. The right holder by his choice determines how the person who has the correlative duty shall act and so he has the power to limit the latter's freedom of action.[6]

Babies and animals cannot exercise such choices, so advocates of this theory think that they cannot have rights (why not say they have rights, but they cannot exercise their rights?). In his article 'Bentham on Legal Rights' Hart admits that the will theory of rights only operates for a sub-class of rights. But in his earlier paper 'Are there any Natural Rights?' he assumed that this theory applied to all rights held by an individual against other individuals or groups. It appears to follow from this last assumption, that on the will theory of rights babies and animals have no rights against other human beings. And Hart in that earlier paper was quite prepared to accept this implication.

Benn too uses the will theory of rights to show that babies have no rights. Such authors beg substantial issues by conceptual decrees, without making perfectionist judgements. They are not saying that animals or human babies have less worth than adult human beings; it is just that they are not the sorts of creatures who have rights. But such attempts at bypassing perfectionist judgements do not work. To say that

[6] 'Bentham on Legal Rights', *Oxford Essays in Jurisprudence,* ed. A. Simpson (Oxford 1973), p. 192.

some creatures have no rights while others have rights is to imply that the claims of the former get trumped by the claims of the latter. For do not rights trump non-rights? It may be that the interests of grown-up human beings should trump the interests of babies and of animals, but such substantial assertions must not be disguised by conceptual decree. Those who believe in the will theory of rights sometimes point to the fact that babies and animals cannot use their rights to further their projects, whereas human beings, by choosing to exercise their rights or waiving their rights, can advance their projects, and exert a kind of sovereignity over the person who has the correlative duties. But why should those beings who cannot, or cannot yet, exercise such powers over others be given lower status than those who can? Of course both Hart and Benn can and do admit that we have duties with regard to babies, but on their view no duties are *owed* to babies. It might be asked why this should matter. It is not the important thing that we ought not do certain things to babies (such as be cruel to them) rather than whether or not babies have rights? To this it can be replied that the virtue of the doctrine of equal right to respect is that if it extends to an individual such as a baby then it gives us a ground for respecting him. We have a duty to respect him because he has a right to be respected. If he does not have a right to be respected, it may still be the case that we ought to respect him, but we need to know the reason. It is sometimes argued that the reason why we should show consideration to babies utilitarian kind'.[7] Elsewhere in this book it is argued that such reasons do not adequately safeguard the interests of babies.

If the utilitarian case for respecting adults is at least as strong as the utilitarian case for respecting babies, and if in the case of adults, there is an added reason for respecting them, namely that they have a right to be respected, then it seems to follow that the adult's interests have greater protection than the baby's interests and that the rights of the adult could trump the interests of the baby. The way to avoid this consequence is to extend the doctrine of right to equal respect to babies, which would

[7] Benn, 'Abortion, Infanticide, and Respect for Persons', p. 101.

involve abandoning the position taken up by Hart and Benn.

The position of Hart and Benn differs in some important respects from Feinberg's views, for Feinberg rightly does not subscribe to the will theory of right that Hart and Benn subscribe to. But the views of Feinberg, Hart, and Benn resemble each other in two important respects: first, they all make conceptual points which tend to block the discussion of substantial issues, and secondly, they all tend to take a static view about rights. On their views an individual can not have (non-contingent) rights, in virtue of possessing the relevant potential. It is this second feature which distinguishes all these static approaches from the dynamic approach.

Views such as those of Benn, Hart, and Feinberg could be reconstructed in such a way as not to involve a conceptual claim but a substantial claim about rights. The problem then would be, why should we not accept the substantial claims implicit in the static approach to rights? The alternative approach that has been sketched here is certainly not obviously true. Its presuppositions, such as the doctrine of transitivity of ends in themselves and the simple view of personal identity, need justification. Why then should we prefer to dynamic approach?

Now I have already said that the static approach is preferable in the case of many rights. What I maintain is that the dynamic approach is preferable in the case of the right to equal respect and consideration. This claim certainly needs justification. In order to justify it, we have to appeal to the reflective equilibrium model.

7

Reflective Equilibrium and Right-based Theories

In this chapter some of the competing right-based theories are tested against the reflective equilibrium model; it is argued that the dynamic approach comes off better than the static one. One of the functions of a right-based approach is to provide moral constraints within which other considerations, such as utilitarian considerations, personal and family commitments, and commitments to traditional forms of life, must operate. It is shown that the simple view (along with the dynamic view) rather than the complex view is needed to provide such moral constraints. For the complex view goes naturally with an unrestricted utilitarian approach.[1] The contractarian attempt, by philosophers such as Mackie, to provide non-utilitarian moral constraints without appealing to the simple view is rejected; it is argued that the denial of the simple view undermines non-utilitarian moral constraints that protect the individual from being sacrificed by utilitarian and other such considerations.

1. More on the static versus the dynamic view and on the complex versus the simple view

On the reflective equilibrium model, according to Rawls, we adjust our moral (and political) principles and our moral instuitions until we get a harmonious fit. I should like to add one more complication to the reflective equilibrium model. The fit has to be not just between our intuitions and our moral and political principles, but also between these and

[1] See also D. Parfit, 'Later Selves and Moral Principles'.

our metaphysical principles. We must examine the metaphysical assumptions and presuppositions of our intuitions and of our moral and political principles and then see whether these metaphysical assumptions are acceptable. In cases where we cannot on reflection accept the metaphysical assumptions, we may have to abandon the intuitions or the moral and political principles whose presuppositions we cannot accept. Rawls is quite wrong to think we can bypass metaphysical (and perfectionist) considerations in constructing a theory of justice. For instance, we saw that his criticism of utilitarianism becomes less plausible if we abandon the metaphysics of the persistent self, which Rawls presupposes. His reason for wanting to bypass metaphysical and perfectionist considerations is that he wants to avoid controversial matters, he wants to arrive at principles that are acceptable to all, irrespective of their metaphysical or perfectionist positions. We have seen that his approach does not tell us why egalitarianism extends to human babies but not to grown-up animals; he includes babies in the club, but leaves out animals, without giving good reasons. It is my contention that such positions cannot be maintained unless one is willing to appeal to perfectionist and metaphysical considerations. Of course, the metaphysical and perfectionist considerations may turn out to be indefensible, but in that case we may have to abandon our views that egalitarianism extends to human beings but not to animals.

One of the attractions of the right-based approach is that it helps to provide moral constraints within which our goal-based policies, such as the pursuit of utility, can be pursued. Now two main versions of the right based approach have been discussed — the dynamic one and the static one. I have argued that the dynamic approach squares better with some of our important egalitarian moral intuitions. In particular, the dynamic approach helps to protect the young children and foetuses. Some of these who take the static approach, such as Benn, seem to think that utilitarian considerations can explain why we should show concern towards children. But I have argued that utilitarian considerations are not adequate for this purpose (see, for instance, chapter 8 section 1). And it was seen in chapter 2 that those, such as Mackie, who adopt the contractarian approach (without presupposing moral constraints) also have similar problems about how to justify the view that there are certain things that we must not do to children. The dynamic approach harmonizes better with our intuition that the doctrine of equal respect and consideration applies to human infants but not to adult animals. On the static approach, such as Feinberg's or Benn's, such an intuition will have to be abandoned. There is another respect in which the dynamic approach is more in harmony with our egalitarian intuitions. Earlier we saw that there is the problem of why we should show greater respect and consideration to human beings than to animals, and there is the problem of why we should show equal respect to all human beings. To answer the first question we may have to appeal to the fact that human life is significant in a way in which animal life is not. But this raises the problem that some human lives seem quite meaningless, the people concerned just drift from day to day, while other human beings seem to lead a much more significant life, and so why should this not be a reason for inequality or respect among human beings? Part of the answer that we can give is that people who drift and lead a meaningless life once had the potential for leading a significant life, even if now they have lost the ability to do so.

It was in virtue of such potential that in the past they got membership of the egalitarian club. And the doctrine of transitivity of ends in themselves ensures that once you are a member of the egalitarian club, you cannot be thrown out of it, even if you lose the qualities in virtue of which you obtained membership, for instance even if you have lost the capacity for leading a meaningful life, through drug addiction or senility or through adverse social conditions. Such considerations can only be relevant as reasons for including such people in the egalitarian club if we take the dynamic approach. On the static view the fact that a senile old man or a drug addict or a psychopath once had the potential to lead a worthwhile life is irrelevant (even if the potential was destroyed through no fault of his own), the only relevant consideration being what his capacities are now. The doctrine of transitivity of ends in themselves presupposes the dynamic view.

Some people would prefer the static approach to the dynamic approach because the former excludes the foetus from the egalitarian club. But for an egalitarian this is not a sufficient ground for preferring the static approach. If this were the only practical difference between what is implied by the two approaches, then it would perhaps have been plausible to prefer the static approach. But the trouble with the static approach is that though it excludes the foetus from the egalitarian club, it excludes, as we have seen, many unfortunate human beings as well. Since it excludes so many people, how can it square with *egalitarian* intuitions?

Now a defender of the static view might appeal to some kind of pragmatic fiction. He may argue that many human beings who are not full members of the egalitarian club (for instance, because they are not leading significant, meaningful lives) should be included as associate members or should be treated as if they were members of the egalitarian club; for not to so treat them would lead to quarrels among human beings as to who is inferior.

Even the dynamic approach (in the version defended in this book) has to appeal to some such pragmatic argument for including congenital idiots in the egalitarian club. But it is a virtue of a theory that it keeps such pragmatic fictions to a minimum. The dynamic approach, unlike the static approach, can harmonize with the view that all human beings (except congenital idiots) really are members of the egalitarian club. This provides a more secure foundation of egalitarianism for all human beings (except congenital idiots) than the static version, which would at best harmonize with the view that egalitarianism is a useful doctrine rather than with the view that it is a true doctrine.

As was pointed out earlier the reflective equilibrium model should not concern itself merely with the mutual adjustment between our intuitions and our moral and political principles. Before using the model to adjudicate between rival theories or principles one needs to see not just how well a theory or a principle squares with our intuitions, but also how should the metaphysical and perfectionist presuppositions of the theory are. For instance suppose (as I believe is the case) the dynamic approach only works if the simple view of personal identity is true, and suppose (as I do not believe is the case) the simple view of personal identity is false, and suppose the static view does not presuppose a false metaphysics. In that case honesty would demand that we abandon the dynamic approach even if it squares better with our intuitions than the static view does; we could then say that some of the intuitions that conflict with the static view may have to be revised, so that the revised intuitions could harmonize with the static view. For instance, we may revise our intuition according to which the doctrine of equal respect and consideration applies to children: and we may have to revise our opinions about young children having greater worth and being more sacred creatures than adult non-human animals.

In fact it has not been shown that the dynamic approach presupposes a false metaphysics. It is true, as was argued earlier, that the dynamic view does presuppose the simple view of personal identity — for without the simple view the dynamic view will not be able to appeal to the doctrine of transitivity of ends in themselves, nor will it be able to show why young children are sacred, for on the complex view the most that would follow from the fact that they (unlike animals) will change into adult human beings is that they have a lot of instrumental worth. But though the dynamic approach presupposes the simple view, the latter has not been shown to be false. I shall not try to prove the simple view; it is not possible to do that. But the simple view is presupposed by much of our moral and practical experience, and it is arguable that if we abandon the simple view this will not only involve the abandonment of the dynamic view, but it will also weaken, if not wholly undermine, the whole right-based approach, according to which human rights set moral constraints within which utilitarian and other goals can be pursued. If this is so then one cannot use the alleged falsity of the simple view as an argument for preferring the static version of the right-based approach to the dynamic version.

The abandonment of the simple view would weaken the idea of right-based theories (whether of the static variety or the dynamic variety). For the reason that there is a need to provide moral constraints against utilitarianism is partly that in the absence of such constraints we could sacrifice the individual for the sake of utilitarian aims. But now if we abandon the simple view of personal identity, then it is not at all clear what is so wrong with sacrificing the individual for the sake of utility. The whole idea that human rights set non-utilitarian moral constraints that must be observed by us in the pursuit of utilitarian goals is weakened if we adopt the complex view. The view that an individual human being is sacred is difficult to defend if one takes the line that considerations of convenience determine whether an individual survives. If considerations of convenience determine which individuals are identical and which ones are not, what is so sacred about an individual human being, why not sacrifice him when that is necessary for the sake of others? Of course there will still be utilitarian reasons why we must not do such things too often, for this may cause insecurity, alarm, and terror among the population, but such reasons would not involve an appeal to non-utilitarian moral constraints. Some of the utilitarian constraints of the kind that rule-utilitarians appeal to could coexist with the complex view; though it is arguable that even utilitarianism would be at least partially undermined by the complex view. For if Parfit's complex theory is correct, if there are no persistent individuals (except in a trivial sense), why should we get so worked up about suffering in the world? Suffering would still be real, but how much worse it is when (intrinsically) the very same individual keeps suffering on and on. Such considerations make one suspect that the complex view is not only incompatible with a right-based approach (which it is for the reasons given in this book) but also with any kind of humane morality. Parfit rightly points out that on his view a person should not be frightened by the prospects of his death, death is not as bad as it appears to the ignorant. He might have added that on his view murder is not such an evil as it appears to the old-fashioned.

Let us grant that even if the complex view is true, human beings would display characteristics such as rationality, humanity, and so forth. We may still be able to appeal to the perfectionist argument that human beings, or rather those human beings who have developed the relevant qualities, are wonderful creatures in a way in which animals are not.

And so we may still be able to appeal to the argument that adult human beings in general have a greater right to respect than animals have, though there are problems about how on the complex view egalitarianism can extend to adult human beings who lead bored and insignificant lives. We saw earlier that the dynamic view (which presupposes the simple view and so is inconsistent with the complex view) can solve such problems, as well as problems about how the doctrine of equal respect can extend to infants. On the complex view, the infant is not in any deep sense the same individual as the adult human being that it will grow into, and it is not easy to see why it should have any more *intrinsic* worth than an animal; the fact that it will in the future grow into something more wonderful than an animal is at best evidence for the view that it has greater instrumental worth. Moreover, on the complex view, even with regard to adult human beings the most that follows is that adult human beings in general are more wonderful creatures than animals are; but the view that the *individual* human being is sacred would have to be abandoned, even in the case of adult human beings. For on the complex view the identity of persons is not a matter of fact but of conceptual convenience and convention. If considerations of convenience determine the identity of a person, then considerations of convenience are an important determinant of the rights of the individual person. But in that case what is so terrible if such individual rights (that have considerations of convenience as their source) are sacrificed when the larger interests of society demand such sacrifice? Why not punish the innocent for the sake of others? Why not replace some human beings by superior ones (see chapter 8)? Admittedly, there are some utilitarian reasons for being cautious before adopting such frightening policies. But the right-based moral constraints against such policies will be weakened if we give up the simple view of personal identity. Nozick says that an individual has only one life and so must not be sacrificed for utilitarian considerations. But if a person's identity is a matter of convenience, then arguments such as Nozick's cease to have much force. Again, Rawls's complaint, that utilitarianism overlooks the separateness of persons, ceases to be an objection if Parfit is right in thinking that on the complex view the separateness of individuals is itself not a deep truth but a matter of convention.

2. The complex view and punishment

In the sphere of punishment non-utilitarian right-based moral constraints will be undermined if we accept the complex view. Retributive theories of punishment seem inconsistent with it. The criminal who is being punished is not intrinsically the same person as the one who committed the crime (in the sense that there is no underlying self common to them both). So why should the later self of the criminal suffer retribution for the deeds of the earlier one? Right-based theories of punishment, such as Hart's, are also incompatible with the complex view. For instance, on the liberal right-based view it is argued that before we are justified in punishing a person for his crime certain non-utilitarian conditions must be satisfied. The person being punished must give us a licence to punish him by voluntarily committing a crime. Even if the institution of punishment is justified on utilitarian grounds, the pursuit of utility is qualified by human rights in the sense that human rights must not be sacrificed for utilitarian goals.[2] An innocent person must not be punished even if it is useful to punish him. Similarly, it is unjust to punish a sick criminal even it it is useful to punish him. Thus Hart has argued that from a utilitarian standpoint it is sometimes useful to punish sick criminals, for a system which excuses sick criminals from punishment may encourage healthy criminals to commit crimes in the hope of bluffing the courts into believing that they were sick and so should be excused. Such punishment of sick criminals may be useful, says Hart, but it is unjust to the sick criminal, who could not have helped what he did.

Such non-utilitarian constraints become much less plausible on the complex view. On the complex view the person who is being punished is not in any deep sense the same person as the one who committed the crime and gave us a licence to punish him. Of course it may, for reasons of convenience, be

[2] See Hart, *Punishment and Responsibility,* and R. Nozick, *Anarchy, State, and Utopia* (Oxford, 1974).

desirable to call him the same individual as the person who committed the crime, but there is no underlying self common to the two. The criminal's later self could no more have avoided what the earlier self did, than a son could have avoided what a father did at a time when the son was not born. So, on the complex view, how can the earlier self be said to give us a licence to punish the later self? We could (for utilitarian reasons) operate a system where the earlier self is deemed to give us a licence to punish the later self, even though there is no underlying self uniting the two. But then so could we (for utilitarian reasons) operate a system where one person is deemed to give us a licence to punish another person — for instance, we could (for utilitarian reasons) operate a system where a person's crime is taken as giving us a licence to punish not only him but also his wife and sons. True, even if the complex view is true, there could be a utilitarian case for a system of punishing the later self for the deeds of the earlier self (for instance because the earlier self is deterred by the thought of what happens to the later self). But then so could there be a utilitarian case for sometimes punishing sons for the deeds of their fathers; such a system could sometimes deter fathers from committing crimes.

Under the complex view there is not a radical moral difference between punishing John Doe for the crimes that John Doe committed earlier, and punishing John Doe's son for the crimes that John Doe committed earlier. True, John Doe's son is innocent of the crimes that his father committed, but on the complex view John Doe is innocent of the crime that was committed by his earlier self. And if you are willing to punish the future self of the criminal even though (on the complex view) the later self could not have committed the crime that the earlier self committed, how can you consider as morally forbidden the punishment of innocent citizens? The complex view seems to undermine the anti-utilitarian moral constraints. And once we undermine such constraints we are on a slippery slope, on the way to the Brave New World.

Often Parfit is aware of the radical implications of his views, but sometimes he is not. Thus sometimes he suggests that the principle of desert could survive the introduction of the complex view: 'when the connections between convicts and their past criminal selves are less, they deserve less punishment; if they are very weak, they perhaps deserve none'.[3] But it seems to me that if the complex view is correct such claims make no more sense than the claim that the tyrant's son deserves more punishment for the tyrant's misdeeds than the tyrant's grandson does. If the complex view is true, then there is no underlying persistent self at all, not even for short periods, not even between my present self and myself yesterday. As Parfit says, talk of successive selves is only a *facon de parler*. So John Doe the convict did not commit the crime and could not have prevented the occurrence of the crime. Admittedly, there may be close psychological connections between him now and his earlier criminal self, closer than the ties between the tyrants and his sons and grandsons. John Doe the convict may well identify himself with the John Doe who committed the crime. Such considerations may make him resent the punishment less than if he did not so identify. But none of this shows that he could on the complex view deserve punishment; at most such considerations may show how he may believe that he deserves punishment.

One might of course decide for utilitarian reasons to have a *system* where people can be punished for what their earlier selves did but not for what their fathers or grandfathers did. It is arguable that under modern conditions a *system* of vicarious responsibility does more harm than good.[4] But nothing is gained by using the language of desert here.

It might be objected that in some ways the complex view could have an opposite effect from the one just suggested; it could provide, in effect, more scope for the anti-utilitarian moral constraints. Thus, Hart insists that a morally necessary condition of punishment is that people should have voluntarily committed a crime for which they are being punished. Now if the complex view is correct, and if the criminal's later self has not really committed the crime that his earlier self committed, then the correct application of Hart's

---

[3] D. Parfit, 'Later Selves and Moral Principles', p. 143.
[4] See J. Feinberg, *Doing and Deserving* (Princeton, 1970), chapter 9.

requirement would be to insist that the criminal's later self cannot be punished. On the complex view, the moral checks against punishing the innocent could still remain; it is just that there are many more innocent people than there are if the simple view is accepted.

But such an objection misses out the fact that the complex view undermines anti-utilitarian moral constraints such as Hart's. For these constraints are designed to protect the individual from being sacrificed for utilitarian ends. But now if the complex view is true, then as we saw the *individual* human being ceases to be important, and so it is not clear why he cannot be sacrificed for utilitarian ends. On the complex view the identity of individuals is rather like the identity of nations. As Parfit tells us, most of us do not bother to treat nations as the primary objects of our duties or as possessors of rights in any deep sense.[5] We regard nations as constructs out of individual human beings. Similarly, if the complex view is true, then the individual human being can be seen as a construct out of individual experiences, and so we may, when we think, morally focus more on the individual items of experience and less on the individual person who has the experience.

It is not being suggested that all non-utilitarian moral constraints will have to be abandoned if we abandon the simple view of personal identity. Some such checks could survive the abandonment of the simple view; but my point is that these remaining checks will not be morally sufficient to preserve some of the basic features of our existing moral system.

There are philosophers, such as Mackie, who do not believe in the simple view of personal identity and yet do not accept utilitarianism. They would argue that we could invent contractarian (or conventional) constraints which our utilitarian policies must not violate. Now I have already discussed the limits of the contractarian approach, for instance that it leaves out those in a weak bargaining position. If we accept the complex view, then the contractarian approach faces further problems. If the contractarian approach is to set adequate moral constraints within which utilitarian

5 'Later Selves and Moral Principles'.

policies can be pursued, it must be able to tell us what is so wrong with sacrificing the individual for utilitarian goals. Now normally the contractarian approach to such issues is to say that on the contractarian model such sacrifices of the individual are not justified because the state has no authority to sacrifice the individual. A contractarian approach has to allow for legitimate sanctions against offenders. For without such sanctions, the rules that enable men to co-operate with and compete with each other in a civilized way will not be able to survive. Now on the contractarian approach, when the state imposes sanctions it could be doing so legitimately provided the offender has given the state a licence to impose the sanction. A murderer, for instance, can be punished because he has forfeited his right to liberty. His punishment is in a sense self-imposed — by breaking the law the murderer has in a sense brought the punishment upon himself. The doctrine *volenti non fit injuria*, according to which no injury is done to one who consents, can be used to show that in such cases the state when it punishes the criminal does not harm the individual. But now this rationale of punishment disappears if we introduce the complex view. For on the complex view the criminal being punished is not the one who has given his consent to the punishment. The crime was committed by an earlier self whereas the punishment is being suffered by the later self; so how can the later self be said to bring the punishment upon himself? One may of course justify punishment on utilitarian grounds, but the problem remains, that if you are willing to punish the later self for the crimes of the earlier self, why not punish an innocent man for a crime he never committed provided it is useful to punish him? Why not have a system that allows us to punish a son for the crime of his father, if such punishment is useful? Even if in our society such punishment is counter-productive there are other closely-knit societies where vicarious punishment may well serve a useful purpose.[6]

There is a sense in which it can, under certain circumstances, be fair to make the son pay his father's debts. Suppose a son inherits wealth from his father. It is quite fair that if the father owed money to others, then the father's debts should

---

[6] See Feinberg, *Doing and Deserving,* chapter 9.

be paid out of the son's inheritance. Similarly one might argue that if the later self inherits all sorts of goods and qualities from his earlier self, is it not fair that the later self should be asked to pay the debts of his earlier self?

This argument has certain important limits. A son is at most morally responsible for his deceased father's debts to the extent that the debts that he inherits from his father do not exceed the capital that he inherits. Similarly, the later self cannot be morally responsible for the debts of his earlier self to the extent that the debts that he inherits exceed the capital that he inherits. Suppose John Doe is asked to pay a library fine of £5 because of some overdue books borrowed by his earlier self. Now in such a case if John Doe were to disclaim responsibility for this debt which he admits was incurred by his earlier self, we could retort, 'Look, you have inherited so much from your earlier self. For instance, the large house that belonged to your earlier self now belongs to you. It is quite fair that if you acquire all his capital, you should pay his debts out of that capital. You cannot claim to be the same as John Doe for the purpose of acquiring all his capital, and at the same time deny that it is you who owe the library money'.

But now suppose John Doe were to commit a murder. Is it fair to severely punish his later self, say, by life imprisonment? Is this not a case where the capital that John Doe inherits from the earlier self is less than the debt that he is alleged to have inherited from his earlier self? And so, if in such a case we were to punish him severely, we would be punishing a person who was, morally speaking, innocent. We may of course decide that for pragmatic reasons we have to punish such people, in spite of their moral innocence. But if so, how can we rule out, on principle, a system which allows us to punish a son for the crimes of his father?

The contractarian approach needs to have sanctions against delinquents if it is to sustain the rules and institutions that it advocates. But now if contractarianism, on the complex view, has to rely on a utilitarian theory of sactions and punishment, then it can hardly provide an adequate check on the pursuit of utilitarian goals.

Contractarians sometimes resort to the device of a hypothetical consent. Even if the convict has not given us his actual consent, he may have given us his hypothetical consent. If he looked at things from an impartial standpoint he would agree that society needs sanctions against criminals. Now it might be argued that such impartial judgements could be made even if the complex view is true. Thus the convict being punished, if he looked at things from an impartial standpoint, would agree that he has to be punished for a crime committed by his earlier self; for let us assume it is the case that such punishment is the most efficacious and economical (in terms of suffering) way of substaining the social order. But the trouble with this reply is that hypothetical consent is not actual consent, it is not even tacit consent. And unless there is actual consent (either explicit or tacit), the doctrine *volenti non fit injuria* cannot apply in the way that we saw that it needs to in order to construct a contractarian theory of punishment.

Contractarians are sometimes aware that hypothetical consent is not real consent. That is why some contractarians appeal to something stronger than mere hypothetical consent. That is why Rousseau distinguished between real will and actual will.[7] The criminal may actually want to break the law, but *qua* citizen his real (or general) will is to obey the law including the law that sanctions punishment against offenders. Critics of Rousseau may argue that his distinction is one between actual wants and hypothetical wants, but I do not think that is how Rousseau saw the distinction. For Rousseau the general will was the real will of the citizens and not their hypothetical will. Again, Rawls appeals to something stronger than hypothetical consent. He believes (or needs to believe) that the criminal, qua his rational or noumenal self has given us his consent.[8]

Now this distinction between the criminal's actual wants and his real or rational wants will be undermined on the complex view. If you accept the complex view because you are empirically minded and suspicious of unobservable

[7] J. J. Rousseau, *The Social Contract and Discourses,* transl. G. D. H. Cole, revised by J. Brumfitt and J. Hall (London, 1973), Book I. chapter VII.
[8] See *A Theory of Justice,* section 40.

and unverifiable entities that are postulated by the simple view, you cannot plausibly combine the complex view with mysterious talk of noumenal or rational or real selves, which go beyond the empirical self.

So we see how the complex view undermines right-based constraints. If that is so, if the simple view is presupposed by the right-based approach, then we cannot prefer the static version of the right-based approach over the dynamic version on the grounds that the dynamic version presupposes the simple view of personal identity.

I do not want to deny the importance of the contractarian approach, but rather to emphasize its limits. It can only work if it presupposes moral constraints. And the dynamic version of the right-based approach helps to explain what these moral constraints are. It will not do to argue that we could bypass such right-based moral constraints by appealing to other considerations, like family considerations. For it can be seen that these other considerations, too, must only be allowed to operate if they presuppose certain moral constraints.

Thus we saw earlier that family considerations, too, need moral constraints. Without such constraints family considerations could lead to the sacrifice of the interests of foreigners to our interests. Some of the shortcomings of the family considerations are similar to the shortcomings of contractarian considerations, and so it will not do to argue that such considerations, in combination, will be able to provide adequate moral constraints. Nor will it suffice if we combine such considerations with utilitarianism. It might be suggested that though future generations and weak foreigners come off badly from the contractarian and family point of view, utilitarian considerations can look after the interests of such people. But this suggestion is not adequate. Utilitarianism when unrestrained by non-utilitarian constraints has serious shortcomings (see chapter 8). If our dealings with weak foreigners are constrained only by utilitarian considerations, then we may be able to justify replacement policies with regard to such foreigners, for instance a policy of painlessly and suddenly killing the weak foreigners, so that we can replace them with superior human beings who are better producers of utility. Or again, we may be able to justify punishing some weak innocent foreigners, using them as scapegoats for our ills, if such punishment serves to promote the general welfare, such that the increase in welfare is enough to offset the suffering involved. Contractarian considerations will not be able to provide sufficient checks. For the weak foreigners may be in a very weak bargaining position, so that contractarian considerations do not apply here; and since they are foreigners, family considerations do now show what is wrong with sacrificing their interests for the sake of the interests of others, especially when these others are more closely related to us than the weak foreigners are.

So we see that family considerations, like contractarian considerations, need to presuppose moral constraints, and so they cannot themselves provide all the relevant moral constraints. We seem to need a theory of rights (such as the view that every human being has a natural right to equal respect and consideration), to provide the necessary moral constraints within which family and contractarian considerations can operate.

3. The Hampshire-Williams argument

An attempt to provide non-utilitarian moral constraints has been made by appealing to the fact that human beings have projects, certain ideals of life. It is these projects and ideals of life that humanize a person and give significance to his life. Now for many of us our conception of the sort of person we want to be does not permit us to do certain things, however useful such things may be. Thus many of us believe that we must not betray our friends and our families, and we must not kill our babies for utilitarian ends. We are committed to ways of life that do not allow us to sacrifice our friends and our family for utilitarian reasons. We cannot be expected to serve utilitarian ends when they conflict with our own ideals of life, ideals without which our own life would lose all meaning. Some such view is found in the writings of Stuart Hampshire and Bernard Williams. Now such a view does provide some checks on utilitarianism but it does not provide sufficient checks. Moreover, this view of Williams and Hampshire is itself in need of checks; our ideals and our projects must operate within moral constraints. Let me explain.

The Hampshire–Williams view does not tell us what is really wrong with a system of utilitarianism which is unrestrained except that it has a proviso exempting people from serving utilitarian ends when this would involve their going against their integrity. Why not have a system where utilitarian parents are permitted to kill their young when this is desirable for utilitarian aims; non-utilitarian parents cannot complain as their children are quite safe, and they are not being asked to kill anyone. Why not have a system where people with utilitarian ideals are allowed to sacrifice innocent people (such as innocent weak foreigners) for utilitarian ends, while people who do not share such ideals are exempt from having to carry out such policies, somewhat as we now exempt conscientious objectors from fighting in a just war?

Such questions can be more adequately answered if we are willing to appeal to a theory of human rights. Thus the reason why one must not allow utilitarian-minded parents, *even if they are in a majority in a given society*, from sacrificing their own children for utilitarian purposes is that children have a right to respect and consideration. The doctrine of rights is needed not only to supplement some of William's and Hampshire's arguments against utilitarianism; it is also required to constrain the Hampshire–Williams argument from being abused. It might be thought that personal commitments are so deep that they are not subject to moral constraints. But this view would be quite wrong. Williams seems to say that unless one is willing to run the risk of breaking these constraints in the pursuit of one's commitments, 'there will not be enough substance or conviction in a man's life to compel his allegiance to life itself.'[9] But why can there not be sufficient substance or conviction in a man's life if he believes that his commitments are subject to moral constraints?

Consider the following conversation:

A. I love you very deeply. I shall do anything you ask.

B. Anything?

[9] 'Persons, Character, and Morality', p.215.

A. Yes, anything, provided it is physically possible for me to do it.

B. Kill C and bring his head on a silver plate to me.

It seems to me that A should never have given such a blanket promise; such an extreme promise is suspect and void to the extent that it violates moral constraints. Perhaps Williams's point could be made plausible if one took him to mean that though our personal commitments are subject to moral constraints, we must be prepared in some very extreme situations to break these constraints. When we break these moral constraints we shall have dirty hands, we shall have done something terrible, but sometimes, in exceptional situations, such a dirty thing may have to be done. This view acknowledges the reality of and the need for moral constraints, even though it allows such constraints to be broken in extreme situations. But how can such moral constraints be spelled out adequately without appealing to a theory of human rights and to perfectionist considerations? In the example just mentioned is it not because C had certain rights that A must not fulfil his commitment to B?

4. The need for the dynamic view

We have stressed the need for a right-based approach, and have dealt with the problem of why, if we adopt the right-based approach, we should prefer the dynamic version of the right-based approach to the static one. It was seen that the dynamic approach squared better with some of our intuitions; but we also saw that the dynamic approach has to face the problem that it presupposes the simple view of personal identity, a view which is controversial. We have not tried to prove the simple view here. but we have argued that the right-based view is seriously undermined if we give up the simple view and adopt the complex view. If this is so, it is not possible for adherents of the static approach to argue that the static approach should be preferred to the dynamic approach on the grounds that the latter presupposes the simple view of personal identity. It seems that if the static approach is to provide moral constraints within which our family considerations, contractarian considerations, and our commitments can operate, then it too must presuppose the simple view. For instance, we have seen that the contractarian model has to work within moral constraints; for otherwise it neglects the people in a weak bargaining position. The way to overcome this deficiency is to postulate that the contractarian considerations must observe the (non-contractarian) rights of all individuals, including those in a weak bargaining position, such as weak foreigners, children, future generations. Now if the right-based approach has to provide such constraints, it cannot do so on the complex view of personal identity. For we have seen that on the complex view, it is difficult to regard an *individual* person as sacred. Although persons can be important, the *individual* person cannot be regarded as sacred, as someone who cannot be sacrificed for the sake of other persons. For on the complex view, the separateness of individuals as well as the unity of the life of one individual is a matter of convention, not reflecting any deep truth.

So if a right-based approach is to set moral constraints within which contractarian and other considerations can operate, and if at least part of the point of these moral constraints is to protect the individual from being sacrificed by the unrestrained operation of contractarian and other considerations, such as utilitarian considerations, family considerations, and the pursuit of one's projects and ideals, then we must postulate the simple view.

We have see that the static approach cannot be preferred over the dynamic approach on the grounds that the latter presupposes the simple view. But may there not be other arguments in favour of the static approach? If so, why not postulate the static approach along with the simple view of personal identity? An objection against the dynamic view might run as follows. Even if we grant the simple view, why should we grant the doctrine of transitivity of ends in themselves or its variants which attach so much importance to the potential that an individual has? The potential that an entity has should only count as being a reason for thinking that the entity has instrumental value, or for thinking that it has contingent rights, not for anything stronger. Suppose we follow William James in this view that human life has significance because human beings, unlike animals, have overall ideals of life that they wish to lead, and then follow such ideals with zest. Human beings, by shaping their lives inaccordance with an ideal, give meaning to their life. Nozick remarks that the notion of meaningfulness has the right feel as something that might bridge the 'is-ought' gap.[10] Perhaps what he means is that if a life is meaningful to the agent, then that life is in an important sense valuable, so statements of value can in such cases be naturally said to follow from the factual statement that the agent's life is meaningful. Now let us see how this applies to the case of the human infant. Suppose it is a fact that this infant will, when he grows up, lead a significant life. Why is that a conclusive reason for thinking that the infant's life is valuable now (except in the sense that it possesses instrumental worth, which is not enough for regarding the infant as sacred)?

What are we to make of this objection against the dynamic view? It seems to me that such arguments do not show why we should prefer the static approach. For such arguments have about equal force against the static approach. Thus, even leaving aside the mentally defective, if we observe adult human beings, many of them drift from day to day, their lives are not governed by any ideal; there are others who have some sort of ideal but do not pursue it with any enthusiasm. Many such people do not lead significant lives, but are bored and try to drown their sorrows in drink and other escapist pastimes. Now on the static view, why should their lives be regarded as sacred? Those who believe in the static approach may reply that even though an adult human being is not leading a significant and meaningful life, he is capable here and now of leading such a life, which is why he is such a sacred creature. But this reply is unconvincing, for it is simply false to claim that all adult human beings (even if we leave aside the mentally defective) who are leading uninspiring lives could by a sudden heroic effort of will start living a significant life right now. As shown earlier the dynamic approach can more easily explain why the doctrine of equal respect should apply to those adult human beings who are drifting from day to day, and not leading meaningful lives.

Admittedly there are all kinds of things that adult human

---

[10] *Anarchy, State, and Utopia,* p. 50.

beings, including those leading bored, insignificant lives can do, which human infants and animals cannot do. Thus many of them can act autonomously, they may be able to kill themselves autonomously, or kill others autonomously. Some adult human beings are incapable of acting autonomously, but they too can do things such as use language in a far more sophisticated way than infants and animals, and so *in a sense* they may be considered more rational than infants and animals. But such considerations cannot rescue the static view from the difficulties that it faces. For such considerations do not provide reasons for granting superior status to adult human beings. Is it not more plausible to argue that things like autonomy and rationality are only good when they are used in the service of significant and worthwhile ends? Something like Moore's doctrine of organic wholes may be relevant here. According to that doctrine there are wholes whose value is greater than the sum of the values of their parts. An autonomous and meaningful life could be much more intrinsically valuable than a life that was meaningful but not autonomous, yet autonomy by itself need have no substantial intrinsic value.

There is another version of the doctrine of rights that is worth discussing. According to this view—let us call it the semi-static view—the individual's right to consideration varies with how near the individual is to realizing its relevant potential, as well as with how wonderful that potential is.[11] This view appears to explain why an adult person in a dreamless sleep has a greater right to consideration than a foetus or a newly-born infant, why an infant has a greater right to consideration than a foetus, why the foetus in the later stages has greater right to consideration than the foetus in the early stages, why the foetus has greater right to consideration than the sperm and the unfertilized ovum. And this view appears to explain why a human infant has greater right to consideration than a grown-up tiger; for though the latter has realized its potential, its potential is of a lower order than the potential of the human infant.

But why should it matter how near an individual is to realizing its potential? Perhaps the reason is this. Other things

---

[11] W. Pluhar, 'Abortion and Simple Consciousness', *Journal of Philosophy*, lxxiv (1977), 159-72.

THE NEED FOR THE DYNAMIC VIEW

being equal the nearer one is to the wonderful state of being an end in oneself, the greater the chances that one will succeed in attaining this wonderful condition. Thus if x will attain Nirvana in ten years, while y has only ten days to go before Nirvana, then y has greater instrumental worth, if only because in the case of x the probability of achieving Nirvana is much less, since all kinds of disasters in the intervening years could prevent x from achieving Nirvana.

What are we to make of such arguments? Such arguments cannot provide sufficient anti-utilitarian constraints. We can conceive of situations where the instrumental effects of human infanticide (with the consent of parents or guardians) are on the whole beneficial—the proviso that there should be consent of the parents can reduce the evil side-effects of such a practice. Suppose there is overpopulation among human beings while the tiger population is in danger of becoming extinct. In that case why not give greater consideration to a tiger cub than to a human infant?

Perhaps the argument under consideration assumes that an individual's intrinsic worth (and not just its instrumental worth) is determined by how wonderful its potential is and how near it is to attaining its potential So an infant has more intrinsic worth than a foetus, it is more of an end in itself than a foetus, the foetus in the later stages is more of an end in itself than the foetus in the early stages. On this view as an individual child develops it becomes more and more of an end in itself until it reaches its wonderful potential. Now it may be argued that this view can show why we should prefer the human infant to a tiger. For the human infant, though it is less of an end in itself than an adult human being, is more of an end in itself than the tiger. So even if there are utilitarian reasons for preferring the tiger to the human infant (for instance, in the case where the tiger population is in danger of extinction, while the world is overpopulated with human beings) we should not prefer the tiger. For the fact that the human infant is more of an end in itself than a tiger sets moral constraints that considerations of utility cannot easily override.

One problem with this view is that it is too strong. It is incompatible with the doctrine of equal respect among adult human beings (even leaving aside the mentally defective). It cannot show why adult human beings deserve equal respect in spite of the fact that some adult human beings lead insignificant lives. Once one is prepared to admit that children have less human worth than adults, it is difficult to deny that some adult human beings have more intrinsic worth than other human adults. On the other hand, if, in order to avoid quarrels among human beings as to who is superior, we decide to treat adult human beings as if they were of equal worth, it is difficult not to extend this egalitarian 'fiction' to cover all human beings (including children) who have not yet attained maturity.

On the dynamic view expounded in this book an individual at the start of his life has just as much *intrinsic* worth as he has when he is at the height of powers. He is just as much of an end in himself throughout his career. And his natural right to respect and consideration remains the same. But this view is quite consistent with the view that there are many specific rights which he may acquire and which he may surrender during different stages of his life.

We should not be worried by the criticism that the dynamic approach presupposes views that are not obviously true. Admittedly, the doctrine of transitivity of ends in themselves, as well as the simple view of personal identity, are controversial doctrines. If such doctines were obviously true there would be no need of the reflective equilibrium model. Rawls attempts to construct his theory without appealing to controversial doctrines. If his attempt had succeeded, it would have rendered the reflective equilibrium model redundant. That his attempt is a failure can be seen by the fact that from time to time he is driven to appeal to controversial doctrines that need to be justified by an appeal to the reflective equilibrium model. Thus earlier in chapter 2 we saw that he allows children to be members of the egalitarian club by appealing to our intuitions. And in chapter 11 we shall see that he appeals to the controversial Aristotelian principle; this principle is far from obvious, and he tries to defend it by showing that it harmonizes with other views that we hold. It is quite legitimate to appeal to the reflective equilibrium model to adjudicate between rival views, but one must abondon Rawls's view that only clear and obvious doctrines should be admitted in the construction of moral and political principles. Failure to appreciate this point has lead Rawls to exclude metaphysical and perfectionist considerations on the grounds that they do not meet his standard of the clear and the obvious.

8

Rights, Utility, and Future Generations

Some egalitarians are utilitarians, but there are others who combine egalitarianism with a right-based approach. This chapter stresses the need for a right-based approach by contrasting it with certain utilitarian doctrines. It is argued that a right-based approach harmonizes better with our egalitarian intuitions than utilitarianism does; it comes off better when tested against the reflective equilibrium model. It is worth stressing that the right-based approach, in the version being defended here, does not deny that utilitarian goals ought to be pursued, but rather sets non-utilitarian moral constraints within which such goals can be pursued. So when right-based theories are contrasted with utiliatrianism, the contrast is intended to be with utilitarianism that is unrestrained by non-utilitarian moral constraints. Utilitarianism may of course have its own constraints; for instance, rule utilitarians tend to admit that there are constraints about killing human beings, breaking promises, and so forth, but they insist that such constraints can be derived from the principle of utility itself.

1. Rights versus utility

Now one trouble with utilitarianism (when not restrained by non-utilitarian constraints) is that it allows an individual to be sacrificed for utilitarian goals. A standard criticism of utilitarianism has been that it allows punishment of the innocent when this can lead to a reduction in crime rate.[1] Another related criticism of utilitarianism is that it does not attach

[1] See Hart, *Punishment and Responsibility*.

moral importance to the distinction between existing persons and potential persons. Utilitarianism makes people replacable. From the utilitarian point of view the reason why it is wrong to kill existing people is that this results in the loss of future years of happiness, but in that case is there not just as strong a utilitarian case for saying that it is wrong to deliberately refrain from conceiving a child? Jonathan Glover, himself a utilitarian, considers the following objection.

Suppose pressure on the world's resources has become so great that it is necessary to place an absolute limit on population size. . . .suppose also that genetic engineering is highly developed so that we have increasing control over what our children will be like. In such a world, it may be that everyone has a faily good life, but advances in genetic engineering suggest that the next generation should have even better lives. One way of increasing the total of worthwhile life in the world might be to kill off painlessly some of the present generation in order to create vacancies in the population for new, happier people.[2]

Why then should a utilitarian not opt for the policy of killing some of the existing people and replacing them with new people who can contribute more to maximizing happiness or the amount of worthwhile life?

Now right-based theories of the kind defended in this book would of course rule out such replacement policies, because such replacement policies violate the rights of existing people; our pursuit of utilitarian goals must not involve a violation of the rights of existing people. Even if rights can sometimes be overrriden when they conflict with other rights, potential people do not have a non-contingent right to be conceived; so in the above example replacement policies would not be justified on a right-based theory, not even a right-based theory that allowed rights sometimes to be trumped by other rights. So does not such an example tend to show that right-based theories harmonize better with our moral intuitions than utilitarianism does?

Glover thinks that utilitarianism can deal with such cases.[3] He thinks that such objections to utilitarianism become less powerful when we consider the adverse side-effects that such policies involve. Glover distinguishes the direct objections to

[2] J. Glover, *Causing Deaths and Saving Lives* (London, 1977), p. 72.
[3] Ibid.

killing which relate solely to the person killed from the side-effects of killing on people other than the one killed. The side-effects of killing a part of our existing population would be that the remaining population would feel, on an extreme scale, grief, resentment, and insecurity. Now it seems to me that such side-effects cannot explain what is really so terrible about killing off some ordinary normal people in order to replace them with people who are better producers of utility. One could construct practices where the side-effects are not so terrible. Why not permit the killing of fairly healthy, normal babies provided the parents or guardians of the babies consent to the killing? The babies could be killed painlessly, and could be replaced by new babies who contribute more to the general happiness. There is no obvious danger involved to the adult population—for the above-mentioned practice would only involve the killing of babies; nor need the adult population feel insecure on account of their babies; for their babies will not be killed without their consent. Glover spends considerable time discussing the infanticide of abnormal babies. But the trouble with utilitarianism is that it could even allow the killing of ordinary babies or of mildly deformed babies—for instance when their parents consented to such killing and when the world is overpopulated or when the babies could be replaced by other babies who could contribute more to the achievement of utilitarian goals.

Utilitarians such as Glover sometimes appeal to other adverse side-effects of such killing, such as the loosening of our inhibitions against killing in general. But there is no guarantee that such utilitarian moves will always succeed in overriding the 'beneficial effects' of infanticide (with the consent of their parents). What is particularly worrying about such a utilitarian approach is that the lives of babies are, morally speaking, at the mercy of extraneous factors, such as whether or not killing them will involve a loosening of our moral inhibitions to an extent that is sufficient to override the beneficial effects of infanticide. As Rawls complains, utilitarians often have to resort to arguments from general facts;[4] the utilitarian tends to deal with objections by appealing to laws of society and of

---

[4] *A Theory of Justice*, p. 160.

human nature that rule out cases that are offensive to our considered judgements.

To be fair to Glover it should be pointed out that he is aware that the argument from side-effects cannot wholly rescue utilitarianism from the sort of objections that we have been considering. He thinks that such talk of side-effects tells part of the story, but not the whole story. He admits that the killing of innocent human beings can be wrong quite independently of the adverse side-effects of such killing. He feels the need to supplement the argument from side-effects by appealing to considerations of autonomy. He thinks that the autonomy principle 'in the case of adults gives existing people preference over potential ones';[5] and again he tells us that the autonomy principle 'will also add to the case against the replacement policy and so may reassure anyone who is reluctant to let that case rest on side effects alone'.[6] Glover attempts to construct a sophisticated version of utilitarianism which does not just attempt to maximize a person's satisfactions, but also tries to give people as much autonomy as possible. He thinks that it is good for a person that he should be allowed to make some important choices with regard to his life even when this may in other respects give him less satisfaction than if the relevant courses of action were paternalistically chosen for him. He suggests that an adequate utilitarianism should allow a trade-off between the value of autonomy and other intrinsically desirable values. Sometimes the value of autonomy should be overriden by other considerations, while sometimes it should not. He thinks that sometimes we could kill people for paternalistic reasons even though their decision is to go on living, but normally we should refrain from paternalistically killing a person if such killing would be against the wishes of that person.

But I do not see how the autonomy principle can come to the rescue of utilitarianism over the replacement problem. Let us (for the sake of argument) grant Glover that his principle of autonomy helps to defend utilitarianism against the charge that it sanctions too many cases of paternalistic killing. What has this to do with the replacement problem? When we

[5] Glover, *Causing Deaths and Saving Lives*, p. 160.
[6] Ibid., p. 161.

kill men in order to replace them with men who are better as contributors to utility, we need not be killing them because it is in their own interest to be killed; and so we need not be going against their own decision about what is good for them. We may even grant that it is in their interest to go on living because that is how they perceive their interests, and yet go on to argue that they must be killed because society would be better off if they were killed and replaced by superior men. No doubt if we kill them then they will not be able to make any more autonomous choices, for they will be dead. But if we replace them with people who will make even more autonomous choices than the dead men (we could choose our victims from among the less autonomous members of our society), then how can Glover's utilitarianism show what is reprehensible about such replacement policies? Why not painlessly and suddenly kill people who live in tribal societies (where human beings lead non-autonomous lives) and replace them with beings whom we can train to become autonomous agents? Again, young children do not lead autonomous lives, and Glover's autonomy principle cannot explain what is wrong with having a replacement policy with regard to them. Nor can his principle explain what is wrong with infanticide as a means of solving the population problem. The adverse side-effects, such as the pain caused to the parents, could be minimized by a system that only allowed infanticide when certain conditions were fulfilled, such as the consent of the parents. Moreover, in a poor overpopulated country the adverse side-effects, such as the loosening of the inhibitions against killing, could, under certain circumstances, be overriden by the beneficial results that would ensue if the policy of infanticide helped to bring the country's population down to the optimum level.

Admittedly considerations of autonomy may help to provide non-utilitarian moral constraints that rule out replacement policies, at any rate among autonomous beings. We may plausibly take the line that even when we pursue utilitarian goals, there are certain things we must not do to autonomous beings, or even to potentially autonomous beings, for such beings have a right to respect, which cannot be overriden by utilitarian considerations. But this would be to adopt a right-based approach.

The trouble with Glover's utilitarianism is that though it allows a role for considerations of autonomy, the role that it allows cannot prevent the utilitarian monster from devouring some of the population. It brings in autonomy at the wrong place, as just another good to be maximized.

One of the attractions of a right-based approach is that it acknowledges the need for providing moral constraints *vis-à-vis* our policies towards the individual. Of course many individuals, such as Bentham and Glover, find talk of rights metaphysical and unhelpful. Glover poses the dilemma that right-based theories are either too extreme or redundant. If one believes in an absolute right to life, then this view is too extreme, for does one not have to allow for exceptional situations where a person's life may have to be sacrificed? On the other hand, if one takes a less absolute position and allows such rights to be sometimes overriden by other considerations, then how is this position different from the kind of utilitarian approach outlined by Glover? For Glover too allows that there is a strong presumption against killing. What then is the value of adding that people have a non-absolute right not to be killed?

There are at least three points worth making in reply to Glover here. First, even if the right to life is not an absolute right, it does not follow that there are no absolute rights. It seems plausible to argue that there is at least one right which we can regard as absolute without making our moral system impractical. It is not impractical to contend that human beings have a right to equal respect and consideration in the design of moral and political rules and institutions. The right to equal respect and consideration does not necessarily imply that an individual who has this right must never be killed.[7] The view that this right is an absolute one is quite consistent with the view that others also have an absolute right to equal respect and consideration.

Secondly, it is arguable that there are other rights, such as the right not to be tortured, which are absolute in an important sense, even though in very extreme situations such a right may have to be violated. The point of saying that such a right is absolute is that even though it has to be violated in extreme situations (for instance, to prevent a social catastrophe),

[7] See chapter 9.

we must admit that the violation of such a right implies that a substantial wrong has been done to the person whose rights were violated. On the utilitarian approach we would have to say that because it was necessary to torture an individual, therefore it was not unjust to torture the individual. On the right-based approach this inference cannot be made. Mill, who adopted the utilitarian approach, considers the example where to save a life it may be allowable to steal or take by force the necessary food or medicine. He thought that in such cases, by a 'useful accommodation of language', we do not say that 'justice must give way to some other moral principle, but that what is just in ordinary cases is, by reason of that other principle, not just in the particular case'.[8] Now I do not deny that in some cases such 'useful accommodation of language' is correct. But there are other cases where it would be most deplorable to go in for such 'useful accommodation of language'. Thus if torture is necessary in order to prevent a social catastrophe, or if it is necessary to punish an innocent man in order to save a social catastrophe, then on the right-based approach such torture or such punishment would involve an injustice and a wrong to the individual concerned, even if such injustice had to be carried out for utilitarian reasons. Nor can this idea of wronging the individual in such cases be reduced to the need for compensating such individuals. No doubt we should compensate such individuals, as much as we can, but the wrong due to them would not necessarily disappear with compensation. In Mill's example of stealing medicine or food in an emergency, it is perhaps possible to fully compensate the victim, which may partly explain why it is permissible to go in for the 'useful accommodation of language' and say that in such a case there was no real injustice involved. But in my examples there is real injustice involved to the individuals, which cannot be eradicated through compensation.

Thirdly, though it is true that most rights, such as the right to life, can be overriden in extreme situations, it does not follow that on the right-based theories individual interests can be overriden as often as they can be on the utilitarian approach. Right-based theories tend to allow the overriding of rights only when the rights of other individuals are at stake.

[8] *Utilitarianism* (London, 1863), chapter V, para. 37.

One striking way of showing the difference between the two approaches is by considering the replacement problem. On the right-based approach, possible people have no non-contingent rights, and we must not sacrifice the rights of existing people for the sake of increased utility that could result from replacing them with new individuals; whereas we saw that it is not easy for Glover's utilitarianism to rule out such replacement policies.

Glover gives us the following example from Parfit. Suppose there are two medical programmes between which we have to choose. In the first one, women would be tested during pregnancy and those found to have an illness which would handicap their children would be cured. In the the second programme the women would be tested before pregnancy and those who have an illness which would handicap their children would be warned to postpone conception. And we assume that other things are equal, and that the handicap involved would not be so severe as to make life not worth living.

Glover uses this example to argue against Narveson's view[9] that tries to place a restriction on the utilitarian principle. I do not want to defend Narveson's version. Rather I shall argue that the sort of right-based approach advocated in this book can deal with Parfit's example adequately. If so, this example would not necessarily support unrestricted utilitarianism (that is to say unrestrained by non-utilitarian moral constraints) of the sort that Glover advocates.

The reason why Parfit's example seems to provide a difficulty for the right-based approach is this. Failure to adopt the first programme will harm some people, that is to say those among the handicapped who would have been normal if the first programme had been adopted. So the failure to adopt the first programme involves a violation of the rights of these people. But failure to adopt the second programme would not violate the rights of those who are born handicapped. For if the second programme had not been adopted, *these* handicapped people would not have been born, and *a fortiori* they would not have been born normal. The individuals who would have been born normal would have been different individuals from the handicapped individuals. So failure to adopt

---

[9] Jan Narveson, *Morality and Utility* (Baltimore, 1967), pp. 46–50.

the second programme cannot be said to make the people who are born handicapped worse off than *they* would have been if the second programme had not been adopted. So on a right-based approach failure to adopt the first programme is worse than the failure to adopt the second programme. But does this not go against our intuition that the case for the two programmes is equally strong?

Right-based theories can survive such criticisms. It is true that on the right-based approach the case for adopting the first programme is stronger than the case for adopting the second programme—because failure to adopt the first programme, unlike failure to adopt the second programme, will adversely affect the rights of the relevant individuals. But this example does not undermine right-based theories. True, the right-based approach does conflict with the 'intuition' some people have that the case for the two programmes is equally strong, but it seems quite plausible to say that this 'intuition' ought to be revised. Glover may think that on the right-based view, there is '*no* case for adopting the second programme, since no one is harmed by our rejecting it'.[10] Now I admit that the view that there is no case for adopting the second programme is a very strange view. But the right-based approach does not imply this strange view. It is quite consistent for a right-based theorist to argue that there is a case for adopting the second approach, though the case for adopting the first approach is even stronger because rights are involved in the first case, while in other respects the two cases are similar. It is important to stress that the right-based approach is consistent with the view that it is good to promote utility; it could grant, for instance, that we have an (imperfect) obligation to promote the good; what it insists on is that the pursuit of the good, whether it be the creation of happy people, or the creation of beautiful paintings, is subject to moral constraints. So a right-based approach could admit that there is a good case for adopting the second programme; it could grant that it is better to produce people without defects than to produce people with defects, other things being equal. In the case of the second programme, where the choice was between postponing conception and not postponing it, whether

[10] *Causing Deaths and Saving Lives*, p. 68; my italics.

the women agree to postpone it or not will not adversely affect the rights of any persons, either in the present or in the future. Since there is a good utilitarian case for postponing conception, and since the pursuit of utilitarian goals here does not involve the violation of rights, or the violation of any other moral constraints, therefore we can, even on a right-based approach, explain why it is better to postpone conception.

Suppose an artist has limited material, which he can either use for painting today or tomorrow. Suppose he knows that if he waits till tomorrow before painting, he is likely to paint a substantially better picture. In that case (and assuming other things being equal) the artist has a good case for waiting till tomorrow. Why should a right-based approach deny this?

2. Moral constraints and the pact to end the human race

There is another problem regarding actual and potential people, which is sometimes taken to constitute a problem for the right-based approach. Consider the following possibility mentioned by Glover: 'Suppose we take a drug which would render us infertile but which would make us so happy that we would not mind being childless. Would it be wrong for everyone now to take it, and ensure that we would be the last generation?'[11] Feinberg, who himself adopts a right-based approach, thinks that a pact to end the human race would not involve any violation of rights and so would not involve any injustice.[12] To some people such a consequence of the right-based approach may well seem a *reductio ad absurdum* of that approach. I shall argue that the right-based approach is consistent with the view that there is something very wrong and terrible about such a pact, even with the view that such a pact is morally void; indeed, it is the utilitarian approach that cannot tell what is especially terrible about such a pact.

Glover, who is, as we have seen, a utilitarian, thinks that it would be terrible if the human race came to an end in this fashion. And he thinks this is because we attach intrinsic value to the lives of the future human beings who would exist if the human race did not come to an end. And he thinks that since we put value on these future possible individuals, and

[11] Ibid., p. 69.
[12] 'The Rights of Animals and Future Generations'.

since we should not have 'time-bias', it is hard not to allow value to the creation of extra people contemporary with us.

Now admittedly there can be value in the creation of extra people either now or in the future. But I do not see why a right-based approach need deny this, any more than it need deny that there can be value in the creation of works of art either now or in the future. In any case, to understand what is especially terrible about the pact to end the human race we have to look deeper than just the loss of the intrinsically valuable future individuals. The pact to end the human race involves an end of the human species, an end of civilization, an end of all that so many people in the present and the past fought for, lived for, and died for. What has given significance to many human lives, to their struggles, in spite of the knowledge of their own imminent death, is that the causes they were fighting for will survive their death. What *right* has this generation to destroy all its heritage, all that is the result of the struggle of the previous generations?

The view defended here does not necessarily imply a narrowly conservative approach. One may want to reform or even radically alter civilization; what is required is that we must not abandon the struggle to improve things. We owe it to the previous generations not to give up the struggle.

Of course one can conceive of situations where it might be permissible to decide to end the human race, for instance if it is the case that there is no hope for mankind because the scarce resources are going to run out, or because a meteor is going to strike and destroy the earth soon. But to grant that in such extreme situations we have a right to go in for a pact to stop procreation is not to grant that we normally have such a right. Perhaps, if you believe, as some Orientals do, that life essentially consists of suffering, then you may be able to justify the pact to end the human race on the grounds that you are preventing the coming into existence of beings who will be miserable. Though if you are impressed with such Oriental doctrines, you are also likely to believe that the suffering that an individual undergoes in this world is a result of his past deeds in previous incarnations, and if a person is doomed to suffer as a result of certain wicked things he did, how then can you prevent his suffering—the law of Karma must take its

MORAL CONSTRAINTS, PACT TO END HUMAN RACE   141

toll, and if we all put an end to the human race, perhaps the individuals who would have suffered as human beings, are now going to suffer as animals!

Admittedly the obligation that we have not to destroy our heritage is a defeasible one. If you have been brought up a Nazi, you have the right to break totally with your heritage. But to generalize and say that we can all abandon our heritage would be wrong. Is *our* heritage like the Nazi one? Though our heritage has evil elements, is that a reason for abandoning the struggle to improve things, a struggle that was begun long before we were born and but for which we ourselves would not have been able to flourish?

There are some neurotic, alienated, unfortunate individuals, who have had a miserable time in the world, and if you remind them of their duties to the previous generations, whose struggles have made possible the society they now live in, they will retort that they owe nothing to society or to the previous generations, since they would have been better off if they had not been born. This retort has some plausibility. But for the ordinary man who has had an enjoyable life, and whose enjoyment would not have been possible but for the struggle of others, for him to deny the debt he owes to his benefactors is ingratitude of the highest order.

I have argued that we have no right to decide to end the human race, partly because of the duties that we owe to the members of the previous generations. Dead persons have rights and interests that survive their deaths. Can utilitarianism incorporate this way of looking at things? One trouble with many versions of utilitarianism is that they are forward looking; they only take the past into account to the extent that by doing so good consequences are promoted in the future. Such utilitarians have a problem explaining why we should not forget about our promises and commitments and duties to the dead. The standard utilitarian answer is that we should honour our commitments and our duties to the dead because such a practice has good consequences. Such a practice enables us to die securely, feeling confident that our interests will be looked after even after our deaths. If we want to benefit from this practice in the future, then we must keep this practice going by honouring our commitments and duties to the dead.

But now such utilitarian arguments have no force at all in the case of our deciding to end the human race. If the race is going to end with us, no one, now or in the future, will suffer from our abandoning all our commitments and duties to the dead. The primary reason that forwarding-looking utilitarians can give for not ending the human race is the kind of reason that Glover gives, namely that there is value in the creation of extra happy people.

There are non-utilitarian reasons that help to explain what is *specially* terrible about ending the human race. There are non-utilitarian moral constraints within which our policies and practices must operate. In the case of the decision to end the human race, this decision violates such moral constraints. It could do so in two ways. First, such a policy could involve us in not honouring our debt to the previous generations and so it could involve us in violating the rights of the members of the previous generations. Secondly, there may be moral constraints upon our policies even though our policies do not involve the violation of any person's right. For example we have no right to destroy a whole species, such as the whale species, even if it is the case that individual members of that species have no right to life. And it could be that quite apart from the adverse effects on the rights of others, we have no right to play god and destroy the human race, even though our contemporaries agree with us in wanting to play god, and join in the decision to end the human race.

A right-based approach is of couse quite consistent with the view that there are limits to what individuals are morally entitled to do, and with the view that some of these limits are so severe that they cannot be removed even if all the relevant parties agree to the removal of these limits. Thus Rousseau, who believed in natural rights, thought that a pact to sell ourselves into slavery is null and void.[13] He thought of course that such a pact was void on the grounds that the agreement could not have been a really voluntary one, for it reflects an act of madness. But he had a deeper reason for thinking that such a pact must be null and void. He implied that even if (*per impossible*) we could voluntarily enter into such a pact, the pact would be null and void because we have no right to

---

[13] *The Social Contract,* Book I, chapter IV.

enter into such a pact in the first place; according to Rousseau, for us to renounce our freedom is to renounce our humanity, which we have no right to do. Now I suggest that the collective pact to end the human race would be equally null and void, for we have no right to play god and end the human species, nor have we the right to sell our soul for the sake of the 'happiness' from a drug of the kind envisaged by Glover, or from the increased availability of resources that would otherwise have been reserved for the use of future generations.

A right-based approach is consistent with the recognition of such moral constraints. There are some extreme libertarian right-based approaches according to which the only moral constraints that we need to recognize are the constraints that result from other people's possession of rights; as long as we do not violate any one's rights, we have a right to do, singly or collectively, anything we like. Now even if we adopt this extreme view, it seems possible to argue that we have no right to end the human race, for as we saw such a policy could adversely affect the rights of previous generations; it would render useless many of the things they struggled for and died for, and it is arguable that our ancestors have a right not to be posthumously harmed in this way. But even if this argument is not a good one, there are other arguments that a right-based approach can deploy. And I shall now turn to these other considerations.

There are less libertarian versions of the right-based approach, which would acknowledge that our right to do things is constrained not just by the rights of the individuals, but also by other moral constraints, such as our duties to look after the planet, our obligation (though imperfect) to pursue the good and shun evil, our duties to God (if there is one), our duties to nature, and so forth. What is essential to a right-based approach is to acknowledge that the rights of other individuals set moral constraints that we must not violate and also sometimes create positive obligations on some of us to enable the right-holders to obtain their rights. But this view is consistent with the view that there are, in addition, other sources of moral constraints, such as the ones mentioned in this paragraph, which we must also respect. So even if Glover is right in thinking that the decision to end the human race does not adversely affect anyone else's rights, even if we neglect the adverse effects that such a pact would have on the interests of people who lived in the previous generations, it would not follow that on a right-based approach we are entitled to end the human race.

The right-based approach is, as was pointed out earlier, consistent with the admission of moral constraints of the kind referred to at the start of the last paragraph. In fact one could say something stronger. The right-based approach goes quite naturally with the existence of such moral constraints. This does not just mean that since human beings have rights, such rights set constraints within which one must act; rather, that since human beings are assumed to have greater status than animals, and to have greater right to respect and considera-tion than animals, human beings also have certain duties to pursue the good. To see this we need to appeal to the source of superior human rights. Earlier we examined the problem of why a human infant has a greater right to consideration than a grown-up (non-human) animal has, and we saw that such a view could be justified, if it could be justified at all, by appealing to perfectionist considerations. Human beings have or had the wonderful potential to lead a significant life in a way that animals do not have. Now if these sorts of consideration are the source of human beings having greater right to consideration than animals, it seems reasonable to insist that human beings have a duty to lead a significant life. There is something immoral about claiming rights on the grounds that we have a wonderful potential and then doing nothing much to develop that potential. Suppose a pleasure machine of the kind envisaged by J. J. C. Smart[14] or a drug of the kind envisaged by Glover could give us lots of pleasur-able feelings, is it all right to sell our humanity for the sake of these pleasurable feelings? Suppose animals too could get just as much pleasure from this drug or from the pleasure machine. Could we still claim that our lives were more significant than animal life and worthy of greater right to consideration? If the pursuit of such pleasures was only part of our end, we could still have other pursuits that were more significant than

[14] 'An Outline of a System of Utilitarian Ethics', in *Utilitarianism For and Against*, by J. J. C. Smart and B. Williams (Cambridge, 1973), p. 20.

animal pursuits. But suppose that we get so 'hooked' on the pleasure machine that we become passive recipients of pleasure from it. How then could we claim to lead more significant lives than animals and claim greater right to consideration? If our justification for claiming superior status over animals is that we have a more wonderful potential than animals (and we saw that without some such rationale it is difficult to claim superior status for human infants over grown up animals or even over ants and bees), then it seems natural to take the view that human beings have a duty to develop their potential, their humanity, in virtue of which they have been given superior status, and that they have a duty not to sell their humanity for the sake of pleaures of the kind that even animals could enjoy. To say this is not to deny that human beings could, without violation of moral constraints, enjoy substantial 'animal pleasures'. But they must do so in a way that is consistent with the duties that they have to develop their humanity.

The doctrine of natural rights, according to which human beings, in virtue of their nature, are entitled to a certain respect and consideration, goes quite naturally with the doctrine of natural duties, according to which human beings, in virtue of their nature, have certain duties that they must perform, in addition to the duties that they have to respect the rights of other human beings. Perhaps a pleasure-oriented utilitarian may quite consistently allow us to sell our humanity, our soul, for the sake of animal pleasure, though even such a utilitarian will have the problem of why we ought to prefer human interests, and why we should not replace the human population by an animal population if it were shown that animals got greater pleasure from the pleasure machine. Be that as it may, a right-based approach must not permit us to do things that are incompatible with our nature, in virtue of which we are entitled to our superior right to respect and consideration.

If human beings, in virtue of their nature, should get superior consideration to the animals, then there is the problem of what is so wonderful about human nature as compared to animal nature, in virtue of which human beings should get superior consideration. It is not enough just to point out differences between human beings and animals. Admittedly, human beings can do all kinds of things which animals cannot, such as autonomously kill on a large scale, or freely choose to become heroin addicts. What is needed is not just to point out the respects in which human beings are different from animals, but to point out that some of these differences are relevant for giving human beings superior consideration. So it will not suffice to merely point out that even when human beings pursue animal pleasures, they remain different from animals. Earlier (in chapter 4) some characteristics that might serve as the relevant ones for giving superior status to human beings were considered. In particular, I stressed that human beings have the potential to lead a significant life. But there is a real danger that our ideas of what tests should be used for deciding whether human beings are worthy of superior consideration compared to animals, are heavily biased in favour of human beings; after all it is human beings who make the decision about whether human beings are superior to animals! Now such dangers are partly, though not wholly, reduced if we take the view that those with superior status also have some extra burdens to carry, such as having to develop their wonderful potential, their humanity, having to look after the planet earth and its inhabitants, including the non-human inhabitants, and so forth. Indeed it might be argued that it is at least partly in virtue of having to carry such burdens that human beings have superior status to animals. For human beings need greater consideration if they are to carry these burdens, somewhat as a king may acquire special rights in order to perform his kingly duties.

If the doctrine of equal respect and consideration applies to all human beings, but not to animals, then human beings have special rights (such as the right to equal respect) which animals do not have; they get superior status to animals. Now the view which says that human beings have superior status to animals as well as having special burdens to carry is more plausible than the view according to which human beings have greater intrinsic worth than animals, but do not have any special burdens to carry. The former view seems less biased in favour of human beings. Of course the danger of self-deception is there even in the interpretation of the former view. The analogy with imperialist countries can be helpful. Many of the inhabitants of the imperialist countries thought that they not only had the right to conquer people whom they thought of as barbarians, they also had the duty to do so. Thus many Englishmen saw themselves as carrying the 'white man's burden'. Now there was a good deal of self-deception in such cases. Very often the imperialists promoted their own self-interest while claiming that their policies were really designed for the good of the natives. It used to be said of some of the imperialists who professed to serve the good of the natives, that in fact they took the goods of the natives!

There is a danger of similar self-deception in man's dealing with animals and nature. We may assume special burdens of being custodians of this planet and claim special rights and privileges that go with our duties *vis-à-vis* animals and lesser beings; but in fact the 'burdens' that we carry could turn out to be in our interest and at the expense of animal interest. For instance, we kill and eat animals, thinking that we are doing them a favour because otherwise they would have met a more painful death in the course of nature. In spite of such dangers of self-deception and bias, the view that we have greater status compared to animals becomes more plausible, or less implausibe, if it is accompanied by the view that human beings also have special burdens to carry out; somewhat as the view that our rulers (whether democratically elected or not) have a right to rule us becomes more plausible if it is accompanied by the view that our rulers have a duty to carry out their function of looking after our interests.

It has been argued in this chapter that the right-based approach, which gives superior status to human beings over animals, goes quite naturally with the view that there are moral constraints that we human beings must observe in our conduct, in addition to the constaints that we have to obey as a result of the rights of other human beings. If a pact to end the human race violates such moral constraints, it is null and void. Now it is quite possible that some of these constraints would be violated by such a pact. For if we have enjoyed superior status to animals partly in virtue of our being custodians of this planet, then we must not abandon our responsibilities to look after this planet.

So there are two main arguments that might, on the right-based approach, be advanced for thinking that the pact to end the world is especially wrong. Firstly, this would involve us in violating the rights of the preceding generations, it would reduce the posthumous significance of their lives. Secondly, we have as human beings certain natural duties to develop our humanity, and our civilization, to look after the planet and other species, and so forth. This second reason can be valid even if the first one is not. In fact this second argument could reinforce the first one as well. For if the previous generations had merely been carrying out some subjective ideals of their own, which had little connection with us, and which they may just happen to have chosen, then it is arguable that it is no great tragedy if their ideals and way of life have been abandoned by us. But to the extent that they shared with us a common humanity and common natural duties and burdens, it becomes plausible to argue that if they have been doing their share of their duty, we owe it to them to carry on the struggle.

9

Some Misunderstandings of Egalitarianism

In this chapter the doctrine of equal respect and consideration is defended against some criticisms and misunderstandings.

According to John Lucas,

To say that all men, because they are men, are equally men, or that to treat any two persons as ends in themselves is to treat them equally as ends in themselves is to import a spurious note of egalitarianism into a perfectly sound and serious argument. We may call it, if we like, the argument for Equality of Respect, but in this phrase it is the word 'Respect' - respect for each man's humanity . . . which is doing the logical work while the word 'Equality' adds nothing to the argument and is altogether otiose.[1]

Now Lucas is quite wrong in thinking that 'Equality' is otiose here. It is a substantial point whether some human beings in virtue of their nature should be given greater respect and consideration than others. To say that they should be given equal respect is to take one side in this substantial controversy; the quotation from Rashdall on p. 2 of the Introduction shows that he took the opposite side. Again, the view that the untouchable's right to respect, in virtue of his humanity, is no less (and no more) than the right to respect of the Brahmin (in virtue of his humanity) is to take a substantial position, a position that is opposite to that taken by some traditional Hindus in the past:

Sir Henry Maine tells us that he has himself heard a high caste Indian declare that it is the teaching of religion that a Brahmin is entitled to twenty times as much happiness as anyone else, and this not upon the ground of individual merit arising from any conduct or mode of life on his part, but because intrinsically, *qua* Brahmin, he is twenty times the superior of those of a lower caste.[2]

[1] J. Lucas, 'Against Equality', *Philosophy*, xl (1965), 298.
[2] W. W. Willoughby, quoted by B. Barry, *Political Argument* (London, 1965), p. 15.

Again, it is a substantial point whether the doctrine of equal respect extends to human infants and whether it extends to animals. Many people think that the doctrine does extend to human infants, but that animals, though they are due considerations, are not due equal consideration to human beings. Whether we agree with such positions or not, it cannot be argued that the word 'equality' is otiose in such debates.

The point of saying that human beings are due equal consideration and respect is that in virtue of their nature human beings are all due equal respect and consideration. This view is of course consistent with the view that you have special obligations and duties to those human beings with whom you have special ties, such as family ties or contractual ties. The doctrines of natural rights (that is to say, rights that we have in virtue of our nature) sets the structure and sets the constraints within which the rest of our moral system must operate.

Perhaps the relationship between the family argument and the doctrine of equal right to respect and consideration is as follows. First, family considerations have to work within the constraints set by the doctrine of rights (for the reasons that we discussed earlier, for instance, that we must not kill foreigners in order to promote the interests of our family or of our compatriots). And secondly, the doctrine of rights leaves certain things unspecified, and the family considerations (along with other considerations) can then fill in the relevant gaps. For instance, human beings have a right to life, and this implies corresponding duties not to kill; it also implies positive duties to provide food for the starving. Now these positive duties are left unspecified in the sense that it is not laid down by the doctrine of rights who all have this positive duty. If a man is starving in America it is not specified that all human beings all over the world must rush to his aid. The family considerations tell us, for instance, that the starving man in America is the responsibility of some American people rather than that of people in India. Again, your child has a right to life, which implies that it has a right to the food that is necessary for it to live. Assuming that you are well off, it is you, rather than I, who has the correlative positive duty to provide food to your child; such conclusions can be reinforced both by examining our legal system and by family considerations, which tell us that, other things being equal, we have greater positive obligations to those with whom we have closer family ties. In such ways family considerations (and also our legal system) help to make specific things that are left unspecified by the doctrine of human rights.

Similarly, we could work out the relationship between the doctrine of rights and other considerations, such as contractarian considerations and utilitarian considerations. The latter work within the constraints provided by the doctrine of rights. The same applies to our personal ideals and commitments.

Egalitarianism is sometimes criticized for being an inhuman and impersonal doctrine; it is criticized for neglecting much that is important in human relationships. But if one constructs egalitarianism in the way suggested in this book, such objections can be seen to be inapplicable. For egalitarianism, in the way constructed here, is quite consistent with the importance of all sorts of special relationships, special duties and special obligations to those with whom one has family ties, or to those with whom one has committed oneself either by a contract or through love and friendship. It is true that egalitarianism does put certain constraints within which these special relationships must operate; for instance, you must not kill a man in order to please the woman you are committed to by family ties or ties of love and affection. But this is a consequence of egalitarianism that we ought normally to be willing to accept,[3] and our special relationships will not be rendered meaningless just because we have to operate within such constraints.

Now it might be thought that the dynamic version of egalitarianism defended in this book is too generous to the senile, to murderers and others, by giving them all equal consideration. But this objection is based on a mistaken idea of the way that the egalitarian doctrine is to be employed. It is not being suggested that murderers should be pampered or that the senile should be pampered, or that the life of human vegetables should be prolonged indefinitely. The doctrine of egalitarianism, as expounded in this book, is quite consistent with the view that a murderer has forfeited his right to life. It is

[3] Notwithstanding Williams, 'Persons, Character, and Morality'.

simply saying that the doctrine of equal consideration applies to an individual even though he is a murderer; other things being equal, the interests of that individual (who happens to be a murderer) must be given equal weight to other people's interests.

We should remember that John Doe the infant, John Doe the rational adult, John Doe the murderer, John Doe the senile old man, are all the same individual. If we forget this we may talk of the interests of the young John Doe, as though he was a different individual from John Doe the adult. No doubt, on certain metaphysical views, for instance on the complex view of personal identity advocated by Parfit, the two are not intrinsically the same; but according to the metaphysical views which are presupposed by our right-based individualistic moral beliefs, John Doe the infant, John Doe the old man, etc. are all intrinsically the same individual. Parfit himself realizes this. He rightly thinks that his concept of a person involves a radical overhaul of our present moral beliefs, for he is aware that the present system of moral beliefs is based on a theory of personal identity that is quite different from his. Parfit's positive views on personal identity are very controversial, but he is right in thinking that our present moral system presupposes the non-Parfitian theory of personal identity; it presupposes that the very same individual persists from infancy to old age. In our existing moral system, when we distribute primary goods, such as wealth and liberty, between different individuals, we have to be fair between individuals, taking their life span as a whole. So it can be misleading to talk of equality between the senile and the young, or between murderers and non-murderers. The equality is rather between individual human beings who may happen to be senile for part of their lives and individuals who may not; and between individuals who may happen to be murderers for part of their lives and individuals who happen not to be.

Suppose John Doe is a human being who has irreversibly become so senile that he has sunk to a level below some non-human animals, though he is still capable of feeling pain and pleasure, and suppose there is another individual John Smith who is a normal rational adult. And suppose they both need a kidney machine in order to survive, but there is a shortage of kidney machines, so that only one of them can have the kidney machine. Now it is quite plausible to say that an impartial application of egalitarianism would lead us to put John Smith on the kidney machine and let John Doe die, assuming that other things are equal. The point is not that egalitarianism is being abandoned or that John Doe is expelled from the egalitarian club when he becomes a human vegetable or when he becomes senile; what happens is that an impartial application of egalitarianism would imply that John Smith should be given priority. If John Smith had been senile and John Doe had been a rational adult, then it is John Doe who would have been given the kidney machine. So the same criterion would be applied in the two cases. Moreover, in arriving at a criterion about what ought to be done in such cases, the interests of the individual John Doe throughout his life, and not just during the senile part of his life, could be given equal weight to that given to other people's interests. We could argue, with the help of perfectionist criteria, that, other things being equal, there is a greater case for spending resources to save a life that is still capable of human endeavour than to save a life that has lost the capacity to act rationally.

So it would be wrong to argue that unless we expelled individuals from the egalitarian club when they become 'human vegetables' we would be involved in pampering human vegetables and diverting too many resources to their welfare. Similarly it would be wrong to argue that unless we expelled an individual from the egalitarian club when he became a murderer, we would be involved in pampering the murderer at the cost of the legitimate interests of other individuals. Egalitarians like Rousseau were not obviously inconsistent when they advocated severe punishment of criminals. No doubt there are complications here. Some criminals have had a hard life, throughout their lives; they are criminals, not so much through their own fault, but due to the appalling conditions in which they were brought up. To punish them severely involves in some case making things even worse for them. Is it fair to inflict a further hardship on them? The solution to such problems involves delicate balancing between the interests of those who happen to be criminals and those who are not. In some cases punishment may be desirable to prevent crime, even though it involves severe hardships on criminals who are morally innocent and who have been driven to crime as a result of unfavourable social conditions. But while the interests of other individuals must be taken into account, it would be callous to expel criminals from the egalitarian club. The legitimate interests of criminals must be taken into account and balanced against the legitimate interests of the law-abiding citizens.

It might be argued that there is a greater case for expelling from the egalitarian club the wicked murderer, who commits the murder not because of the unfair conditions in which he was brought up, but because of his own autonomous choice; such a person, it may be argued, has forfeited his membership of the egalitarian club. An alternative view, which I follow, is that of Vlastos who thinks that such a person (if he exists) would have forfeited certain rights, such as the right to life or to liberty, but he should still be treated as a member of the moral community, as an end and not merely as a means.[4] As suggested earlier in this chapter, the view that he is not expelled from the moral community (or from the egalitarian club) does not imply that he is to be pampered at the expense of other human beings.

Of course the moral community could be wider than the egalitarian club. Many people, such as Rashdall,[5] would think that animals are members of the moral community but not of the egalitarian club. For they are due moral consideration, though their interests do not carry as much weight as human interests do. Now it might be suggested that when a human being voluntarily and wickedly commits a murder, he is expelled from the egalitarian club, even though he is still a member of the wider moral community. Why not treat a wicked murderer like we treat a dog? Vlastos is quite right when he says that we have no right to be cruel to a cruel person, we have no right to beat or lynch a murderer. But such considerations would at most show that the wicked human being is not expelled from the moral community; they would not show that he is not expelled from the egalitarian club. After all we have no right to beat or lynch a dog, nor

---

[4] G. Vlastos, 'Justice and Equality', p. 48.
[5] *The Theory of Good and Evil,* i. 239.

do we have any right to be cruel to a dog; so why not treat the murderer much as we should treat a dog, and allow him to be a member of the moral community but not of the egalitarian club?

I would contend that murderers are not expelled from the egalitarian club. Such views cannot be proved, but one can try to refute some of the arguments against such a view and point out some considerations in its favour. The main argument in favour of expelling wicked murderers from the egalitarian club is that if they remained members of the egalitarian club, they would get too good a deal. This argument is based on a misunderstanding of the way in which egalitarianism works. Although as a human being each person gets equal respect and consideration, this does not imply that there should be no punishment of serious criminals. Moreover, there are pragmatic-cum-moral arguments that can be given for not expelling wicked murderers from the egalitarian club or for treating them as if they are not expelled. We have seen that in the case of murderers who have become criminals because of unfavourable social, economic, psychological, or other such conditions, such individuals have had a raw deal from society. Punishment of such individuals involves a further hardship for such people. And while the punishment of such individuals may sometimes be necessary for crime prevention (for the interests of the law-abiding population must be taken into account too), it would be too harsh to expel them from the egalitarian club for crimes that they committed because of conditions outside their control. Now in fact it is in general very difficult to distinguish really wicked autonomous criminals from individuals who have become criminals due to unfavourable social and economic, psychological, or genetic conditions; so there is a case for not expelling any criminal from the egalitarian club, for not treating any criminal like a dog. While punishment of criminals may be necessary for crime prevention, no such social aim is achieved by expelling them from the egalitarian club. So why risk being unjust to them by expelling them from the egalitarian club?

There is also the Kantian view according to which the criminal's right to dignity must be respected; he must not be treated like a dog but as an autonomous agent. That view too does not lead to expulsion of the wicked murderer from the egalitarian club (or from the kingdom of ends), though it does allow for punishment of criminals.

We can deal in a similar fashion about the complaint that our egalitarianism is too generous to the claims of the foetus. It is true that on our view the doctrine of equal respect applies to all who are members of the egalitarian club, and so it applies as much to the foetus as to the mother. This may appear inhuman to some people. They would say that we have all sorts of special relationships with the mother which we do not have with the foetus, whom we have not even seen. Now as was pointed out earlier, the doctrine of equal respect does not deny that such special relationships carry weight. Rather it sets constraints within which such special relationships must operate.

Egalitarians can vary in the way in which they relate their egalitarianism to other moral and political principles and rules that they believe in. There are several versions. First, there is the radical version according to which other principles and rules are not only subordinate to the principle of equality in the sense that they must not violate the constraints set by it, but they are also derivative from the principle of equality. Secondly, there is the moderate version according to which other principles and rules subordinate to the principle of equality, but not all of them are derivative from the principle of equality. Thirdly, there is the 'dirty hands' version of egalitarianism, which is like the moderate version except that it concedes that in very extreme situations you may be morally compelled to break from the egalitarian constraints. It does not deny the existence of these constraints, even in the extreme situations; it says that when you break from those constraints you have done something terrible even though you were morally compelled to do so. Applying this to the problem of abortion, if for the sake of the life or health of the mother you decide to have the foetus killed, then you have done something terrible, even though, given your special relationships with the mother, this had to be done. It is arguable that society has special relationships with the mother, in a way in which it does not have with the foetus. And so it is understandable if society allows the foetus to be occasionally sacrificed for the sake of the mother; when it allows this sacrifice it sanctions something terrible, even though it is morally compelled to do so. Similarly in very rare cases our society may decide to override the legitimate interests of civilians abroad in order to save a social catastrophe at home, for instance, suppose civilian bombing abroad is the only way to prevent the war from carrying on indefinitely and causing social catastrophe in our society, and suppose that our cause is just and the enemy's cause is unjust.

Critics who reject egalitarianism for being too inhuman and radical, seldom bother to examine the non-absolutist versions of egalitarianism, such as the 'dirty hands' version of egalitarianism. Of course there are some good people who never want to dirty their hands. They would argue that we should never sacrifice an innocent person for the sake of others. If one combines such an absolutist stance with egalitarianism, then this may well commit us to a very rigid and inflexible view about not killing foetuses and innocent civilians. Those who think that such an approach is too rigid should realize that the cause of the rigidity is found not in egalitarianism, but in absolutism.

PART III

LIBERTY, PERFECTIONISM, AND SOME IMPLICATIONS OF EGALITARIANISM

10

Autonomy, Perfectionism, and Paternalism

The doctrine of equal respect and consideration faces problems about its foundations which were discussed in the earlier chapters; it was argued that perfectionist considerations have to be appealed to in order to provide the foundations of egalitarianism. Another related set of problems is about the implications of egalitarianism. In this chapter it is argued that perfectionist considerations have to be appealed to in order to work out the liberal implications of the egalitarian doctrine. Rawls on the other hand implies that all such appeals to perfectionism should be bypassed.

Many egalitarians, such as Rawls, think that their doctrine of equal respect and consideration commits them to respecting the autonomy of every human being; and they tend to be liberals because they think that everyone should be allowed to choose and pursue his own plan of life, as long as he allows similar liberties to other people. And they think that no person's plan of life should be considered of any greater *intrinsic* worth than another person's plan of life, and so perfectionism is bypassed as a political principle.

I agree with R. Dworkin in thinking that Rawls's model can be seen as an attempt to work out the implications of egalitarianism.[1] But in this chapter (and the next) it is argued that Rawls does not succeed in his attempt at deriving a liberal set up from egalitarian premises without resort to perfectionist considerations. Admittedly, Rawls only claims that this derivation works if we assume a society where people are materially well off. But for reasons given in this chapter, even if we

[1] R. Dworkin, *Taking Rights Seriously.*

assume that people are materially well off, the argument from egalitarianism to liberalism would still need to be supplemented by perfectionist considerations. And even when a liberal state is set up we would still need to appeal to perfectionist considerations in order to operate it, for instance in order to decide which forms of life to encourage among the young (see the last section of this chapter) or in order to show why some liberties are more important than others (see chapter 13).

Rawlsian views are explained in section 1 of this chapter, and are critically examined in sections 2-5.

1. Outlines of Rawls's Theory

As was seen in chapter 2, some contractarian approaches face the problem with regard to people in a weak bargaining position; such people tend to get exlcuded from the contractarian club. One of the charms of Rawls's model is that it tries to ensure that all human beings, including weak ones, get a fair deal. He constructs an imaginary or hypothetical social contract, which assumes that every human being is due equal respect. In real life if a slave owner opts for the continuance of the system of slavery, we may suspect him of being biased. If the mighty and the powerful reach an agreement with the meek and the downtrodden, we may suspect an unfair bargain. In order to remove such biases and bargains, Rawls asks us to simulate an imaginary and original contractarian position where equal human beings meet, behind a veil of ignorance: 'Among the essential features of this situation is that no one knows his place in society, his class position or social status ... his intelligence, strength and the like . . . the parties do not know their conception of the good or their special psychological propensities.'[2] The veil of ignorance ensures that no one can tailor principles to his advantage.

In real life certain kinds of knowledge can, as we have seen, be a source of bias and unfair bargains; but so too can ignorance and false consciousness; for instance, suppose a slave opts for the continuance of slavery, because he has been indoctrinated to believe that he is a slave by nature and that

[2] *A Theory of Justice,* p. 12.

civilization would collapse without slavery. So in order to reach a fair and just agreement we need to assume not only that the parties in the original position are confronted with the veil of ignorance over those things that set them at odds with one another but also that they should be provided with relevant knowledge. What knowledge is relevant in order to ensure that the agreement is not unfair will depend upon what practice is under discussion. Rawls constructs his contractarian theory as a four-stage sequence, at the first stage of which the parties are to choose the principles of justice. At this stage 'the only particular facts known to the parties are those that can be inferred from the circumstances of justice. While they know the first principles of social theory (and of other theories when relevant) the course of history is closed to them; they have no information about which kinds of society presently exist.'[3] Having chosen the principles of justice, the parties then move on to the second stage, the constitutional convention where they are to choose a constitution that satisfies the principles of justice already chosen. After choosing the constitution, they then go on to the third stage, the legislative stage. At the second and third stages, the parties know the general facts about their society, such as its size and level of economic advance, its institutional structure and natural environment, and so on, but the particularities of their own condition is still unknown to them. The last stage 'is that of the application of rules to particular cases by judges and administrators and the following of rules by citizens generally. At this stage everyone has complete access to all the facts.'[4]

Rawls assumes that the parties in the original position are rational and he attempts to show that the theory can be derived from the theory of rational choice. But how do the parties choose rationally in the original position when they do not even know what their conception of the good is? Rawls replies that, though the parties do now know which rational plan of life they have, the details of their aims and interests, yet they do know, even at the first stage of the four-stage sequence, that they have some rational plan of life. And it is assumed that the parties in the original position try to further and safeguard their aims and interests in so far as they can ascertain

---

[3] Ibid., p. 22.   [4] Ibid., p. 199.

them. Which conception of justice would they find it rational to opt for? To answer this problem Rawls appeals to his theory of primary goods. Primary goods are goods that any rational person is presumed to want whatever else he wants. These goods normally have a use whatever a person's rational plan of life. He divides primary goods into (a) social primary goods such as self-respect, rights and liberties, powers and opportunities, income and wealth, and (b) natural primary goods such as health, vigour, and intelligence. Natural primary goods, though they can be influenced by the basic structure (the way in which major social institutions distribute fundamental rights and duties and determine the division of advantages from social co-operation) are, unlike social primary goods, not directly under the basic structure's control. Rawls argues that the parties in the original position would find it rational to get as large a share as possible of social primary goods.[5]

Now Rawls has to face the objection that it may be rational for the parties in the original position to take a gamble and opt for unjust practices; for instance, they may opt for a slave society in the hope that they will turn out to be slave owners rather than slaves. Part of his reply to this is that such gambles are irrational when so much is at stake and when they have to take into account the fact that their choice of principles should seem reasonable to others, in particular to their descendants, whose rights will be deeply affected by it.[6] In view of such considerations, Rawls claims it would be rational for the parties to choose in accordance with the maxi-min rule, which tells us to rank alternatives by their worst possible outcome. The parties would therefore find it rational to opt for a system of equal distribution of all social primary goods except where the inequalities lead to the maximization of the long-term expectations of the worst off group in society. This constitutes the *general* conception of justice. Rawls then claims that, assuming favourable economic and social conditions, the parties would find it rational to opt for the *special* conception of justice which consists of the following two principles. The first principle of justice is the principle of liberty, according to which each person is to have the most extensive basic liberty compatible with a similar liberty for others. The

[5] Ibid., pp. 142–3.   [6] Ibid., p. 155.

second principle has two elements: the fair opportunity principle and the difference principle. According to the fair opportunity principle, social and economic inequalities should be
attached to offices and positions open to all under conditions
of fair equality of opportunity. According to the difference
principle, such inequalities should be arranged to the advantage of the worst off; inequalities that do not lead to the maximization of the expectations of the worst off are to be rejected.

Rawls argues for the priority of liberty, which implies that
the first principle should get priority over the second and that
a basic liberty (for instance, freedom of conscience, freedom
of association, political freedom, freedom that is protected
under the rule of law) should never be sacrificed for the sake
of anything except liberty. He does not count 'freedom from
poverty' as a liberty.

The contractarian model can be constructed in different
ways and, if we set it up differently, with different assumptions and constraints, we could derive different principles
from it. How then does one justify constructing the model in
one way rather than another? Rawls replies that ultimately
the superiority of one theory over another depends upon how
well the principles that follow from it match our considered
and intuitive judgements of justice, or extend and revise them
in an acceptable way. The theory should provide a 'deep
structure' of our confident but intuitively held judgements,
such as the judgement that religious intolerance is unjust; it
can then give an acceptable ruling in controversial cases where
our intuitions are not so clear, for instance, on how to distribute wealth and authority. Rawls's book can be seen as a
heroic attempt to show that his theory performs these functions better than its rivals. Various forms of utilitarianism and
perfectionism are considered and rejected; unlike many other
critics of such theories, Rawls attempts to put in place of the
rejected theories a theory that is also unified and comprehensive, at any rate within the field of justice.

The feature of Rawls's theory that needs to be stressed is
that he attempts to construct it without appealing to perfectionist considerations. He assumes that from the contractarian
standpoint a life dedicated to the pursuit of art and beauty
has no more intrinsic worth than a life devoted to pushpin

and to the eating of one's excrement. The parties in the original position would, he claims, reject perfectionism as a political
principle.

Rawls does, however, value autonomy very highly and he
appeals to this value at several points. For instance, his argument for the priority of liberty, once a certain level of material
comfort has been reached, is based on our 'fundamental
interest in determining our plan of life'.[7] He stresses that we
have an interest in choosing our plan of life, not just in carrying out the plan of life that we happen to have. It will be
argued in this chapter that Rawls brings in perfectionism
through the back door; the view that an autonomous life is an
essential part of human well-being is a kind of perfectionism.

In order to understand and evaluate Rawls's attempt to
bypass perfectionism it is worth referring to a suggestive
distinction that Brian Barry made and that Rawls takes over,
between want-regarding and ideal-regarding theories. The
former take wants as the basis of social evaluation. Barry
defines want regarding principles as principles which take as
'given the wants which people happen to have and concentrate
attention entirely on the extent to which a certain policy will
alter the overall amount of want satisfaction or on the way in
which the policy will affect the distribution among people of
opportunities for satisfying wants'.[8] He then goes on to define
ideal-regarding considerations as the 'contradictory of want
regarding principles, the two being jointly exhaustive of the
possibilities'. If, for instance, a principle is concerned with
how the wants arose (for instance were they acquired autonomously, or were they implanted?), what the wants are
aimed at (for instance, are they aimed at the higher forms of
life or not?), then the principle is an ideal regarding one.
Ideal-regarding principles, unlike want-regarding principles,
do not take wants as given, but judge wants according to how
they arose, what they are aimed at, and so forth.

Now Rawls takes over this distinction and claims that his
own theory is an ideal-regarding theory. Barry, however,
insists that Rawls's theory is a want-regarding theory, for the
theory does not allow an appeal to any standard of excellence

---

[7] Ibid., p. 543.
[8] B. Barry, *Political Argument*, p. 38.

or perfection.[9] Barry also argues convincingly against some of Rawls's reasons for regarding his (Rawls's) theory as an ideal-regarding one. But I think that there is one feature of want-regarding theories that Rawls does not share, namely the importance that the former attach to existing desires or wants. Rawls's theory has a more Kantian flavour, he appeals to what we would choose *qua* rational beings, which is different from what we want or choose as we happen to be. Those, such as Rawls, who love autonomy dislike the manipulation of wants, and to them it is very important whether or not a given want was autonomously acquired; such concern is alien to the spirit of want-regarding theories.

Rawls does however, face an important problem. He wants to reject perfectionism as a political principle and yet his own liberal theory needs to appeal to ideal-regarding considerations. He is therefore committed to the defence of the view that not all ideal-regarding theories are perfectionist theories. He is not against appeals to excellence as such. Those ideals that would be approved from an impartial, rational, neutral, Archimedean standpoint are admitted by Rawls in the construction of his liberal theory, while those ideals which cannot be justified by an appeal to rational considerations but which depend for their justification upon appeals to considerations of intrinsic worth or other controversial considerations are ruled out.

2. *Criticisms of Rawls's theory*

This chapter shows some of the ways in which liberalism has to appeal to ideal-regarding or perfectionist considerations. The next chapter examines whether liberalism can be constructed by appealing to ideal-regarding considerations that do not presuppose perfectionism; it will be shown there that this distinction between non-perfectionist ideal-regarding judgements and perfectionist judgements cannot be sustained in the way that is required by Rawls and that consequently perfectionism cannot be bypassed.

The doctrine of equal respect does not automatically commit us to a liberal society. In order to show why a liberal society is superior from an egalitarian standpoint to a hierarchical

[9] B. Barry, *The Liberal Theory of Justice* (Oxford, 1973).

society, a tribal society, or to a Brave New World, we would need to appeal to certain perfectionist ideals. The egalitarian argument in favour of liberty has to be supplemented by such perfectionist considerations. In order to show this we can try to see why, in the absence of perfectionism, egalitarianism may be compatible with non-liberal set-ups, even assuming material comfort.

You can be an egalitarian at what in chapter 2 was called the deepest level, which involves your giving equal weight to everyone's interests. This is, under certain circumstances, compatible with your recommending to the public a society where there are considerable inequalities of things like income, and educational opportunities. For there are at least two variants of egalitarianism: strict egalitarianism and maxi-min egalitarianism. A maxi-min egalitarian wants to improve the position of the worst off as much as possible. He is willing to allow departures from strict equality, provided such departures help the interests of the worst off. The strict egalitarian is not prepared to allow such departures; he adheres to equality even when doing so hurts the interests of the worst off. Maxi-min egalitarians, like Rawls, believe in equality of respect and yet allow inequalities of income and wealth. There are some, including Rawls, who are egalitarians with respect to a good x (such as self-respect), and yet allow unequal distribution of some other good y (such as income).

But there is another kind of position that is also possible. One may be an egalitarian with regard to x at the deepest level and yet be a non-egalitarian with regard to x at the level of what doctrine to present to the public (Rawls neglects this possibility). Thus it may be that the right to equal consideration and respect is something that ought to be valued at the deepest level. But this may under certain circumstances commit one to a denial of the public acknowledgement of this same right.

Anti-utilitarians sometimes criticize utilitarianism on the grounds that it may involve a kind of deception. Utilitarianism at the deepest level may commit one to producing a race of non-utilitarians. For if people are brought up as utilitarians this may (as a matter of fact) make them do actions that lead to bad results from a utilitarian point of view. But now there is a similar paradox in the case of egalitarianism. It may be that even if egalitarianism is true, preaching it and implementing it under certain social conditions may create so much havoc that it harms the egalitarian cause; it may raise people's expectations far beyond what the state can satisfy, and lead to misery, envy and violence. In a hierarchical society where the lower castes have not just less liberty but also are acknowledged to have less worth than the top ones it is quite *possible* that, even from the point of view of self-respect, the worst off are better off under such a society than they would be in a society where egalitarianism was publicly acknowledged and where there was much dissatisfaction. Now under such conditions a maxi-min egalitarian (though not a strict egalitarian) may well find the caste society the lesser of the two evils.

Of course many moralists, such as Kant and Rawls, would think that any moral doctrine that is true at the deepest level, but cannot safely be turned into a public moral code, is an immoral one. Now such thinkers disvalue deception very strongly. Rawls follows Kant in stressing what he calls the publicity condition: the true political principles, according to Rawls, should be the basis of public charter. But now Rawls is also an egalitarian at the deepest level; the conditions of his original position are designed to ensure this equality. It is not obvious to me why the publicity condition must be accepted by egalitarians. Rawls uses the publicity constraint to construct his model, for 'the parties assume that they are choosing principles for a public conception of justice. They suppose the everyone will know about these principles all that he would know if their acceptance were the result of an agreement';[10] this condition automatically (that is to say, without considering the relevant merits and demerits) rules out 'such devices as Plato's Noble Lie in the Republic'.[11] But why must we accept the publicity condition as a universal constraint on the model? Rawls points out that the publicity condition is natural. But if it is so natural it should be possible to derive it from the rest of the contractarian model rather than have it as a separate and universal constraint on the

---

[10] *A Theory of Justice*, p. 133.
[11] Ibid., p. 454.

model. The truth is that it is no more difficult and unnatural to construct an egalitarian model that has the other constraints (such as the veil of ignorance) but not the publicity constraint. Rawls tends to justify his constraints by appealing to their reasonableness. And he does point out some important advvantages that follow from it. But there are also important disadvantages that he neglects. Suppose under certain conditions the lot of the worst off would be much worse without something like the 'Noble Lie'. Suppose, for instance, that under certain circumstances certain false beliefs about the basis of society and the state, along with other conditions, help to keep people contented and in their place, and help to prevent the envy, insecurity, and widespread disorder that sometimes follow when people begin to assert their right to equality. In such circumstances may there not be a case for permitting such useful falsehoods to be believed in? A perfectionist may well say that it is better to be a discontented and despairing liberal who is aware of the truth about the way things are than to be a contented and ignorant man whose contentment is based on a Noble Lie. But those such as Rawls who do not appeal to perfectionist considerations cannot demonstrate why the doctrine of equal respect commits us to a belief in a liberal and open society.

Admittedly, Rawls's publicity condition does go naturally with a liberal outlook. Thus Rawls believes in autonomous liberals, each following his own plan of life, respecting each other's forms of life, achieving self-respect as a result of obtaining other people's respect, and so forth. An autonomous life goes naturally with a life based on knowledge rather than ignorance, and so the publicity condition would seem to go naturally with such an ideal. But though the publicity condition does go naturally with a liberal–egalitarian outlook, why does it go naturally with an egalitarian outlook? We cannot assume that egalitarianism at the deepest level commits one to a liberal–egalitarian position.

Of course the parties in the original position should have access to the general facts about society, about human nature, about economic theory, and so forth. But it does not follow that they would never under any conditions opt for a system which permits such devices as the 'Noble Lie'. For on the egalitarian theory of the kind that Rawls appeals to, the test of the justice of a society is not that members of that society should freely consent to the relevant practices (if that were the test, the publicity condition would be essential), but that free and rational persons who surveyed the system from the original position would find it rational to opt for it.

It seems to me that maxi-min egalitarians may under certain empirical circumstances be committed to rejecting the publicity condition and preferring a hierarchical society where some people have less *acknowledged* worth than others. There are two kinds of hierarchical societies, half-hearted ones and full-blooded ones. A maxi-min egalitarian (at the deepest level) may under certain circumstances prefer a half-hearted hierarchical society where some people have less power, income, liberties than others; but where any individual has the same acknowledged worth as any others. American society, at least until recently, was an example of such a society. Or one could have a full-blooded hierarchical society, like the Indian caste system in the past, where there are not only inequalities of wealth, liberties and power, but also a public denial of the view that all human beings have (or ought to have) equal worth and equal human rights.

Now under certain empirical conditions, the (non-perfectionist) egalitarian may prefer a hierarchical society to a liberal society; he may even under certain conditions find it not unreasonable to prefer the full-blooded one. For it is possible that under certain circumstances the full-blooded hierarchical society satisfies the interests of the worst off better than a half-hearted one does. For the latter could be less stable, and have more tension. The publicly proclaimed ideology may cause the worst off, as well as others, to be dissatisfied with their lot for they will see how far their condition deviates from what they appear entitled to even under the publicly proclaimed ideology; and once they become conscious that things could be much better for them, this may make them feel humiliated and lacking in self-respect and incite them to revolt against the existing order of things. Of course, such a hierarchical society may deserve to be got rid of, and sometimes the change may take place in an orderly fashion. But conditions are also conceivable when the dissatisfaction and envy leads to a bloody revolution, and even if things were to improve after the revolution, this will not necessarily compensate the worst off who suffered and died during the transitional period.

Of course many progressives will think the half-hearted hierarchical society less evil than the full-blooded one, for the former contains the seeds of its own reform or destruction, whereas the latter will be more evil precisely because it is more stable. But how can these progressives, who want to reject the full-blooded hierarchical society, rule out *a priori* the possibility that under certain conditions the worst off may well be better off in a full-bloodied hierarchical society, for instance where they have got a benevolent despot, who is regarded as divine and has more acknowledged worth than the people he rules?

If a maxi-min egalitarian wants to reject such a full-blooded hierarchical society he may have to supplement or qualify his egalitarianism with some form of perfectionism. A person who has supplemented his egalitarianism with perfectionism could argue that the people in the above-mentioned whole-hearted hierarchical society are leading degrading or sub-human lives.

3. The Brave New World and autonomy

One of the best ways of seeing the limitations of a non-perfectionist approach is to examine some of its implications. Would it, for instance, involve an acceptance of some form of Brave New World? It will be argued in this section that one cannot reject all the evil features of the Brave New World unless one is willing to appeal to perfectionist considerations. By the 'Brave New World' I mean a non-autonomous society where the following conditions obtain. Suppose we have a society that conditions very effectively the wants of its citizens when they are very young. Suppose that in this society the aims and interests that people have when they grow up depends upon the way that they were conditioned when they were young; they do not, when they grow up, autonomously choose their final aims. Suppose that the conditioning is done in such a way that the citizens grow up to have aims and wants that are internally consistent, that they do not set their aims and aspirations high but are content and happy because they have aims that are easy to satisfy; they do not strive for any of the higher forms of self-realization. Also suppose that their anti-social desires have been largely suppressed if not eliminated as a result of the conditioning, so that they live at peace with themselves and with each other. They still have some minor conflicts of interest; for instance more people may want to go on holiday during the summer season than can be allowed; so problems of justice still arise. But they resolve these conflicts in a peaceful manner, without any substantial friction. And let us assume that such a system of conditioning has abolished, or almost abolished, severe mental problems. This supposition goes quite naturally with the other suppositions we have made. For, provided the conditioning of the young was successful, severe mental troubles would become a rarity.

Now such a system of conditioning could have considerable advantages from the point of view of the parties in the original position. One of the goods that is neglected by Rawls and that has a good claim to be considered a primary good, in so far as it makes sense to talk of primary goods, is mental health in the sense of absence of mental illness, serious mental and emotional troubles and despair. Rawls does consider health in general to be a primary *natural* good. But it seems to me that mental health is at least as much under control of the basic structure, as, say, self-respect, which Rawls considers to be an important primary social good. Mental health is sometimes used in a stronger sense to imply that the agent who is mentally healthy has some sort of freedom and autonomy. I am not using mental health in this strong sense but in the weak sense that merely rules out the sort of conditions just referred to. It is mental health in this weak sense that is likely to carry much weight with the parties in the original position. Those who suffer from mental and emotional troubles include not just the mentally ill but also those who hover between illness and sanity and those who are prone to despair or to mental and emotional dissatisfaction. Perhaps in some cases despair is followed by elation, by some worthwhile achievements, and even by bliss. But if we are concentrating on the worst off, we must think of the plight of those who go through a life of mental dissatisfaction or of despair without any ensuing substantial compensations such as bliss. It is arguable that in very poor societies the worst off are the economically poor rather than the mentally distressed; but as societies get less and less poor a point is reached when, from the contractarian standpoint, the prevention of mental distress gets priority over the goal of economic advancement of the worst off. This argument is at least as good as Rawls's argument that beyond a certain point the basic liberties would get priority over economic advancement of the worst off. Even in the case of very poor societies, one of the chief reasons why extreme poverty would cause concern to the parties in the original position is that such poverty results in, or is accompanied by, much mental and emotional distress. The plight of the Yogi who is very poor but mentally happy should not worry the parties in the original position.

A system of effective conditioning of people's wants, such as the one briefly described earlier, would have the advantage from the contractarian standpoint that it would lead to much less mental dissatisfaction, envy, and despair than would be found in a free and autonomous society that did not go in for such conditioning. It might be asked: would it not be better from the contractarian standpoint to opt for an autonomous and liberal system with the proviso that those suffering from despair and other mental troubles could be given treatment? But this suggestion is not convincing. For let us suppose that the prevention of despair by large-scale conditioning of the kind described earlier is much more effective in reducing the incidence of such mental dissatisfaction and despair than a system of attempting to cure such cases after they have been allowed to occur. Some other considerations would reinforce the desirability from the contractarian standpoint of such conditioning. Thus Rawls emphasizes that our choices in the original position should not appear unreasonable to our descendants and that in making such choices we should be guided by the requirement that we must be able to honour our commitments: 'There must be a rational assurance that one can carry through.'[12] Such considerations would, from the contractarian point of view, weigh in favour of the non-autonomous society where we and our children would have

[12] *A Theory of Justice*, p. 175.

been suitably conditioned to enjoy (or at least endure) life even if we found ourselves amongst the worst off. Admittedly, under existing conditions, conditioning is never completely successful, and in a hierarchical society and in all other conditioned societies that have existed in the past or present there are always at least some individuals left who have not been properly 'fixed' and who find life under such a society quite unbearable. But the better the system of conditioning the less serious this problem will become.

One of Rawls's arguments against a hierarchical society and against non-autonomous societies is that 'in such a society the basic structure is said to be already determined, and not something for human beings to affect. On this view it misconceives men's place in the world to suppose that the social order should match principles which they would as equals consent to.'[13] This argument rests on a confusion. The contractarian model does not require actual consent of its members, but hypothetical consent, that is to say consent from the original position. A conditioned or hierarchical society may prevent its present members from giving free consent to its practices, but it does not necessarily make it impossible for the people in the original position to have given their consent to its practices.

Rawls may argue that all forms of the Brave New World would be rejected under the contractarian experiment, for such a world would conflict with the publicity constraint. But to this defence one could make two replies. First, as we saw earlier, it is not at all obvious why we must accept the publicity constraint as a universal constraint. Secondly, even if we accept the publicity constraint, we can construct a non-autonomous society in such a way that it satisfies the publicity condition. It may be that in fact hierarchical societies and other conditioned societies have been based on falsehoods, but this is not a necessary feature of them. We could have a society that conditions some of its young in such a way that when they grow up they wholeheartedly desire to go into certain 'inferior' positions. Some people would claim that even in some 'liberal' societies many girls are conditioned (for instance, by giving them dolls to play with and in other more

[13] Ibid., p. 547.

important ways) in such a way that when they grow up they really prefer to be housewives; moreover, even after they have been educated and the fact of their past conditioning and the advantages of the alternative ways of life have been pointed out, they still prefer to be housewives, though had they been brought up differently they would have had quite different preferences. Such forms of conditioning are consistent with the letter if not with the spirit of the two principles of justice that Rawls thinks can be derived from the contractarian model. In any case, even if they are not, this does not show the un-desirability of such conditioning from the contractarian stand-point; for it may be that in some situations the advantages to the worst off of such conditioning may carry more weight from the contractarian standpoint.

It is conceivable that a non-autonomous society is consis-tent with Rawls's first principle. For assume that the legal and political liberties exist; some people will still not use their liberties for certain purposes for the simple reason that they have been brought up as children not to have such purposes. Thus, suppose that women are given the liberty to vote, free-dom of association, freedom of expression, and so forth, but prefer not to use these liberties for the sake of 'liberating' themselves; and suppose that this preference would not have been there had they been brought up differently. Similarly we can imagine some societies where some people when they grow up genuinely prefer to aim at the 'lower' professions, such as coal-mining, which carry fewer rewards and privileges.

There is the problem about whether such conditioning necessarily involves a violation of Rawls's fair opportunity principle. The answer would depend upon how widely one stretches the term 'opportunity'. Normally opportunity is used in a sense that does not include motivation and wants: for instance we say he has every opportunity of doing x, but does he want to do x? However, one may say that the person who has been brought up (at home, in schools, and in other such places) in such a way that he wants to go into the 'inferior' jobs has in a sense been prevented by his upbringing from wanting to go into certain 'superior' offices, even though these offices are formally open to him. Now from the contractarian standpoint such conditioning may be desirable provided it satisfies the requirement that the worst off under such a system are better off than the worst off would be in that society if there were no such conditioning. But this requirement could be satisfied by a system of conditioning that violates human freedom and autonomy. Assume that society requires that some 'inferior' jobs, such as coal-mining, have to be done; is it not better from the contractarian standpoint that those who fill these jobs are doing things they want to do, rather than doing them in a discontented spirit, wishing they were doing something else?

It is true that from the contractarian standpoint it is rational to attach importance to freedom in the sense of capacity to get what one wants. For without such capacities people's interests would suffer. Now if one attaches importance to this capacity, it can help to prevent those forms of conditioning that reduce this capacity. But there would still be other forms of conditioning that would be consistent with the importance attached to this capacity. The condition of the worst off, from the contractarian standpoint, can be improved not just by giving them what they want and by not preventing them from getting what they want, but also by bringing them up in such a way that their aims and aspirations are easy to satisfy, that they do not set their aims high, and do not have mental and emotional troubles. Now such conditioning of people's aspirations and goals may be objectionable on the grounds that it interferes with the human personality, with freedom and autonomy, and with self-realization; for instance, if you get rid of the possibility of despair from human beings, you also deprive them of the possibility of certain worthwhile experiences. But freedom and self-realization are not regarded as intrinsic goods by the parties in the original position and they will only be relevant to the extent that they help to protect human interests, especially the interests of the worst off. But does not concern for human interests include a concern for freedom and autonomy in a sense that includes men freely choosing their own final aim? To this objection one can reply that from the contractarian point of view the parties are concerned with protecting and furthering as far as possible the aims that they will find themselves possessing, once the veil of ignorance is removed. The parties have no reason to think that when the veil of ignorance is removed they will find that they value rather than dis-value freedom and autonomy; it may turn out that when the veil is removed what they really want is to lead a life of peaceful and unquestioned submission to a primitive religious order that they have been brought up to believe in. Many ordinary people (who are neither children nor lunatics), such as some housewives, regard autonomy as a burden that they do not want to carry. They would prefer to carry on pursuing their conception of the good, which they have been brought up to believe in, and would resent the idea that they must 'decondition' themselves and freely choose their final ends. Of course freedom in the sense of capacity to do what one wants would still be valuable to such people. Also, it is true that the parties in the original position would not approve of the compulsory conditioning of their aims, once the aims have been formed. For to allow such conditioning would involve jeopardizing one's conception of the good and one's integrity. But such contractarian considerations will not show what is wrong with forming our aims in the first place by a system of conditioning that prevents us from becoming autonomous when we grow up. Nor can we argue that we must always take the wants and aims of human beings as given. This point should become clearer when paternalism with regard to the young is discussed in the last section of this chapter.

Rawls does devote section 78 of *A Theory of Justice* wholly to a discussion of autonomy and objectivity. He tries to show that freedom and autonomy can be derived from the contractarian model, but his arguments are not convincing. He believes that from contractarian standpoint no one's moral convictions should be the result of indoctrination in a well-ordered society;[14] he would presumably extend this point to prohibit other forms of indoctrination as well, such as religious indoctrination. Moreover, in order to rule out the kind of conditioned society we have described, he would have to rule out not just indoctrination in the sense which involves implanting of a false belief, but also conditioning and 'fixing' of the wants of its citizens without implanting such false beliefs. Now Rawls believes that such indoctrination (and such condi-

---

[14] *A Theory of Justice*, p. 336.

tioning) is bad because it violates the duty of mutual respect.[15] But the duty of mutual respect can be interpreted in different senses. There is first the Kantian version, which implies that we should respect each other's autonomy; but there is a second version which does not carry this implication. Accordint to this second version, we can respect each other by respecting each other's way of life and conception of the good, without necessarily respecting each other's autonomy; of course, in those cases where such autonomy is part of the person's conception of the good, our respecting of his conception of the good will commit us to respecting his autonomy. Now it would seem that the most that can be derived from the contractarian model is the second version, which would not rule out the conditioned society of the kind we have described. Moreover, even if the Kantian version of the duty of mutual respect could be derived from the contractarian model, this duty would at best be a *prima facie* duty and not an absolute duty[16] and so it would not be able to rule out such a conditioned society.

According to Rawls, the parties in the original position are concerned with protecting their autonomy.[17] But how does this concern relate to their concern for protecting and furthering their conception of the good, whatever it turns out to be? For, as we saw earlier, the two concerns may conflict. Perhaps Rawls's position is that the parties try to protect their conception of the good, provided this conception is freely and autonomously chosen. But this suggestion has some difficulties for a non-perfectionist. For a non-perfectionist such as Rawls cannot assume that autonomy is intrinsically good. A non-perfectionist contractarian has to construct his model without assuming that autonomy is intrinsically good; he has to try to ascertain how far we can derive the worth of autonomy from the original position, without assuming that autonomy is intrinsically good. But for the reasons given in this chapter it is not at all clear why the parties in the original position would put such a high value on autonomy.

Rawls seems to think that a person's autonomy is part of his interest, that a person has an interest in choosing his final aims and in preserving the conditions that allow him to alter his final aims if he wishes to do so. Now Rawls may argue that even if the parties in the original position do not assume that autonomy is intrinsically good they will want to protect their autonomy, since it would be in their interest to do so. But how does this answer the problem arising from the fact that it is possible, if we look at things from a non-perfectionist standpoint, that the worst off, even if they have attained material comfort, may be better off in a non-autonomous society where they have been suitable conditioned than they would be in an autonomous society. Let us grant that if I were an autonomous being, then I would be miserable in a non-autonomous society, and that I would be better off in a liberal set-up. But this does not show why I would be worse off if I was brought up since birth in a hierarchical, conditioned society, so that I had no desire for an autonomous life when I grew up. Nor will it do to say that such an upbringing is unfair to the autonomous way of life, for as Rawls rightly says fairness has to be to individuals, not to ways of life. The lover of autonomy will have to show that individuals would be better off under conditions of autonomy. Can this be shown without appealing to perfectionist considerations?

Rawls argues that a liberal society encourages different forms of life to compete with each other, and this enables human beings to choose the form of life that is most suited to them; the unsuited ones will disappear. But critics of Rawls could point out that such advantages have to be balanced against the advantages that come from having a non-autonomous society, such as increased psychological security as a result of not having the burdens of choice. Moreover, it is questionable whether in liberal societies the most suitable forms of life will triumph.

Rawls uses the argument that a society that goes in for indoctrination (or conditioning) of the aims and interests of its citizens would be involved in an unfair exploitation of human weakness in order to advance the interests of the people in authority.[18] If so, such conditioning may be rejected by the contractarian model. But suppose we construct a conditioned society where the conditioning is from the contractarian standpoint benefiting the citizens, especially the worst off,

[18] Ibid., p. 515.

for instance in the way that we saw earlier by eliminating
serious mental troubles, by forming their aims and wants in
such a way that they are not set high and are mutually consistent. Such a society would be considered desirable from
the contractarian standpoint, yet it would not be acceptable
to the 'common-sense' morality of many of us; for, if we elimi-
nate the possibility of despair, this may involve the elimination
not only of freedom and autonomy but also of many worthwhile moral, artistic, or religious experiences. As we saw earlier,
from the contractarian standpoint a very high priority would
be given to the elimination of despair, for since the parties in
the original position concentrate on the plight of the worst
off, they have to think of those individuals who go through
a life of despair that is not followed by any substantial worthwhile experiences.

It might be replied that our supposition that the worst off
in the conditioned, non-autonomous society are likely to be
better off than they would otherwise be is in fact false. As
a matter of fact conditioned societies invariably result in the
people at the bottom being, from the contractarian point of
view, much worse off than they otherwise would be, for they
are exploited by the rulers. Now this reply on behalf of Rawls
relies on an argument from general facts which Rawls rightly
admits is a fallacious argument.[19] If it can be shown that a
theory (whether it is Rawls's theory or any other theory such
as utilitarianism) implies that x (for instance, a conditioned
society of the kind we constructed earlier) would be desirable,
and if we can show that x would be regarded by our ordinary
morality as undesirable, then we have shown that the theory
does not square with out ordinary morality. And this conclusion would not be affected by whether or not x does exist,
has existed, or will exist. It is sufficient if we can suppose it
to exist.

It might be objected that for the parties in the original
position the possibility that there might be some good hierarchical societies would be irrelevant. For the contractarian
parties, being cautious, would be more concerned with guard-
ing themselves against the possibility that the hierarchical
society might turn out to be a bad one. But this suggestion

[19] Ibid., p. 160.

seems unfair to the case for hierarchical societies. For Rawls
constructs an ideal variety of a liberal society, and it would
be fairer to compare his Utopia with a hierarchical Utopia.
Perhaps the latter is more likely to degenerate than Rawls's
liberal Utopia. This could be one important argument in
favour of the Rawlsian Utopia, assuming that it could be established. It would not be a decisive argument in favour of the
liberal–democratic forms of government that are likely to
exist in fact. The Weimar Republic did after all degenerate,
giving way to Hitler.

Rawls's view seems to be that in the well-ordered liberal
state that he envisages people will not be prone to much envy,
and they will feel self-respect and self-esteem as a result of
possessing equal liberties. The envy, despair, and other undesirable features of existing liberal societies will, he thinks, not
be present in his liberal Utopia. But this raises the real problem
of whether his liberal utopia is realistic and can be established
and prevent itself from degenerating. Like Plato's Republic,
Rawls's liberal Utopia seems to be an ideal that cannot be
exactly reproduced in real life. The most that one can do is
to adopt a set-up that is closer to it than other set-ups are.
But now if one takes a realistic approach one may find considerable envy and despair in liberal egalitarian set-ups. Indeed,
it has been pointed out that in societies where equality of
opportunity prevails those at the bottom will feel even more
envy for they will no longer have the excuse of being denied
fair opportunity to rise up the ladder; it will be galling for
them to realize that their lack of success is due to their own
limitations.[20]

There are two kinds of considerations that could be advanced against a non-autonomous society. Firstly, since freedom and autonomy are intrinsic goods, therefore such a society
involves an intrinsic evil. Secondly, one can try to show the
various bad effects of such a society on the interests of the
citizens. Now non-perfectionist approaches cannot rely on the
first argument at all. They will therefore have to rely wholly
on the second line of argument, which would not be as strong
as it would be if it were backed up by the first argument. One
will have to study the various effects, good and bad, of such

[20] See M. Young, *The Rise of the Meritocracy* (London, 1958).

a non-autonomous society on the interests of the citizens, especially on the interests of the worst off. And in those cases where the expected good effects of such a society (for instance, improvement in mental health of the citizens) outweigh the expected bad effects of such a society, it could be rational for the parties to opt for such a society, assuming that the parties opt in accordance with the maxi-mini rule.

In fact the second line of argument is not powerful enough. The experience of totalitarian countries shows that economic, technical, and scientific progress is quite compatible with the denial of human freedom and autonomy. Those such as Mill[21] who assume that the autonomous life on balance has good utilitarian effects in such fields have a rather naïve picture of man, according to which either man develops his autonomy and individuality or he remains a puppet or a machine incapable of any kind of creativity. What believers in this false dichotomy overlook is that a person who is non-autonomous in the sense that he does not choose his final aims and ends could be capable of considerable achievements in scientific and technical fields. Admittedly progress in such fields requires considerable freedom in *such fields*; if the scientists take their scientific views from their political rulers they will not become good scientists. But even hierarchical and other non-liberal societies can provide their experts with the requisite degree of freedom and privileges in order to pursue their scientific and technical interests.

Of course, liberal societies do possess some advantages compared to non-liberal societies. The Lysenko affair[22] would not perhaps have occurred in a liberal set-up. But then so do non-liberal societies possess advantages compared to liberal societies; for instance they can be ruthless in dealing with vested interests and other obstacles (such as strikes) in the way of economic and technical progress.

So we can see that to make a really good case for an autonomous society we would have to resort to the first line of argument, or at least to supplement the second line of argument

[21] See *On Liberty*.

[22] Lysenko was a Russian geneticist whose unscientific and dogmatic views about the inheritance of acquired characteristics harmonized with Stalinist ideology and received support from the Soviet state, while the scientific study of genetics was virtually outlawed. The result was disastrous for Soviet agriculture.

with the first. And so we would be committed to a perfectionist approach which asserts that an autonomous life is an essential constituent of human well-being. Unless it is supplemented by perfectionist considerations, egalitarianism (especially in its maxi-min version) cannot rule out a non-autonomous society such as the Brave New World or some kind of hierarchical society.

4. Rawls and paternalism

Another related way of showing the need for a perfectionist approach is by examining the problem of paternalism. Can a non-perfectionist approach deal satisfactorily with the problem of paternalism? Rawls thinks that it can. He thinks that in cases of paternalistic interference the parties will be guided by the individual's own settled preferences and interests in so far as these are not irrational or, failing a knowledge of these, by the theory of primary goods.[23] Now critics of Rawls can point out that the theory of primary goods is not applicable to certain sorts of people. If you give too many basic liberties or too much money to a child or to certain lunatics, this can ruin them. Also, there have been certain societies, such as certain tribal societies, where a large number of its ordinary members, and no just the lunatics and the children, were not well-equipped to make use of basic liberties: where, if you gave them basic liberties, you would destroy their happiness and the whole fabric of their traditional society. Of course, to say this is not to deny that such people may be very developed in many other ways; nor is it to imply any form of imperialism, for it is quite consistent to maintain that a society that is not ready for or suited to the basic liberties, such as freedom to vote, should none the less be free, in the sense of being a sovereign society not ruled or exploited by foreign societies.

Rawls does consider the case of persons who for religious or other reasons may not want primary goods such as liberty or money.[24] He wrongly thinks that from the contractarian standpoint such considerations can be neglected, for people who do not want any particular primary good will not be

<hr>

[23] *A Theory of Justice*, p. 249.   [24] Ibid., p. 143.

compelled to make use of it. His point would at best apply to the case of the strong-minded person who can control the temptations presented by the presence of more primary goods. But what about those who are weak-willed and would succumb to and be tortured by the temptation? His view that ordinary people can *never* suffer from an overdose of the primary goods such as liberty[25] is clearly false. While the introduction of more primary goods may satisfy a person's existing wants more effectively, it may also create new burdens and duties, new aims and aspirations. To say that a man is better off when he begins reaching for the sky involves a perfectionist judgement.

Rawls says that in the original position the parties assume that in society they are rational and able to manage their own affairs;[26] the parties choose the ideal conception on this assumption, making appropriate modifications to cater for the special cases. But the trouble is that in the case of some societies this assumption does not just require a little modification but is radically wrong. For as we said earlier there have been societies where many of the ordinary members (and not just the children and some lunatics) are not capable of looking after their own political, religious, or other important interests, where they may be better off (from the contractarian standpoint) in some kind of non-autonomous society. In societies where the average man is capable of benefiting by the basic liberties, it may be rational, from the contractarian standpoint, to opt for a system of basic liberties, and one could then exclude certain categories of people such as children from these basic liberties. But for those societies where the average man is not ready for the introduction of the basic liberties, it may be better from the contractarian standpoint to prefer some kind of paternalistic or hierarchical social system in spite of the dangers involved in such a system.

The parties in the original position are trying to advance and protect their interests as far as possible. Now this raises the problem about whether the parties should protect what is objectively in their interest or what they will regard as their conception of the good once the veil of ignorance is removed. Often Rawls's position seems to be that the parties are trying

<hr>

[25] Ibid.   [26] Ibid., p. 248.

to protect and promote whatever their conception of the good turns out to be. But suppose taking a lot of drugs forms part of my conception of the good, and suppose that such a pursuit will certainly ruin me, that I do not want to be ruined, and that though I am neither a child nor a lunatic yet out of immaturity or cussedness I do not heed any of the warnings about the dangerous effects of the drugs. Now should someone in the original position always try to protect and promote his conception of the good whatever it turns out to be? In view of the example just mentioned, one is tempted to answer— No, not always. Yet in order to give an adequate justification of such cases of paternalistic interference one may have to resort to perfectionist considerations!

5. Paternalism towards the young

That perfectionist considerations would be required to give an adequate justification for paternalistic interference can also be seen by considering the conditioning of the young. Rawls points out that paternalistic interference is to be guided by an appeal to the individual's own settled preferences and interests in so far as these are not irrational.[27] Now this principle cannot guide us in those cases where the individual's settled aims and values are obviously irrational or where, as in the case of the young, the individual has not yet got any really settled preferences and aims. Perhaps children do in a sense have fairly stable aims and preferences, but it would be silly to assume that our interference with the lives of children's should be guided solely with a view to advancing the aims that children happen to have as children.

Rawls would at this point refer us to his other guide for paternalistic interference, namely the theory of primary goods.[28] Now we have already seen some important flaws in this theory. In any case, it is difficult to avoid appealing to perfectionist considerations here. In deciding how to bring up children, the interests of society are taken into account, but the good of the children is at least one of the important considerations to be kept in mind. But how do we decide adequately what is for their own good without resort to

[27] Ibid., p. 249.   [28] Ibid., p. 249.

perfectionist considerations? When we are bringing up children we do not just provide them with primary goods like money or liberty; many of our decisions will influence, though not necessarily determine, the very aims and preferences that they will have when they grow up and the different weights they will give to different preferences. Now in order to deal with the problem of the direction in which we should influence children's growth we shall need to decide what is really good for them. But we cannot adequately decide what is really good for a person whose aims have not yet been formed without resort to perfectionist considerations. For instance, some people think that it is for a child's good that he should be a free and autonomous agent when he grows up, so that when he grows up he can freely choose his final ends and his way of life. But this position cannot be justified merely by appealing to the contractarian standpoint, for as has been shown in this chapter people in the original position may not reject a conditioned society of the kind described earlier.

One of the tests of the morality of paternalistic interference that might be suggested[29] is that the individual, after his rational powers have been restored or developed, should freely approve of what we did for him and to him in the past. Now this test would rule out a non-autonomous society, for though a non-autonomous creature can approve of what we did for him, he cannot *freely* approve of anything. But it is not at all clear why the parties in the original position must accept this test. For one thing, this test is too strong. Even in cases where we have brought up people in such a way that they will grow up as autonomous men, some of them may, when they have developed their rational powers, refuse to approve of what we did for them, for they may resent having to carry the burdens of an autonomous life. Now can we, without conditioning them appropriately, ensure that children will, when they develop their rational powers, approve of what we are doing now for them and to them? We could perhaps condition them to accept the burdens of an autonomous life, but in that case they will not be able to give us their *free* approval of the conditioning that we enforce upon them. In order to overcome such objections, one might modify the test so that

29 Ibid.

it requires only that the individual, after his rational powers have been developed or restored, should be *able* freely to approve of the past paternalistic interference. This would not require that they should in fact freely approve of such past interference, only that it should be possible for them to do so. This test would reject a conditioned society. But in view of the advantages of the non-autonomous society to the parties in the original position, why should the parties agree to this as a universal requirement?

If we try to bring up a child so that he becomes an autonomous agent, we shall in a sense be influencing him; we shall be helping to make him a different sort of person from what he would be if he were not an autonomous agent. The view that autonomy is among the constituents of a person's good is a kind of perfectionism. A person who has been conditioned in the Brave New World may also have freedom in the sense of capacity to fulfil his wants and aims, though he will not have the freedom to choose between alternative ways of life. Indeed if he has been suitably conditioned (so that he does not aim too high) he may also find it much easier to satisfy his wants and aims than the autonomous agent who may be pursuing aims that are difficult to attain. We cannot show that the non-autonomous creature would be worse off than the autonomous one by appealing to contractarian considerations alone; those who think that the education system should aim at turning out autonomous agents will probably have to reject Rawls's view[30] that perfectionism must not serve as a political principle.

Rawls does realize the limitations of the test according to which paternalistic intervention is justified if the person being interfered with will approve of such interference after he has been subjected to it. If such a test were sufficient, it could sanction brainwashing as long as the brainwashed person approved of what had been done to him after he had been brainwashed. In order to overcome such undesirable consequences, Rawls supplements this test with the following necessary conditions that must be satisfied: paternalistic interference is to be justified by the evident failure or absence of reason and will, and it must be guided by the principles of

[30] Ibid., p. 329.

justice and what is known about the subject's more permanent aims and preferences, or by the account of primary goods.[31]

Now the trouble is that at any rate in the case of young children these Rawlsian consraints are not adequate. For in the case of young children there is 'absence of reason and will', and so the constraint that there must be absence of reason and will does not tell us what we must not do to such people; later in chapter 12 it will be shown that this constraint does not solve problems in the case of adults either. And we have already seen that the requirement that we should take into account the permanent aims and interests of individuals has little relevance in the case of individuals whose aims and interests have not yet been formed. Nor will the theory of primary goods and of justice solve all the problems. Admittedly a non-perfectionist theory such as Rawls's does imply that certain virtues ought to be inculcated in the young. For example, the young ought to be encouraged to develop a sense of justice[32] and to enjoy the fruits of social co-operation.[33]   But such considerations do not uniquely determine what form of life to encourage among the young. They do rule out certain forms of life, but they do not help us with the problem that of the many forms of life that are compatible with the theory of justice which do we encourage among the young? Should we, for instance, encourage our children to become mystics, or should we encourage them to practice the life of polymorphous sexuality and polymorphous perversity as recommended by Marcuse, who celebrates sexual perversions and who suggests that from childhood onwards there should be far less repression and far more experimentation in sexual matters than exists in our society,[34] or should we encourage them to pursue more staid forms of life? To answer such problems we shall have to study the child's nature and to make perfectionist judgements about what is good for him.

Nor will talk of autonomy rescue the non-perfectionist here. For firstly, as we have seen, an appeal to the value of autonomy involves an appeal to perfectionist considerations. And secondly, even if we assume that an autonomous life is

---

[31] Ibid., p. 249.   [32] Ibid., pp. 514-15.
[33] Ibid., pp. 570-1.   [34] H. Marcuse, *Eros and Civilization* (London, 1969).

essential for human well-being this will not solve all the problems. Admittedly, the view that the aim of education is to turn out autonomous and just adults does have substantial implications. Thus it can rule out taking hard drugs and adopting other soporific forms of life. Some forms of life are clearly more congenial than others to the powers of autonomy, critical thinking, and sense of justice. But the fact remains that several forms of life are compatible with such requirements about autonomy and about justice. And how do we choose between such forms of life? How, for instance, do we decide whether or not to encourage children in a life of polymorphous perversity?

Sometimes certain forms of life, such as the life of sexual promiscuity, are contingently linked with habits, such as drug addiction, which impair autonomy. But, one may still ask, why not allow sexual promiscuity among the young and only forbid the use of things (such as hard drugs) that impair autonomy?

If you are living in a puritanical society then it is advisable not to encourage your daughter to enjoy a promiscuous life, for if she does then she is likely to looked down on by others, and this could in the long run damage her self-respect and self-esteem. But such considerations do not show what is wrong with encouraging the young in general to indulge a promiscuous sexual life; for if such practices became widespread, the censorious social attitudes towards individuals who indulged in such practices could also alter and become less inimical to the growth of self-esteem and self-respect.

So though there are some useful Rawlsian guides and constraints for paternalistic interference, such guides and constraints do not solve the problem of how we should choose, for the purposes of bringing up children, between forms of life that are compatible with the existence of such constraints and guides. In order to make this choice we shall have to appeal to perfectionist considerations and maintain that some forms of life are more suited to certain human beings than others are. It might be suggested that instead of appealing to perfectionism here, one could appeal to tradition. But it seems to me that though we can and should learn much from our experience and our traditions about what forms of life are suitable for the young, it would be wrong to think that we could bypass perfectionism here. For traditions have to be adapted to modern conditions, and we must make judgements about which of our traditions are worth preserving and encouraging and which are not.

Rawls is aware that several forms of life are compatible with his theory of justice. He thinks that it is an advantage of a liberal set-up that it allows these forms of life to compete with each other on fair terms, so that the most suitable ones will emerge eventually on top, and the unsuitable ones will disappear. This view of Rawls will be examined in Chapter 11; it will be argued that his choice criterion of value does not succeed in bypassing perfectionist considerations; for the choice criterion can only operate if we assume certain values.

Some people think that though society has the right to impart its wisdom to the young, the state should not interfere with the education of the young. For it has no authority to interfere. So the state can be neutral and can bypass perfectionism by doing little or nothing in the matter of education except perhaps acting as a kind of referee or umpire.

What are we to make of this objection? Now admittedly it is not easy to show that the state has the right to use compulsion against the young. But then is it any easier to show that anyone, even parents, have the right to use compulsion against the young! Since children seem in need of help and paternalistic intervention and since they are not as yet autonomous agents, nor are capable of managing their own affairs, one can defend the use of compulsory paternalistic measures with regard to them without violating their autonomy. Of course, sometimes there is good evidence that the state is so inefficient or corrupt or attached to outmoded dogmas that it may ruin the minds of children. In such cases one should try to keep state education to a minimum until one has improved the state. But such considerations do not show that the state is never entitled to provide education. Private schools too can in certain circumstances provide degenerate education. Such facts are consistent with the view that educational authorities, whether state or private ones, have a duty to provide *good* education and to create a morally healthy environment in which children grow up. There are some good arguments against giving the state a monopoly over education. But such arguments do not show why the state should not be one of the important educational agencies. And as long as the state has an important role to play in the upbringing of the young, it cannot bypass perfectionist considerations.

Choice and Values

It is one of the main contentions of this book that at several points a liberal-egalitarian theory has to appeal to ideals. Now this creates a problem for liberal-egalitarians such as Rawls who want to bypass perfectionism as a political principle; they have to show that though they appeal to ideals, their ideals are not perfectionist ideals. In order to solve such problems, Rawls appeals to the Aristotelian principle and to the choice criterion of value.[1] According to Rawls, the Aristotelian principle and the choice criterion of value help us to find out what ideals human beings in fact follow under normal conditions; such ideals can he thinks be justified from a neutral, impartial standpoint and do not involve an appeal to perfectionist values. So Rawls would claim that though liberalism does need to resort to ideals, its ideals can be justified without resort to perfectionism.

In this chapter such attempts at bypassing perfectionism are rejected and the limitations of the Aristotelian principle and the choice of criterion of value are pointed out. Also in this chapter, there is a comparison of some of the ideas of John Stuart Mill and Rawls. Rawls is one of the greatest liberal philosophers since Mill. In some respects the two have remarkably similar ideas, in spite of the fact that Mill was a utilitarian, whereas Rawls is openly hostile to utilitarianism. Both subscribe to some version of the choice criterion of value. Rawls compares his own position to that of Mill and suggests that he and Mill arrive at similar conclusions through different routes.[2] But a closer reading

---

[1] *A Theory of Justice* and 'Fairness to Goodness', *Philosophical Review*, lxxxiv (1975), 536–54.
[2] *A Theory of Justice*, pp. 209–11.

of Rawls would show that even the routes that the two
follow (or need to follow) and the moves they make in order
to forestall objections have similarities. Both Rawls and Mill
adopt a somewhat high-minded and morally elevating stance,
not only with regard to the virtues of liberalism but also in
their preference for what they regard as the superior forms
of life. And, as we shall see, they both attach great importance
to the choice criterion of value, to what people would prefer
under conditions of liberty.

1. The Aristotelian principle

Rawls commends the Aristotelian Principle according to which

> human beings enjoy the exercise of their realized capacities (their
> innate or trained abilities), and this enjoyment increases the more the
> capacity is realized, or the greater its complexity . . . human beings
> take more pleasure in doing something as they become more profi-
> cient at it, and of the two activities they do equally well, they prefer
> the one calling on a larger repertoire of more intricate and subtle
> discriminations.[3]

He then illustrates this principle by saying that chess is more
complicated and subtle than checkers (draughts) and so
people who can do both generally prefer chess to playing
checkers; and for similar reasons he thinks algebra would
be preferred to arithmetic.

Now the Aristotelian principle plays an important part in
Rawls's system. Rawls rejects perfectionism as a political
principle; he takes this to imply that from the point of view
of the parties in the original position, no form of life is
intrinsically better (or worse) than another form of life,
pushpin is assumed to be intrinsically no worse than poetry.
He has to face the objection that if we reject perfectionism
as a political principle, many undesirable consequences
will follow. For instance, it is difficult to see, without perfectionism, why the parties in the original position should attach
the high value to autonomy that Rawls thinks they should.
If the parties in the original position, cannot assume that
autonomy is intrinsically valuable, it is not clear how they
can reject the Brave New World (see chapter 10). Though

[3] *A Theory of Justice*, p. 426.

Rawls tries to bypass perfectionism, Hart correctly points out that Rawls does harbour

a latent ideal of his own . . . The ideal is that of a public spirited citizen who prizes political activity and service to others as among the chief goods of life and could not contemplate as tolerable an exchange of the opportunities for such activity for mere material goods or contentment. This ideal powerfully impregnates Rawls's book at many points . . . It is, of course, among the chief ideals of Liberalism, but Rawls's argument for the priority of liberty purports to rest on interests, not on ideals.[4]

Hart goes on to complain that Rawls's argument, if it is based purely on interests does not succeed in establishing the priority of liberty.

In order to answer such objections, Rawls needs to appeal to the Aristotelian principle. He needs to appeal to certain ideals, in order to defend liberalism. Since he cannot defend his ideals with the help of perfectionist considerations, he tries to defend them by appealing to the Aristotelian principle which is for him a kind of stand-in for perfectionism. The Aristotelian principle is, according to Rawls, a principle that human beings *in fact* follow to an important degree; according to him the Aristotelian principle, unlike perfectionist principles, does not assume that some values (or ways of life) are intrinsically superior to others; it merely tells us that some ways of life are in fact preferred to other ways of life.

We have seen that Rawls has to face the problem as to why we should value autonomy and reject the Brave New World. The Aristotelian principle, if true, may be used with some plausibility to show why a Rawlsian should value autonomy and so reject the Brave New World. For in the Brave New World human beings will not be fully stretched; and the parties in the original position would prefer to lead an autonomous life which is more creative and challenging.

Again if the Aristotelian principle is true it may be used with some plausibility to defend the doctrine of the priority of liberty over income. Rawls believes that 'since the Aristotelian principle ties in with the primary good of self-respect,

[4] H. L. A. Hart, 'Rawls on Liberty and its Priority', in *Reading Rawls*, ed. N. Daniels (Oxford, 1975), p. 252.

it turns out to have a central position in the moral psychology underlying justice as fairness'.[5]

According to Rawls, beyond a certain point it becomes irrational to prefer the satisfaction of material wants over cultural and spiritual aims, and over our desire to determine our plan of life.[6] When people are too poor to exercise their spiritual and cultural aims, it is reasonable for them to concentrate on giving priority to the production of more wealth and income. But once they can exercise in a fruitful way their cultural, religious, and moral interests, it becomes irrational for them to sacrifice such interests for the sake of increased material welfare. The priority of the spiritual, cultural, and autonomous life over the material life appears to Rawls to be a consequence of the Aristotelian principle: 'it follows from the Aristotelian principle (and its companion effect), that participating in the life of a well ordered society is a great good.'[7]

According to Rawls,

perhaps the most important primary good is that of self-respect . . . (which) includes a person's sense of his own value, his secure conviction that his conception of his good, his plan of life, is worth carrying out . . . without it nothing may seem worth doing . . . all desire and activity becomes empty and vain, and we sink into apathy and cynicism. Therefore the parties in the original position would wish to avoid at almost any cost the social conditions that undermine self-respect.[8]

He then goes on to argue that when our activities fail to satisfy the Aristotelian principles, our self-respect is undermined; for when our activities do not satisfy the Aristotelian principle, 'they are likely to seem dull and flat, and to give us no feeling of competence or a sense that they are worth doing. A person tends to be more confident of his value when his abilities are both fully realized and organized in ways of suitable complexity and refinement.'[9] Moreover, according to Rawls, there is the companion effect to the Aristotelian principle; when our activities are subtle and complex and so satisfy the Aristotelian principle, they are more likely to get us the admiration of other human beings; which is vital for us for 'unless our endeavours are appreciated by our associates

[5] *A Theory of Justice*, p. 33.   [6] Ibid., p. 543.
[7] Ibid., p. 571.   [8] Ibid., p. 440.   [9] Ibid.

it is impossible for us to maintain the conviction that they are worthwhile . . .'.[10]

Rawls is aware of some of the limitations of the Aristotelian principle, but he does not realize the significance of these limitations for his theory. He claims that the Aristotelian principle is borne out by the behaviour of adults, of children and of higher animals. He thinks complicated and intricate activities are preferred because they allow us to get pleasure and delight from the variety, the novelty, the spontaneity, and the occasions for ingenuity and invention that such activities provide. On the other hand simple activities tend to get dull and boring as we do them over and over again. Moreover, unlike with complicated and skilled activities, simple activities do not get us the admiration of our fellow men, and so they tend to leave us without self-esteem, since the respect and admiration of other people is essential for our self-esteem. Evolution too is likely to favour people who follow the Aristotelian principle.

Rawls is aware of some of the burdens of acting in accordance with the Aristotelian principle, the strain and difficulty involved in pursuing complex and intricate activities. And so he thinks that a balance must be struck between the gains of pursuing complex activities and the strains of pursuing them. Since there are various hazards and risks involved in the pursuit of complex activities, the Aristotelian principle 'formulates a tendency and not an invariable pattern of choice and like all tendencies it may be overridden'.[11] However, he goes on to say, in spite of such considerations, that the tendency postulated by the Aristotelian principle 'is relatively strong and not easily counter-balanced . . . and . . . in the design of social institutions a large place has to be made for it, otherwise human beings will find their culture and form of life dull and empty . . .'.[12]

At least at times, he seems only to be defending a fairly modest version of the Aristotelian principle. Thus, as we just saw, he is not saying that it is rational to stretch ourselves as fully as we can; he admits that the charms of doing so must be balanced against the hazards. Moreover he seems to admit that the Aristotelian principle does not imply that

[10] Ibid., p. 441.   [11] Ibid., p. 429.   [12] Ibid.

we must reach a high level of excellence and pursue complex and intricate activities in all important areas:

> It will normally suffice that for each individual there is some association (one or more) to which he belongs and within which the activities that are rational for him are publicly affirmed by others . . . In a well ordered society, anyway, there are a variety of communities and associations, and the members of each have their own ideals appropriately matched to their aspirations and talents . . .Thus, what is necessary is that there should be for each person at least one community of shared interests to which he/she belongs and where he/she finds his/her endeavours confirmed by his associates.[13]

Now, although the modest verion of the Aristotelian principle that he defends may be substantially true, it will not suffice for the purposes of his theory of justice. He needs a stronger version. Yet the trouble is that a stronger version is much more difficult to defend against criticisms. In other words, the element of truth in the Aristotelian principle is not sufficient to give Rawls's theory the support that he needs. For instance, Rawls attaches a lot of importance to the value of autonomy. Now the problem for him is to justify the high value he places upon it. He cannot appeal to perfectionist considerations so he needs the support of the Aristotelian principle.

Rawls suggests that one of the important reasons why our 'fundamental interest in determining our plan of life' assumes a prior place is because of the crucial role of 'self-respect and the desire of human beings to express their nature in a free social union with others'.[14] But it seems to me that people could have self-respect without being autonomous, without autonomously determining their plan of life; indeed Rawls modest version of the Aristotelian principle must allow this. Thus, as we saw earlier, the modest version of the Aristotelian principle does not require that the individual must stretch himself in all important directions; as long as he pursues some complicated and intricate activities, a person could get the necessary approval from other human beings and feel self-respect.[15]

Rawls's modest version of the Aristotelian principle cannot show why we should reject the Brave New World where people have been brought up in a non-autonomous way; it

---

[13] Ibid., pp. 441–2.   [14] Ibid., p. 543.   [15] Ibid., pp. 441–2.

is not clear why people in the Brave New World will feel that their lives are dull and empty and lacking in self-respect. The modest version of the Aristotelian principle requires only that 'there should be for each person at least one community of shared interests to which he belongs and where he finds his endeavours confirmed by his associates.'[16] It is not clear why the non-autonomous Brave New World could not satisfy this requirement. You can indulge in complicated and intricate activities, even if your way of life is not autonomous, even if you do not choose the final aims of your life. In feudal societies where people automatically joined the professions of their fathers (and so did not choose their professions autonomously), some of the professions involved complicated and skilled artistry. And similarly in the Brave New World the people can pursue fairly complicated and subtle activities, such as games which involve skill. So it is not clear why the inhabitants of the Brave New World will feel that their lives are dull and empty and lacking in self-respect; they could belong to associations where some of their activities are publicly affirmed by others.

Rawls has other arguments to show why the parties in the original position would reject a non-autonomous society, but none of them are conclusive. We can only make his arguments work if he allows autonomy as an intrinsic good, but to do would pose other problems for his system, for it would involve admitting perfectionism as a political principle.[17]

So we see that if Rawls is to succeed in bypassing perfectionism as a political principle, he needs the Aristotelian principle in some strong form, and not just in its modest form. But how can the Aristotelian principle in a strong form be defended? Are there not many exceptions to it? We shall deal with this problem shortly.

There is an interesting difference between the way that Mill characterizes the lower life and the way that Rawls does. Mill allows that the person who pursues the lower life (that is to say the life that does not involve the exercise of the higher faculties) could be contented, more so than the

---

[16] Ibid., p. 442.
[17] See Haksar, 'Autonomy, Justice and Contractarianism'.

person pursuing the higher life; the former will be more easily satisfied and contented because he will have fewer wants and because he will be 'unconscious of the imperfections' that he suffers from.[18] According to Rawls, however, the person who leads the lower life, the life in accordance with the Aristotelian principle, will be bored and will feel that his life is empty and dull; he will realize that he is not respected by others around him and therefore he will feel that his own life is rather worthless.[19] So it would follow from Rawls's views that the person pursuing the lower life will be discontented and dissatisfied. Now Rawls exaggerates the boredom and the tedium of the simple life. One needs to distinguish the simple life from a sensual life. It is perhaps true that an undiscriminating pursuit of sensual pleasures leads to boredom; for instance, His Highness Sir Bhupinder Singh, The Magnificent, The Maharaja of Patiala, had three hundred and fifty concubines and is said to have died of boredom![20] But it would be quite wrong to infer that the simple life is necessarily boring and tedious. There are plenty of people who lead well-regulated simple lives without becoming bored.

In spite of such differences, Rawls's Aristotelian principle has similarities to Mill's idea that higher pleasures are superior to the lower ones. The arguments used by Rawls and Mill in favour of their positions are also similar. Thus, while Rawls thinks that people who can, for instance, play chess and checkers will prefer the former, Mill argues that those who have experienced the higher and lower pleasure will prefer the former and therefore the higher pleasures are more desirable.

Now Rawls has to face the following criticism.[21] Either the Aristotelian principle is put forward as an empirical generalization, in which case it is false; for at least in some cases, people who can, for instance, play both chess and checkers will prefer the latter. Or it is really a perfectionist recommendation about what constitutes rational behaviour, appealing not to what *all* human beings in fact choose but to what they should choose in order to promote certain ideas

---

[18] *Utilitarianism*, chapter II, para. 6.
[19] *A Theory of Justice*, p. 429 and pp. 440 ff.
[20] See L. Collins and D. Lapierre, *Freedom at Midnight* (Glasgow, 1975).
[21] See Barry, *The Liberal Theory of Justice*, p. 28.

of human excellence; but in that case Rawls would have to abandon his claim that perfectionist considerations are not allowed to enter into the contractarian model.

Mill has to face a similar dilemma. Thus either his claim, that the higher pleasures are more desirable than the lower ones, is based on a false empirical generalization, for many people who have experienced the higher and the lower pleasures prefer the latter; or Mill is just making a perfectionist recommendation of what people ought to prefer in order to pursue certain human excellences, but in that case he is abandoning the choice criterion of value.

Probably those like Mill and Rawls who use the choice criterion of value are making an empirical claim. For on the choice criterion of value, if A is more valuable than B, then A would be preferred to B by the relevant people. So if enough of the relevant people (that is to say, those who have experienced both A and B) do not prefer A to B, then it will not be the case that A is more valuable than B. So Mill's view, that the higher forms of life are more valuable than the lower ones, does involve an empirical claim about what the relevant experts will prefer.

So Rawls and Mill both appear to be committed to some empirical generalization about what the relevant people do prefer. Now this leads to the objection that the empirical claims made by Rawls and Mill are false. In order to see how Rawls can deal with this, it is instructive to see how Mill dealt with it. Mill had to face the objection that there were exceptions to his generalization that those (or most of those) who have experienced both prefer the higher to the lower forms of life. Mill replied that the alleged counter-examples are not really counter-examples. For though some people who have experienced both opt for the lower pleasures, this is because the test for deciding which pleasures are better is not being conducted fairly. Certain conditions have to be satisfied before Mill's tests can be fairly carried out. For instance, the experts must be 'equally acquainted with and equally capable of appreciating and enjoying both', they must be 'equally suceptible to both classes of pleasure'.[22] Mill insists that unless these conditions are satisfied the

[22] *Utilitarianism*, chapter II, paras. 6–7.

relevant choices by the experts are not voluntary ones. He points out that people who have experienced both and 'choose' the lower pleasures have become incapable of the higher pleasures. According to Mill, the higher forms of life need cultivation like tender plants, without which they can easily be stifled by 'hostile influences and by mere want of sustenance . . . Men lose their high aspirations as they lose their intellectual tastes . . . and they *addict* themselves to inferior pleasures, not because they deliberately prefer them but because they are the only ones to which they have access or the only ones they are any longer capable of enjoying'.[23] So in this way Mill argues that the alleged counter-examples to his theory are not really counter-examples, they are not cases where the experts voluntarily and deliberately choose the inferior pleasures.

Now Rawls, at least implicitly, makes a similar move to defend himself against counter-examples to the Aristotelian principle. He considers the example of the intelligent and skilled person who prefers to count blades of grass 'in various geometrically shaped areas such as park squares and well trimmed lawns.'[24] rather than exercise his skills and talents. Rawls suspects that such a person is perhaps 'peculiarly neurotic and in early life acquired an aversion to human fellowship, and so he counts blades of grass to avoid having to deal with other people'.[25] So his suggestion seems to be that a person who acted voluntarily (which would exclude his being 'peculiarly neurotic') and under fair and normal conditions, would not choose simpler to more complex and discriminating forms of activities. The counter-examples to the Aristotelian principle then could be explained away as arising from abnormal conditions, such as neurosis. This method of dealing with counter-examples is used by many thinkers who go in for generalizations about human nature. For instance, Hume claimed that benevolence was natural to human beings. When confronted with counter-examples such as Nero's cruelty, Hume suspected that such cases were not cases of voluntary behaviour but of perversions.[26]

[23] Ibid para 7.   [24] *A Theory of Justice*, p. 432.   [25] Ibid.
[26] *Enquiry concerning the Principles of Morals,* reprinted in *Hume's Enquiries,* ed. L. A. Selby-Bigge (Oxford, 1902), pp. 169–323, para. 184.

Again, Rousseau believed that no one would freely choose to be a slave. When confronted with alleged counter-examples, he replied that such cases are not cases of free choice: 'slaves lose every thing in their chains even their desire for escaping from them: they love their servitude . . . If then they are slaves by nature, it is because they have been slaves against nature'.[27] '. . . we cannot therefore from the servility of nations already enslaved, judge of the natural disposition of mankind for or against slavery; we should judge by the prodigious effort of every free people to save itself from oppression.'[28] Rousseau's position is similar to Mills's. Rawls mentions Mill's argument that men normally desire to be free, and when they do not desire to be free this is because of abnormal circumstances, such as the presence of apathy or despair. Rawls says that such arguments are forceful;[29] and he appears to support Mill's choice criterion of value.[30]

So Mill, Rawls, and Rousseau would all agree that for the choice criterion of value to work, the choice has to be a free choice, a choice made under conditions of liberty. Now this requirement creates some very important problems for the choice criterion of value. First, how do we ensure that all the relevant conditions of liberty have been met? Moreover, are not concepts like 'freedom' and 'voluntary' at least partly normative? Since they are,[31] in order to decide that the choice is a free one, or a voluntary one, we would already have to presuppose some values. Therefore the choice criterion cannot be used as a criterion for all the values. This criticism would not by any means render the choice criterion useless; but it would reduce the scope of the choice criterion. We could, assuming certain norms or values, use the choice criterion to validate or reject certain other norms or practices. I shall come back to such complications later.

Rawls believes that his well-ordered society sets the conditions of liberty that are required for the choice criterion

[27] *The Social Contract*, Bk. I, chapter II, in *The Social Contract and Discourses*, transl. G. D. H. Cole, revised by J. Brumfitt and J. Hall, p. 167.
[28] Rousseau, 'Discourse on the Origins of Inequality', in *The Social Contract and Discourses* p. 93.
[29] *A Theory of Justice*, p. 210.
[30] Rawls, 'Fairness to Goodness'.
[31] See Haksar, 'Coercive Proposals', *Political Theory*, iv (1976), 65–79.

of value to operate.[32] Now he is in danger of arguing in a circle. For he wants to set up his well-ordered society without an appeal to perfectionist considerations, and he needs the Aristotelian principle as a stand-in for perfectionism; he cannot construct his well-ordered society without appealing to the Aristotelian principle. But the Aristotelian principle has to be defended against counter-examples, and in order to defend it against counter-examples Rawls has to appeal to the choice criterion of value, for he needs to argue that the alleged counter-examples are not cases of really free choice. So the Aristotelian principle has to be defended by appealing to the choice criterion of value, and yet the Aristotelian principle is needed to construct a well-ordered society without which the choice criterion of value cannot operate! Is this not circular?

But can it not be replied that those for whom the Aristotelian principle is not suitable are neurotic or abnormal in other ways, so that the Aristotelian principle applies to all normal people? Now for this reply to work it is necessary (though not perhaps sufficient) that the relevant evidence should be forthcoming, viz. the evidence that those who do not act in accordance with the Aristotelian principle are abnormal. Moreover, this evidence must be of a non-circular kind. If you ask for the evidence for the view that the person who prefers the simpler activities (such as counting blades of grass and checkers) to complicated activities (such as chess and algebra) is abnormal, you must not give as your evidence the fact that he violates the Aristotelian principle and is therefore abnormal. You must not presuppose the truth of the Aristotelian principle in order to defend the Aristotelian principle against counter-examples! Now is such non-circular evidence forthcoming? It may well be that if you study people who spend most of their time counting blades of grass, they are as a matter of fact neurotic in some clinical sense. But can the same be said of those who prefer, say, checker to chess, or arithmetic to algebra, or reading second-rate philosophers to reading Rawls?

Next, there is the problem that if in order to operate the choice criterion of value, we have to create conditions of

---
[32] Rawls, 'Fairness to Goodness', p. 549.

liberty, this may involve our loading the dice in favour of the free and autonomous life. Rawls and Mill both need to avoid this danger. Thus Mill says that people practicing the higher life, even if dissatisfied would not consent to become contented fools.[33] And Rawls implies that people under conditions of liberty would choose to lead the autonomous life.[34] Now such arguments are not necessarily circular. It is logically possible for autonomous people to opt for a non-autonomous life, so the view that autonomous people prefer the autonomous life involves a substantial, non-tautologous assertion. Sometimes what Rawls says would reduce such an assertion to a triviality, for instance, when he says that acting autonomously 'is acting from principles that we would consent to as free and equal rational beings'.[35] In the index under the entry 'autonomy' Rawls seems to imply that the above assertion about autonomy is a definition of autonomy.[36]

Now as a definition of autonomy, the above definition is very inadequate. A definition of autonomy should allow for the logical possibility that the people in the original position may (from a position of equal liberty) opt for a non-autonomous life, so that if it is the case that the parties opt for an autonomous life, this should be a substantial result and not something that is made trivially true by definition. But though such inadequate definitions of autonomy can be avoided, and the view that free (or autonomous) people would in fact opt for a free (or autonomous) life may not be circular or trivially true, it may still be suspect for other related reasons. For instance, may it not be that free people are biased in favour of the free life?

Autonomous people sometimes find autonomy such a burden and cause of despair that they might be willing to opt for a non-autonomous life. Mill and Rawls would have to say that in such cases the presence of the excessive burden of autonomy showed that the choice for a non-autonomous life was not made under normal conditions. But how do we specify 'normal conditions' in a neutral way? Just as Rawls and Mill

---

[33] *Utilitarianism*, chapter II.
[34] *A Theory of Justice*, section 78; see also 'Fairness to Goodness'.
[35] Ibid., p. 516.
[36] Ibid., p. 589.

would say that when autonomous people opt for a non-autonomous life, this is because their choice in such cases was loaded against the autonomous life, could not the critic of Rawls and Mill argue with equal plausibility, that when autonomous people opt for the autonomous life, they are biased in favour of the autonomous life?

2. The choice criterion of value

Even if free people prefer the free way of life, this may only show that the free way of life is suited to free people; but how does it follow that it is suited to non-autonomous people, for instance to people living in tribes? And if people in tribal societies (who have never observed the free way of life) insist that they want to stay on in the tribal way of life, it is not at all obvious that they are being irrational.

But do not free, autonomous people have more knowledge on which to base their decision regarding which form of life is better? Knowledge of alternative forms of life may not be a sufficient condition of a wise choice between the alternative ways of life, but it is a necessary conditon. But now there is the complication that those who fulfil this necessary condition of the application of the choice criterion of value, become radically different in the processs, and so what is good for such experts is not necessarily good for others, nor even good for them had they not become experts (experts being those who have acquired knowledge of different forms of life).

Some philosophers who are very impressed with problems of culture relativity, would go further and claim that in order to get knowledge of alternative cultures, we have to get this knowledge from the inside, we have to actually participate in the life-style before we can understand it fully. But one does not have to believe in such extreme culture relativity in order to be sceptical of the choice criterion of value. For let us grant, at any rate for the sake of argument, that a free man does not have to become a tribal person in order to observe what life is like for a tribal person; he could learn a lot about tribes from spending a lot of time with them, provided he is intelligent and sympathetic. But even if this is so, it is not clear how the choice criterion works impartially. For when one obtains knowledge, even as an intelligent and sympathetic onlooker, one becomes different after acquiring this knowledge from what one was before acquiring it. So the choice criterion of value is faced with a dilemma. Either the choice criterion is applied by someone who does not fully know about different forms of life, but in that case there is no free choice, and the 'choice' of one's own form of life does not reflect the superiority of one's own form of life; or the choice criterion is applied by the autonomous man who has acquired knowledge of the different forms of life between which the choice has to be made, but in that case the form of life that is chosen is not necessarily suited to non-autonomous people. So the Good for Man (in general) remains elusive—let us call this the dilemma about the elusiveness of Good.

Small acquisitions of knowledge are consistent with the personality remaining much the same. For instance, if you move from university X to university Y, you can be in a better position after you have acquired knowledge of both these universities to say which of them is more suited to you. But if a member of a tribal society, who has been leading a sheltered life, leaves his society and goes to observe an autonomous society, either he will get only a superficial picture of the autonomous society, or alternatively if he does get an intimate picture of such a society, the acquisition of this knowledge will be likely to change his tastes, character, and so forth. So if after observing the autonomous society, he says he prefers it, this may only show that the autonomous society is more suited to him after his change of personality, and it does not follow that it is more suited to men in general, or to other members of the tribal society, or would have been more suited to him before he underwent the trauma of living in the autonomous society.

Would similar considerations apply to a person who leaves a liberal society to go and observe a tribal society? Now it is part of the liberal ethos that a liberal must be allowed to choose between different forms of life; if a liberal who is exposed to a tribal form of life prefers the tribal form of life (where there are no civil liberties), then this suggests that he may be more suited to the tribal form of life. Though there is the complication that the social and other conditions that were present against which he made the choice may have been unfair. Thus it may be asserted that under normal conditions a liberal would not wish to give up his way of life for a tribal way of life; this move is similar to a move, discussed earlier in this chapter, whereby if a free man decides to become a slave this is because of the presence of abnormal conditions. The difficulty with such moves is in enabling us to explain normal conditions in a neutral, impartial way, without resorting to normative or perfectionist considerations.

In any case, in fact, at most only some liberals who have been exposed to tribal forms of life prefer the tribal form of life, while others would prefer to continue living under a liberal set-up; so it is not clear how we can decide from such considerations whether or not liberalism is more suited to man. The most that might follow is that liberalism is more suited to those who have been brought up in a liberal set-up, though even here there is, as we have seen, the problem of what to do with those liberals who prefer the tribal set-up, where there are no civil liberties.

The above-mentioned difficulties involved in the operation of the choice criterion of value need to be distinguished from a related but less forceful objection, namely the objection that the choice criterion of values involves brainwashing in the sense which implies deliberate inducements of beliefs and desires by some manipulator or manipulators. This last objection can be dealt with by ensuring that the person who observes and chooses between different forms of life does not have his beliefs or desires manipulated by any individual or set of individuals. But the objection we have mentioned cannot be dealt with so easily, for how do we prevent the person who has to choose between different forms of life from being altered by his knowledge? So we have a dilemma about the elusiveness of the good for man. On the one hand, to operate the choice criterion of value the experts have to be provided with the relevant knowledge. On the other hand, providing them with this knowledge can change their tastes and preferences, and what the experts choose as good for the experts may not be good for more primitive people. It might be suggested that the experts are better off than the primitive man and that therefore the rational thing would be to provide the primitive man also with the extra knowledge, so that the gap between what is good for the experts and what is good for others vanishes. But how can we (without resorting to perfectionist ideals) assume that the experts are better off than the primitive men? It is quite consistent to maintain that a person who leads a sheltered life in a tribal society is better off (for instance, because of greater psychological security) than are people who live in autonomous societies, even if it is the case that once he has been exposed to the autonomous forms of life, he will be worse off in his tribal set-up. Compare: it is quite consistent to maintain that non-smokers are better off than smokers, even if it is the case that once one has become habituated to smoking, one is better off smoking than being deprived of smoking.

Jonathan Glover says that in the case of those who undergo a prolonged state of withdrawal, 'The best evidence can only be provided by those who have experienced both normal life and the state of withdrawal. Since people in the withdrawn state are normally unwilling to discuss it, we must turn to those who have experienced it and then been cured. It is only because they are glad of the change that we have any right to describe it as a "cure".'[37]

Now Glover's argument is probably a sound one, but it is crucial to his argument that people in the state of withdrawal do not claim to be well off, they just do not communicate, and so we have to rely on other evidence in order to make judgements about their welfare. But in the case of tribal societies many of the members of such societies are quite willing to talk and to claim that they are well off, and do not want to opt for the autonomous life. Similarly, many of those who indulge in what Mill would regard as the lower pleasures are willing to defend their form of life. That is why Mill feels the need for the expert's verdict. So we are still left with the dilemma about the elusiveness of the good for man.

Mill attempts to see which form of life is better by seeing what form of life his experts will choose. For Mill the experts must not only have knowledge of different forms of life (for otherwise how can they rationally say that one form of life is better than another?); they must also be equally susceptible

[37] *Responsibility* (London, 1970), p. 124.

to different forms of life. Presumably, this last requirement is there because Mill wants to compare different forms of life from an impartail standpoint; if a person is more susceptible to the higher forms of life, then his choice of the higher forms of life may just reflect his temperament, and the experiment will be biased against lower forms of life. Now Mill's requirements do not solve the problem about the elusiveness of the good for man. It is not at all easy to see how we decide when this requirement about equal susceptibility has been satisfied. And to the extent that we appear able to operate his test of equal susceptibility, we would get involved in strange forms of arguments. Suppose it is the case that homosexuals think that homosexuality is the best form of sexual life, heterosexuals think that hererosexuality is the best form of sexual life and bisexuals think that bisexuality is the best form of sexual life. Now in this example bisexuals satisfy the equal susceptibility requirement better than the others do, and so it would follow from Mill's theory that what they choose, namely bisexuality, is the best form of the sexual life for man. But this is an absurd argument. One fallacy in this argument is that since bisexuals satisfy the equal susceptibility requirement better than the others do, they are in the relevant respects rather different from the others; what is good for the former is not necessarily good for the latter; even if bisexuality is suitable for those who are equally susceptible to homosexuality and heterosexuality, it does not follow that bisexuality is suitable for those who do not satisfy the equal susceptibility test. Such non-perfectionist attempts to find the Good for Man (in general) appear doomed to fail!

Mill also mentions the requirement that of two pleasures, 'if there be one to which all or almost all who have experience of both give decided preference, irrespective of any feeling of moral obligation to prefer it, that is the more desirable pleasure'.[38] Now the reason why he does not allow feelings of moral obligation to be used in the application of the choice criterion of value, is that he wants to avoid biases. If people prefer a certain pleasure because of a moral feeling, then their preference may reflect their moral training, and if they had had different moral training, their preferences might have been

---

[38] *Utilitarianism*, chapter II, para. 5.

different. So to admit moral feelings would make the test
subjective. Nor would Mill, without circularity, have allowed
the correct or objective moral feelings to determine the preferences of the experts. For his expert test was meant to
provide the test of morality and so it could not presuppose the
correctness of any particular moral feeling.

Now though precautions such as not letting moral feelings
affect the deliberations of the experts seem necessary for the
working of the choice criterion of value, they are not sufficient
to ensure fairness. To be fair between different forms of life
requires a choice from some sort of neutral value-free standpoint, but such an idea is not a coherent one. Later, I shall
criticize the idea that autonomous choices are somehow
neutral between different forms of life and therefore can be
used to operate the choice criterion of value.

There are several versions of the choice criterion of value.
Here are two of them. First, there is what I shall call the
hypothetical choice criterion of value (or of justice) according to which to find out what is valuable (or just) we have to
appeal to what a hypothetical observer (or agent) would choose.
Secondly, there is what I shall call the categorical choice criterion of value, according to which in order to find out what
is valuable we have to allow people in real life freely to choose
between different forms of life. The best form of life will
emerge from open and fair competition between the different
forms of life; the undeserving ones will become extinct.

Now this distinction between hypothetical and categorical
choice criterion is of some importance in understanding problems of liberalism, as well as in understanding the views of
quite a few political philosophers. Many of the sophisticated
contractarian philosophers, such as Rousseau and Rawls,
appeal to a hypothetical choice criterion of value. Rousseau
appeals to the hypothetical choice criterion of value in his
rejection of slavery (see the quotation from him given earlier
in this chapter). When Mill (as interpreted by Rawls)[39] suggests
that the best form of life will emerge from open and fair
competition between different forms of life, he is appealing
to the categorical choice criterion of value. Rawls, like Mill,
uses the categorical choice criterion of value in order to find

[39] 'Fairness to Goodness', section 5.

out the Good.[40] But, unlike Mill, he uses the hypothetical choice criterion to construct a well-ordered society,[41] which provides a fair background against which the categorical choice criterion of Mill's can operate. Later we shall see that Rawls uses two versions of the hypothetical choice criterion.

There is another equally important distinction. This is the distinction between applying the choice criterion of value to ultimate values, and applying it at the non-ultimate level. If you presuppose some values and then operate the choice criterion of value, you are operating it at a non-ultimate level. If, however, you do not presuppose any values, and yet apply the choice criterion of value, then you are applying it at an ultimate level, you are using it to try to establish ultimate values. Now if the choice criterion of value enables us to establish ultimate values, then it can successfully bypass perfectionist considerations. But for reasons given in this chapter the choice criterion of value (whether in its categorical or its hypothetical version) cannot be applied at the ultimate level; at best it can be applied at the non-ultimate level.

That the categorical choice criterion cannot be applied at the ultimate level can be seen from the following considerations. When we set up a fair system for the categorical choice criterion to operate, the system itself cannot without circularity be justified by an appeal to the choice criterion. This point can be illustrated by a reference to Rawls. Rawls says that his well-ordered society sets a fair background for the operation of Mill's choice criterion of value.[42] Now it would be circular if Rawls were to try to justify his well-ordered society by appealing to Mill's choice criterion of value (and indeed earlier we saw he gets in danger of circularity when he uses the Aristotelian principle to construct his well-ordered society). Probably Rawls would try to get out of such a circle, by claiming that the well-ordered society is justified by an appeal to a hypothetical choice criterion, and not by an appeal to a categorical choice criterion such as Mill's. The principles of fairness that help to construct the well-ordered society set the stage for the operation of Mill's categorical choice criterion,

---

[40] Ibid.

[41] *A Theory of Justice*, section 3, and 'Fairness to Goodness', section 6.

[42] 'Fairness to Goodness', p. 579.

are the principles that would be chosen by people in the original position; since the original position is a fiction, the choice
of the principles of fairness is hypothetical; Rawls refers to
what people would choose *if* they were in the original position.
But hypothetical choices, too, if they are to carry the weight
that they have to in Rawls's system, must be made against
a fair background (otherwise, why should anyone pay heed
to such choices?), and so we are still left with the problem of
how to construct a fair background against which the parties
in the original position must choose. If we try to answer this
last problem by appealing to what people would choose we
would get involved in a circle or a regress. Rawls himself
seems to avoid such difficulties by appealing to our intuitions.
Thus he rightly realizes that the contractarian model can be
set up in different ways, with different constraints, and that
the choices that the parties in the original position make
could vary with the way in which the model has been set up.
He then has to face the problem of why we should set up the
model in one way rather than another. To answer such a
problem Rawls is driven to appeal to our intuitions. That way
of constructing the model is best which gives the best fit with
our intuitions in reflective equilibrium. Our intuitions help to
set up a fair background against which the parties in the original position can make their choices. So the choice criterion
of value would here be used at a non-ultimate level; it would
presuppose (at least provisionally) the values revealed by our
intuitions.

Rawls would admit that the categorical choice criterion
does operate against the background of a well-ordered society,
and so it does presuppose what is Right and Just. Now if one
uses values in a broad sense to include not only the Good but
also the Right (and Just), then it follows that the categorical
choice criterion presupposes the value of Right or Just, and
is designed only to find out the Good. But does it even succeed
in telling us how to find out the Good? Does it not presuppose
some substantial idea of the Good in order to work? Later in
this chapter it will be argued that it does, and that the categorical choice criterion at best can only tell us what is valuable
if it already assumes certain substantial ideas of Good.

Rawls appeals to a hypothetical choice criterion (for

instance, when he tells us what the parties in the original position would choose), but he also appeals to a categorical choice criterion; he appeals to the latter somewhat in the way that Mill and Hart do. Rawls believes that if a form of life deserves to survive, it must survive in open and fair competition against rival forms of life;[43] if it does not survive under such conditions its demise is not to be lamented. Here his position is similar to Mill's, who believes that a civilized community should not impose its way of life on a barbaric community by force: 'If civilization has got the better of barbarism when barbarism had the world to itself, it is too much to profess to be afraid lest barbarism, . . . should revive and conquer civilization. A civilization that can thus succumb to its vanquished enemy must first have become so degenerate . . . [that] the sooner such a civilization receives notice to quit the better.'[44] Here Mill is talking about one community not imposing its way of life upon another, but it is clear from his writings that he believed that within the same society also the state should not protect civilized forms of life by barring other forms of life (as long as the latter are not harming other people they should be allowed to co-exist with the civilized forms of life). Indeed, it has been argued that Mill's choice criterion of value requires a liberal society in order to work; for the choice to be a criterion (or evidence) of value, it must be a choice under conditions of liberty.

There is a similar idea in Hart who considers Burke's 'wisdom of the ages' argument, according to which 'the social institutions which have slowly been developed in the course of any society's history represent an accommodation to the needs of that society which is always likely to be more satisfactory to the mass of its members than any ideal scheme of social life which individuals would invent or any legislator could impose.' Hart thinks that such an argument could only work if the social institutions have developed as a result of the 'free, though no doubt unconscious adaption of men to the conditions of their lives. To use coercion to maintain the moral *status quo* at any point in a society's history would be artificially to arrest the process which gives social institutions

---

[43] 'Fairness to Goodness', p. 549.   [44] Mill, *On Liberty*, chapter IV, last para.

their value.[45]

The Mill–Hart–Rawls view can be contrasted with that of Rousseau, for instance. Rousseau used a weaker criterion and implied that if the legislators freely banned a practice for several generations, this would tend to show that the practice was worth banning.[46] He believed in a weak version of the categorical choice criterion of value; he wanted the legislators to choose a form of life freely or under conditions of liberty, but unlike Mill, Rawls, and Hart, who believe in a stronger version of the categorical choice criterion of value, he did not think it necessary that virtuous forms of life should be made legally to co-exist with their rivals. The legislators on Rousseau's views could freely ban a form of lfe that they thought was a rival to the virtuous form of life. On the stronger version of the categorical choice criterion of value, the law should allow open and fair competition between rival forms of life; the different forms of life were allowed (by the law) to be practised. On the weaker version of the choice criterion of value, there is freedom to discuss the pros and cons of various forms of life; but that is weaker than the freedom of practice diffferent forms of life.

Briefly, and roughly, the difference between the weak and the strong version of the categorical choice criterion of value can be characterized as follows: the former requires freedom of discussion, whereas the latter requires in addition to freedom of discussion, freedom to practice the rival forms of life. Now the strong version of the categorical choice principle cannot be used to defend all values, for the reasons given in this chapter. At the political level, the strong version of the categorical choice principle cannot be applied to the constitution which sets the fair background for the operation of the categorical principle (in its strong version). There is normally no room for two competing constitutions to co-exist simultaneously in the same state, applying to the same area. It may be that in some transitional situations it is not clear which constitution is binding; it is not clear whether the old constitution still applies or whether the new one has taken over; and for a time we may have two constitutions, both

---

[45] *Law, Liberty and Morality* (London, 1963), p. 75.
[46] *The Social Contract*, Book III, chapter XI.

competing with each other for acceptance. But once one of them is accepted, the other one does not apply. It would be strange to argue that we should not have only one constitution, on the grounds that we must carry out experiments in living with several constitutions.

Now we can see a mistake that Hart makes in his discussion of 'the wisdom of the ages' argument. The 'wisdom of the ages' argument can work if the citizens, or at least the wise among them, are allowed to have considerable influence on how the laws and institutions should be adapted to the needs of society. Without such influence, there is no reason to think that the current institutions and laws incorporate the wisdom of the ages. If you have a history of tyrants ruling the country, tyrants who take no heed of the prevalent wisdom, there is no reason to think that our current laws and institutions, however old they are, represent the wisdom of the ages. Free discussion too (at any rate among the wise) is probably essential if the citizens' judgements are to be informed and wise. But such requirements are weaker than the requirements that Hart (mistakenly) thinks are essential for the working of the 'wisdom of the ages' argument. For as we have seen, Hart not only insists on freedom of discussion, but freedom to practice different forms of life. The point is not that Hart may not be right in insisting on the legal freedom to practice different forms of life, but rather that such legal freedom is not necessary for the 'wisdom of the ages' argument to work. One could quite consistently side with Devlin in the Devlin–Hart controversy[47] about the enforcement of morality and yet believe in the 'wisdom of the ages' argument.

Indeed, if Hart's strong version of liberalism were essential for the 'wisdom of the ages' argument to work, it would follow that the basic constitution of the country, even though it has been amended from time to time, in response to the prevailing wisdom of the time, could not incorporate the wisdom of the ages. For a society can only have one constitution at a time. And while people can freely discuss the pros and cons of rival constitutions, they cannot allow rival forms of constitution to legally co-exist, simultaneously. If you think (as

[47] See Hart, *Law, Liberty and Morality,* and P. Devlin, *The Enforcement of Morals* (London, 1965).

THE CHOICE CRITERION OF VALUE 217

I do) that it makes sense to say that a country's constitution incorporates the wisdom of the ages (for instance, because the constitution has been adapted from time to time in response to wise and informed criticisms), then you cannot agree with the view that the 'wisdom of the ages' argument *only* works when a law or an institution has been competing with its rivals.

All the liberals are involved in the problem of having to justify their ground-rules, the framework of justice within which different forms of life can flourish. Rawls's principles of justice have been disputed by other thinkers, even by fellow-liberals such as Hart. And Rawls himself admits that people can disagree about what principles of justice can be derived from his contractarian experiment. Again Mill lays down certain ground-rules that all ways of life must satisfy if they are to be permitted by law to compete with other forms of life. Thus he too would not allow infanticide to be legally permissible on the grounds that it was a valuable experiment in living, without which people could not reach a rational decision about the best form of life. His ground-rules were provided by his harm principle: 'the only purpose for which power can be rightfully exercised over any member of a civilized community, against his will, is to prevent harm to others.'[48]

Now people disagree about the correct formulation of the harm principle.[49] Even liberals cannot agree on what the ground-rules should be. We have seen that the strong version of the categorical choice criterion does not apply to the ground-rules; and since the question of what the ground-rules are, is controversial, how do we identify the sphere where it is legitimate to operate the strong version of the categorical choice criterion of value? Compare the following suggestions:
1. Those who want to beat their wives should be allowed to do so. Then we shall have experiments in living that will enable us to decide whether wife-beating is a superior form of life to non-wife-beating. If the practice of non-wife-beating deserves to survive, it must survive in open competition with the practice of wife-beating.
2. Parents who want to kill their infants should be allowed to

[48] Mill, *On Liberty,* chapter I, para. 9.
[49] See J. Feinberg, *Social Philosophy* (Englewood Cliffs, 1973).

do so. Then we shall have experiments in living that will enable us to decide whether infanticide is a superior form of life to non-infanticide. If the practice of non-infanticide deserves to survive, it must survive in open competition with the practice of infanticide.

3. Women who want abortions should be allowed to have them. Then we shall have experiments in living that will enable us to decide whether abortion is a superior form of life to non-abortion.

4. Those who eat meat and have animals killed should be allowed to do so. Then we shall have experiments in living that will enable us to decide whether these forms of life are superior. If vegetarianism deserves to survive, it must survive in open competition with meat eating.

5. Collectivist and individualist ways of life should be allowed to openly compete with each other. If collectivist ways of life deserve to survive, they must be able to survive in open competition with rival forms of life.

6. We must have experiments in living in different forms of education and the upbringing of children. Some schools should concentrate on the 'higher' forms of art, culture, and so forth; other centres should concentrate on the charms of pornography, polymorphous perversity (as recommended by Marcuse), masturbation competitions, and so forth. The best form of life can emerge from such open competition between different forms of life.

It is obvious that liberals such as Rawls and Mill will not allow practices such as 1 and 2. 'Experiments in living', like other desirable activities, have to be carried out within certain moral constraints. We have no business to sacrifice the welfare of individual women in order to find out whether the practice of wife-beating is suited to the human race, or in order to prevent the view that wife-beating is wrong from becoming a dead dogma. But what some liberals do not realize is that similar moral constraints may be operative in the case of practices such as, for instance, 3, 4, 5, and 6. No doubt if some people are vegetarians while others are meat eaters, we can learn an enormous amount about the value or non-value for human beings of eating meat; for instance, we can compare the health of meat-eaters with that of vegetarians, and try to discover whether eating meat is associated with certain illnesses, and whether lack of meat is associated with certain other illnesses, or deficiencies. But those who believe in animal rights will insist that such experiments in living are subject to moral constraints, that animal rights must not be sacrificed lightly for the sake of other desirable goals.

Again, experiments in different forms of education may well lead to many desirable ends, but such experiments are subject to moral constraints. For instance, the interests of children who get less desirable forms of education must not be sacrificed, merely because such experiments will help us to discover the best form of education. Human beings have just one life, and if an individual child is ruined by a bad education, it is not sufficient compensation for him to be told that other children in the future will benefit from the experiments that were conducted with him. He must not be treated merely as a guinea-pig. Rawls says (with considerable plausibility) that the important thing is to be fair to individuals, not to ways of life.[50] I suggest that an unnoticed but important corollary of this view is that we must not be unfair to some individuals in order to be fair to different forms of life; for instance, we must not sacrifice the interests of children by sending some of them to hippie schools in order to be fair to the hippie way of life! So this important point about being fair to individuals rather than to ways of life, is not so helpful to a person such as Rawls who wants to argue for equal liberites to the various way of life!

There are of course other hazards in pursuing 'experiments in living'. Even from a consequentialist viewpoint, too many options can lead to neurosis, instability, and insecurity, and some people may well be much better off in an environment where they were less burdened with the agonies of choice. But here I have stressed the moral constraints or the ground-rules that must constrain our pursuit of liberal practice such as 'experiments in living'. The point about the agonies and burdens of choice makes one wonder whether it is worthwhile preferring a liberal society to a non-liberal society. But even if we go in for a liberal society, we shall be limited by the kind of considerations just stressed, as well as by the undesirable

[50] 'Fairness to Goodness'.

effects of too many choices (for even if we opt for a liberal society, there can be enormous variations in how many options we allow).

The view that the categorical choice criterion of value cannot serve as a criterion for what is ultimately good can be reinforced by the following considerations. Barry makes some important remarks about fairness of contests, which in my opinion have serious implications for the categorical choice criteria of value, though Barry himself does not work out these implications. Barry rightly points out that the idea of a contest is to test the competitors for the possession of some quality or qualities, and he suggests that one 'can define fairness in a contest as that which makes it more likely that the competitor with the greater amount of the quality which is being tested will win'.[51] This gives us a rough idea of how to apply fairness to cases of boxing matches, intellectual examinations, and so forth; if the desired quality is intellectual effort, we will have one kind of examination, if the desired quality is to test intellectual ability, we shall have another kind of examination. But now when liberals like Rawls talk of fair competition between different forms of life, how can they specify the desired qualities that they are seeking for in such a contest, without presupposing some substantial idea of the Good?

It is true the aim of the categorical choice criterion of good is to discover the most suitable form of life. But this does not tell us anything sufficiently specific about the desirable qualities that we should look for in the 'contestants'. Compare: suppose examiners are told to set out an examination that is suitable for the students; this would not be a sufficiently precise guide to the examiners as to what constitutes a fair examination. On the Rawlsian liberal view we are in the dark about the Good; and yet we see that without presupposing some substantial ideas of the Good we cannot arrange a fair contest between different forms of life and so we cannot operate the categorical choice criterion of value. Perhaps the way out of this circle would be to assert that the categorical choice criterion has a more modest role; it does not tell us about what is ultimatley good; but assuming certain values,

[51] Barry, *Political Argument,* p. 304.

it can help us to find out which forms of life are unsuited to human beings under certain conditions. Thus suppose under certain conditions the dominant form of life cannot survive in open competition with fringe forms of life; in that case it may be that such a form of life is not suited to human being under those conditions.

In fact Rawls does appeal to certain ideals of the person,[52] and these along with his principles of justice help him to set up his well-ordered society. The well-ordered society is set up from the point of view of the original position, which is meant to be a neutral and fair standpoint. And Rawls would claim that the well-ordered society would set a fair background within which different forms of life can compete. But this does not get us out of the difficulties in the way of setting up a fair contest between different forms of life, without presupposing substantial ideas of the Good. Rawls's well-ordered society cannot be set up without appealing to perfectionist ideals; for instance, we have seen that the view that autonomous life is essential to human well being is a kind of perfectionism; and the view that animal interests count for less than human interests commits us to perfectionism in the strong sense. Moreover, the most the well-ordered society does is to tell us which forms of life should not be allowed to compete for our allegiance? For instance, the well-ordered society would rule out forms of life, such as fascism, which violate the principles of justice. But the well-ordered society does not tell us how to arrange fair competition between those forms of life that are eligible to compete with each other for our allegiance. What constitutes fair competition between forms of life that encourage polymorphous perversity, and the forms of life that encourage a more puritanical upbringing? What constitutes fair competition between the mystic way of life and the materialistic form of life? How much influence should each form of life have in the upbringing of children? Should we go by some kind of numerical weighting, so that those ways of life with 90 per cent support in the population are encouraged in 90 per cent of the schools, while a fringe form of life which has a following among 0.01 per cent of the population, gets 0.01 per cent of the schools. But this may be

[52] *A Theory of Justice,* p. 262.

'unfair' to the fringe form of life. For the fact that only 0.01 per cent of the population believe in the fringe form of life may be a reflection of the raw deal that such a form of life has received in the past, so how can we get a fair starting-point how can Rawls argue that if a form of life disappears in open competition with rival forms of life, 'then its passing is not to be regretted'?[53]

One of the important problems facing the categorical choice criterion (in its more ambitious version) is that this criterion only works (if it works at all) in the case of autonomous and knowledgeable individuals. If heteronomous (or ignorant) individuals prefer a form of life, such a preference may just reflect their conditioning, and cannot be taken as evidence of the suitability of that form of life for human beings in general. For the choice criterion to work, the choice has to be by individuals who are autonomous and knowledgeable about different ways of life; that is why Mill resorted to his expert criterion (according to which that form of life is best which the experts prefer rather than what the people at large prefer). Now children are not autonomous creatures and so the choice criterion of value will not work with children. Nor will it work with the bulk of grown-up people who are not experts. The fact that many prejudiced grown-ups reject a form of life does not imply that that form of life was not a good one.

To operate the hypothetical choice criterion, we do not have to create or operate a system where experts (who are autonomous agents with competence to choose between different forms of life) choose between different forms of life. Similarly, the original position (as described by Rawls) does not have to exist; it could suffice that we simulate it. But to operate the categorical choice criterion we have to actually create and operate an actual society that is full of experts. But how do we do that? By force or by liberal means? Certainly we cannot rely upon just finding a society that is full of experts, for if we examined any existing society only a small minority would be experts. So how can we operate the categorical choice criterion? And unless we can operate this criterion how can we argue that because a way of life was rejected by our society, therefore it deserved to be rejected.

[53] 'Fairness to Goodness', p. 549.

For it may be that the decision to reject it reflects the ignorance of the masses.

There are certain forms of life, such as the highest form of mysticism, that require enormous cultivation and discipline. All or almost all who have experienced the highest forms of mysticism, prefer the mystical form of life to our ordinary materialistic way of life. If we use Mill's experts' test of value, the experts being those who have experienced the different forms of life that are being compared, the test would, if anything, show that the mystical forms of life are superior. Yet such superior forms of life way well disappear in a liberal-democratic society where the experts are in a minority. The bulk of the population, being ignorant (since they have never experienced the charms of such a form of life), may be put off by the discipline and hard work required in the initial stages. It may happen that as the experts in this sphere die out, they are not replaced. Suppose their children are educated in schools that are devoted to more materialistic ways of life, or suppose that with increasing urbanization people do not grow up in an atmosphere that is congenial to the development of the mystical personality. Now if, because of some such conditions, the masses in a liberal society reject the mystical form of life, would a Rawlsian be right in inferring that such forms of life deserved to become extinct, 'that their passing is not to be regretted'? The mystical form of life has been used here only as an illustration. Similar points could be made about other forms of life that are, as Mill would say, like tender plants and require cultivation.

There is the added problem that even the experts' choice is not an unbiased one. Even if the individual is an autonomous agent, which way he chooses will be influenced to some extent (even though it is not determined) by the way he was brought up. So we have a dilemma. The categorical choice criterion cannot work in the case of children for they are immature and non-autonomous. Yet by the time one is an autonomous individual one has already acquired preferences in favour of certain ways of life. Thus most autonomous individuals in our society would reject the life of polymorphous perversity. But had they been brought up by people who were more sympathetic to the life of polymorphous perversity, they might now, consistently with retaining their autonomy, have preferred the life of polymorphous perversity.

The autonomous man differs from the heteronomous man in not automatically accepting the way of life that he has been brought up in. He reflects upon the customary way of life and compares it with the alternatives. But even the autonomous man does not choose his final aims in a vacuum. Which way of life he will choose after reflection will depend at best partly upon the way he was brought up, and upon the prevailing social conditions. His choices depend not only upon knowledge of the alternative life-styles, but also upon his emotions and his imagination. And his emotions and imagination may depend at least partly upon the way he was brought up, upon the kind of schools he went to, his home life, and so forth. Suppose people have been brought up in rural surroundings congenial to mysticism, in the company of mystical gurus and mystical music and so forth. If a person has been brought up in such surroundings when he was young, when he grows up he may autonomously reject alternative ways of life; even after the pros and cons of alternative life-styles have been pointed out to him, he may genuinely prefer the mystical way of life. Yet it is quite possible that had the same individual been brought up in a different way and in a different setting his autonomous preferences when he grew up would have been quite different. Thus, had he been brought up in an urban, materialistic culture it may be that his capacity for the mystical form of life would have been destroyed, and as a grown-up he would autonomously reject the mystical form of life.

Even if we assume liberal–democratic forms of government, which forms of life will flourish will depend at least partly upon such factors as the amount of urbanization and industrialization. So how do we decide what is a fair starting-point? A rural setting or an industrial setting?

Perhaps the most that one might argue is that *assuming* certain values x, y, z (for instance, the values of an industrialized, materialist society), if certain forms of life do not survive in a liberal society which is dominated by values x, y and z, then such forms of life are not suitable. But of course if we abandon the assumption that the dominant values of a society are good, then the mere fact that a form of life does not survive in that society would not show that such a form of life did not deserve to survive.

There is also an element of truth in the view that the dominant form of life should be able to survive in open competition against rival forms of life, and that if it cannot survive in such open competition, then it does not deserve to survive. But it does not follow from this that if, say, a non-dominant form of life does not survive in open competition, it did not deserve to survive. It might be that the fringe form of life, unlike the dominant form of life, did not have a chance to assert itself. The element of truth in the categorical choice criterion of value cannot enable it to bypass perfectionist considerations.

3. The hypothetical choice criterion of value

So we see that the categorical choice criterion of value operates within a basic framework; it assumes certain ground-rules. The ground-rules themselves cannot be established by the categorical choice criterion of value. Rawls would probably agree with this. He thinks that his contractarian model sets up a well-ordered society which provides a fair background within which the categorical choice criterion of value can work. So then there is the problem of how we establish this fair background. We cannot without circularity use the categorical choice criterion to establish it; Rawls uses, instead, the hypothetical choice criterion to establish his well-ordered society. Having constructed the well-ordered society, the stage is set for the operation of the categorical choice criterion of value, which helps to discover the Good. So the hypothetical choice criterion is relevant (according to Rawls) in order to find out the principles of Right; and then the categorical choice criterion comes into help us find the Good.

Now the hypothertical choice criterion cannot really by itself do the work that Rawls wants it to do. The basic ground-rules of the well-ordered society cannot be set up without an appeal to perfectionism which reinforces the point that the hypothetical choice criterion does not, any more than the categorical choice criterion, work at the level of ultimate values; rather, it presupposes certain ultimate values. Even if the hypothetical choice criterion enables us to find out what is good for man, it cannot tell us why human interests should be given greater weight than animal interests.

However, I do not deny that the hypothetical choice criterion can work if we assume certain values (or goals). Thus suppose a person has certain worthwhile permanent aims and interests, and out of ignorance, or temporary insanity, he wants to do something that (unknown to him) goes against his professed aims and interests. In that case, we can use the hypothetical choice criterion to show that what he is doing is not really good for him.

Sidgwick uses a test that is similar to the hypothetical choice criterion. He considers the suggestion that a person's good is what he actually desires; but he is impressed by the objection that people, out of ignorance, desire all sorts of things that are not really good for them. He then considers the suggestion that a person's good is what is desirable, not in the sense of what ought to be desired but in the sense of what would be desired (and chosen) 'if it were judged attainable by voluntary action, supposing the desirer to possess a perfect forecast, emotional as well as intellectual, of the state of attainment of fruition'.[54] Sidgwick's discussion is mainly in terms of 'desires', but his discussion applies *mutatis mutandis* to 'choices' also; indeed sometimes Sidgwick explicitly talks of what a person desires and *seeks* which suggests that he would be willing to make similar statements about what a person chooses.[55]

Sidgwick distinguishes his own hypothetical test of good from another hypothetical test of good. According to this latter test a way of life is good for a person if he is not averse to it after he has been exposed to it. Sidgwick rightly rejects this test:

Indeed we commonly reckon it among the worst consequences of some kind of conduct that they alter men's tendencies to desire, and make them desire their lesser good . . . and we think that it is the worse for a man . . . if he is never roused out of such a condition and lives till death the life of a contented pig, when he might have been something better.[56]

---

[54] H. Sidgwick, *Methods of Ethics* (London, 1874), p. 111.
[55] Ibid.   [56] Ibid.

He thinks that his own hypothetical test can avoid such drawbacks. He thinks that in order to avoid such an objection a man's future good is what he would now desire and seek on the whole if all the consequences of all the different lines of conduct open to him were accurately foreseen and adequately realized in imagination at the present point in time.

Sidgwick insists that the alternatives must be not only foreseen but also fore-*felt*.[57] He points out that the 'notion of Good thus attained has an ideal element in it'; for the good is not always actually desired, and aimed at, but the ideal element is always interpretable in terms of fact, either hypothetical or actual, and does not involve any judgements of value.

Sidgewick uses the hypothetical choice criterion of good rather in the way that Rawls does; for Rawls, too, uses the hypothetical choice criterion to establish certain ideals; we saw earlier that he needs ideals to construct his liberal Utopia. Rawls, too, is not impressed by what many ignorant people in fact want;[58] he is more impressed by what they would want if certain appropriate conditions were fulfilled. And though Rawls appeals to ideals,[59] he too, like Sidgwick, wants to do this without appealing to perfectionism or to judgements of intrinsic value. The hypothetical choice criterion is meant to provide the ideal element without resorting to perfectionism. The choice criterion in the way it is used by Sidgwick and Rawls is meant to provide a criterion of value, and is not itself allowed to presuppose any values. But how can such a choice criterion (which does not presuppose values) work? My earlier discussion of the hypothetical choice criterion applies, *mutatis mutandis,* to Sidgwick's criterion also.

How do we apply Sidgwick's test? Suppose the problem is to find out the good for the ignorant man who leads a non-autonomous life. Take, for instance, the case of a person who worships the monkey god because he has been brought up to do so; he has been brought up to believe that the monkey god will save him from illnesses and other calamities. Suppose that if he became fully informed about the nature of religion he would cease to believe in the monkey god and would believe instead in one of the more sophisticated world

[57] Ibid., pp. 110 ff.   [58] *A Theory of Justice*, section 64.
[59] Ibid., pp. 261-2.

views. Now if the problem is, what way of life is good for this ignorant primitive man, we must beware of arguing that because a way of life would be suited to him if he were knowledgeable, therefore it is suited to him in his primitive state. Many Hindu philosophers as well as some European ones, such as Spinoza, have rightly stressed that a form of life, the value-system, that is suited to the wise is not necessarily suited to the ignorant.

Once a person acquires knowledge and freedom he becomes a different kind of creature from what he was before he acquired it. The view that he is a superior creature compared to the primitive person is not one that can be established by the choice criterion of value. And even if we grant that the free or autonomous man is superior to the primitive man, it still remains true that the way of life that is suited to the free man is not necessarily suited to the primitive man.

But now suppose we apply the hypothetical choice criterion in the following way: what is good for a primitive man is what he would choose if he had the relevant knowledge, imagination, and so forth, the choice being in the interests of him, as a primitive man. Suppose, for instance, that a primitive man is given a pill that gives him knowledge and imagination for a short time; he knows that very soon the effects of the pill will wear off and he will go back indefinitley to his old state; he has now, while he still has the knowledge and the imagination, to choose the form of life that is suitable for him in his primitive state; his good in his primitive state is what he would choose in his knowledgeable state, the choice being made for himself in his primitive state. But now it is not clear what role the choice criterion of value is performing here; one could get just as good a result by introducing the benevolent, knowledgeable, and wise spectator. The good for a primitive man is what a wise and benevolent spectator (who knows all about the consequences of various ways of life) would recommend for the primitive man. This test could be generalized to cover non-primitive people as well—the good for an individual is what a wise, well-informed, and benevolent spectator would recommend for that individual. Let us call this the wise man's test. The wise man's test can be extended to cover social good also: the good for society is what the wise will recommend for that society. We can have a categorical version of the wise man's test and a hypothetical version; the former would go by what the wise in fact have recommended (or chosen), the latter by what they would recommend or choose.

The choice criterion cannot be used at the ultimate level. Assuming certain values, such as the happiness of the primitive man, the hypothetical observer or chooser can prescribe what is good for the primitive man, somewhat as a wise doctor prescribes the correct medicine, assuming that the health of his patient is a good.

Rawls uses both the categorical and the hypothetical choice criterion of value. And he uses the hypothetical choice criterion in two ways. First, he uses it to try to derive the principles of right and of justice, he uses it to construct the well-ordered society, within which the categorical choice criterion of value can operate. Secondly, he uses the hypothetical choice criterion to tell us about what an individual's good is,[60] and here his use of the hypothetical choice criterion of the individual's good, is, as he admits, very similar to Sidgwick's. My discussion of Sidgwick's hypothetical choice criterion will apply, *mutatis mutandis,* to Rawls's hypothetical choice criterion (in its second sense), just as the discussion of Rawls's hypothetical choice criterion applies, *mutatis mutandis,* to Sidgwick's criterion.

It has been argued in this chapter that the hypothetical choice criterion of value cannot be safely used when the person's values would have radically altered as a result of his acquiring more knowledge. But this is consistent with saying that in less radical cases something like this test can be used; for in the less radical cases we could assume those values of the agent which remain constant before and after the change in his knowledge; we could then talk about whether a particular course of action is in a person's interests by seeing whether the course of action coheres with the agent's value system. Take a person who wants to cross the bridge that he does not know is dangerous. Though he wants to cross the bridge, he would not choose to cross it if he knew the facts about the bridge; his hypothetical choice in such a situation

[60] *A Theory of Justice,* section 64.

may well be a better guide to his interests than his actual (ignorant) choice to cross the bridge is likely to be. But even in such cases, the hypothetical choice criterion, though it can work, seems redundant. We could just as well say that the good for the agent is what the wise and well-informed benevolent spectator would recommmend for the agent, assuming the scale of values that the agent has. Thus a wise spectator who assumes that the agent does not want to get injured could tell us that crossing the bridge is not in the agent's interest. It may be objected that the wise man's test has a more paternalistic flavour than the hypothetical choice criterion does; and so is it not more dangerous to liberty than the latter is? But it seems to me that this alleged superiority of the hypothetical choice criterion is based on an illusion. If two tests give the same results, it is not clear why one of them should be more dangerous to liberty. Even if a test tells us how to distinguish what is good for a person from what the agent thinks is good for him, this does not necessarily permit us the use of compulsory paternalistic measures. For, as Mill stressed, more harm than good may come out of using coercion in such cases. There are also (and Mill did not stress this) non-utilitarian limits to our right to interfere with a person for his own good; even when we can do him more good than harm we may not have the moral right to interfere with him.

Of course, it is possible to abuse the wise man's test in such a way that people's liberties are sacrificed; we could 'force people to be free' by appealing to the wise man's test and this could lead to a despotic system. But then so could we abuse the hypothetical choice test to justify a despotic system; the despot could, by appealing to the hypothetical choice test, claim to know more about the person's good than the person knows himself, and he could go on to claim, 'If only you were knowledgeable you would agree with the compulsory measures that I propose to take against you, for your own good.' The fact that such tests can be abused by despots is not a conclusive argument against a proper employment of such tests. One way to prevent such tests from being misunderstood is to stress that even when the authorities know more about the person's good than he himself does, this does not automatically give them a right to use paternalistic measures against the person. There are two related problems involved in paternalism. First, under what conditions do the authorities have the right to interfere paternalistically with the individual? Secondly, when the authorities do have the right to interfere paternalistically with an individual, what are the considerations that they should bear in mind in order to ensure that they exercise this right wisely? Tests like the hypothetical choice test or the wise man's test are of more help in answering the second question. The first question, in the case of people in the maturity of their faculties, is to be answered by appealing to the consent, actual or presumed, of the individual being interfered with; such actual or presumed consent is quite different from hypothetical consent (see chapter 12).

We have seen in this chapter that the choice criterion of value cannot succeed in bypassing perfectionist conditions. The categorical choice criterion has to work within certain moral constraints. And how can we fully spell out these moral constraints without appealing to perfectionist judgements? Nor can the hypothetical choice criterion anable us to bypass perfectionism. For at most the hypothetical choice criterion attempts to tell us what is good for a person; it does not even begin to tell us why a person's good should count for more than an animal's good.

4. Two conceptions of good

There are two conceptions of the good in Rawls as well as in Mill: the high-minded conception of good and the ordinary conception of good. Liberalism (at least of the egalitarian variety) seems to need both these conceptions of the good and it is not an accident that they are both found, though not in exactly the same form, in Mill and in Rawls. Mill subscribed to the high-minded conception of the good when he used his expert criterion of what is valuable, when he claimed that it is better to be Socrates dissatisfied than a fool satisfied.[61] And he subscribed to the ordinary conception of the good when he said that a person's own mode of existence is the best not because it is best in itself but because it is his own mode; and when he implied that persons who indulge in the

[61] *Utilitarianism,* chapter II.

lower pleasure should be left free to pursue their way of life
even though they have not voluntarily chosen the lower forms
of life.

Rawls subscribed to the high-minded conception of the
good when he uses the Aristotelian principle to show that it
is better for human beings to indulge in cerebral activities like
algebra and chess rather than in simpler activities such as
arithmetic and checkers. Rawls also subscribes to the ordinary
conception of the good, for he defines the good 'as the successful execution of a rational plan of life'.[62] He asks us to imagine
a being who is intelligent and skilled in things like mathematics
but 'whose only pleasure is to count blades of grass in various
geometric shaped areas such as park squares and well-trimmed
lawns'.[63] He allows that in such a case the good for this person
will centre around the activity of counting blades of grass,
assuming that there is no feasible way to alter his condition.

Liberalism needs both the high-minded conception of the
good and the ordinary conception of the good. It needs the
high-minded conception of the good because, as we have seen
in earlier chapters, it presupposes a certain ideal of a person.
But it also presupposes the ordinary conception of the good,
for without that it could degenerate into intolerance and
paternalism of the strong kind which sanctions forcibly
liberating non-autonomous people for their own good.

Now there is nothing inconsistent in appealing both to
the high-minded conception of the good and to the ordinary
conception of the good. For it is quite consistent to maintain
that a form of life A is better than a form of life B and yet to
take the line that the form of life B is suited to people who
have lost (or never had) the potential to enjoy form of life A.
Or again, it is quite consistent to maintain that though A is
inherently superior to B, the fact that a person has chosen
B for himself makes it better (all things considered) for him
to be allowed to pursue B than for A to be forcibly imposed
on him.

Mill and Rawls are probably right about the need for the
high-minded conception of the good. But Rawls and Mill (as
interpreted by Rawls) are wrong in using the mechanical and
facile method for establishing the high-minded conception of

[62] *A Theory of Justice*, p. 433.   [63] Ibid., p. 432.

the good, namely the method of appealing to the choice criterion of value. I would contend that the high-minded conception of the good involves perfectionist judgements, it involves controversial judgements about what form of life is inherently suited to human beings.

One of the reasons why liberalism needs the high-minded conception of the good is that it needs to make judgements about what is good for the coming generation. One may adopt the ordinary conception of the good with regard to people who have already formed their aims and values, but the ordinary conception will not be of much help in dealing with individuals whose aims and values have not yet been formed. Nor, as we have seen, will the choice criterion of value solve this problem. It is one of the tasks of the state to create a morally healthy environment in which the young may grow up. The higher forms of life have to be encouraged from the start otherwise people are likely to lose their potential for them. So, even at the political level, we shall have to make judgements about what forms of life are good for the coming generation. We saw in chapter 10 that it will not do to take the line that the state has no authority to take part in the education and up-bringing of the young.

The view that I defend in chapter 14, according to which the doctrine of equal liberty does not extend to inferior forms of life, is closer to Mill's substantial views about liberties than to Rawls's, though I agree with Rawls in rejecting Mill's utilitarian foundations. Mill, unlike Rawls, did not want to give equal status to different forms of life (that were not anti-social); Rawls's anti-perfectionism seems to commit him to not giving inferior status to a form of life on the grounds that it was degrading or unsuited to human beings. Mill's liberal society was, in effect, heavily biased in favour of the customary morality. He was willing to allow society to use the higher or rational morality in its dealings with the young. He seemed to think that in practice this would involve giving society the right to use its customary morality to educate the young, though his hope was that society would use the rational morality.[64] His doctrine of liberty does not commit him to giving equal status to all forms of life.

[64] Mill, On Liberty, chapter IV, para. 11.

Even in the case of adults, Mill allowed us to have contempt for the inferior forms of life and pity for those who are practising such forms of life. He was quite aware that his principle of liberty does not apply to children. He was not committed to allowing children to experiment with all kinds of unconventional life-styles. He does not deny society the right to use its knowledge of good and evil in making decisions about how to bring up children what sort of moral environment they should grow up in. He does not seem to object to society having 'absolute power over them [its members] during all the early portions of their existence'.[65] Mill rightly does not deny that we learn from our previous experience, as well as from the experiences of previous generations, not only in scientific matters but also in moral matters. He admits that experience does provide a presumption that one mode of existence is preferable to another and that people should be trained in youth 'to know and benefit by the ascertained results of human experience'.[66] And his view that the higher forms of life are like tender plants that need protection from hostile and corrupting influences, also implies that we should give preference to some forms of life over others in our dealings with children. Since Mill allows the state to educate children,[67] the state can hardly fail to encourage some forms of life over others. Sometimes, however, Mill talks as if education would be quite neutral.[68] He attempts to avoid bias by insisting that education only imparts facts without predisposing students in favour of any doctrines. But is Mill seriously suggesting that moral education, for instance, should aim to be neutral between different forms of life? Do not children, while they are children, need more guidance in moral matters than merely to be told about the beliefs that other people happen to hold? Does not Mill's own doctrine about the higher forms of life being like a tender plant require that people should be encouraged in such forms of life from the start? If so, why should the state be neutral between the higher and lower forms of life?

Mill admits that we have a presumption from past experi-

---

[65] Ibid.   [66] Ibid., chapter III, para. 3.
[67] *Principles of Political Economy* (London, 1848).
[68] *On Liberty*, chapter V, para. 14.

ence that some modes of existence are better than others, though he admits that this presumption can be defeated. So my suggestion in chapter 14 that some forms of life should be given lower status than other forms of life, though adults should not be forbidden from practising the lower ones in private, is in harmony with some of Mill's ideas. The presumption that some forms of life are inferior to others provides a reason for giving the former lower status, especially in our dealings with children. The possibility that the presumption can be defeated should provide us with one, though not the only, reason for tolerating the alleged lower forms of life and for allowing free discussion about which forms of life are inferior.

Rawls is right in rejecting Mill's utilitarian foundations. Rawls points out certain dangerous consequences of utilitarian approaches:

Whenever a society sets out to maximise the sum of intrinsic value or the net balance of the satisfaction of interests it is liable to find that the denial of liberty for some is justified in the name of this simple end. The liberties of equal citizenship are insecure when founded upon teleological principles.[69]

The substantial view of Mill's that I have supported is the view which gives lower status to some forms of life than to others. This view can be defended on a right-based approach. I have *not* defended the view that some citizens should have less of the essential liberties such as freedom to vote, freedom of discussion, and so forth than others; Rawls is right in thinking this view to be obnoxious and also in thinking that it is not easy for utilitarians to rule out this view.

---

[69] *A Theory of Justice*, p. 211.

Paternalism Towards
Sane Adults

This chapter considers the problem of paternalism with regard
to sane adults. It shall not be concerned with paternalism
towards children (which was discussed in chapter 10) or
towards mental defectives. Paternalism towards children, as
was shown in chapter 10, involves an appeal to perfectionist
ideals. Now it is sometimes thought that in the case of sane
adults, paternalistic intervention should not involve an appeal
to perfectionist ideals, but rather that it should be based on
the agent's own value system. While not denying that we
should whenever possible respect the agent's own value system.
I shall contend that even in the case of sane adults an adequate
account of paternalistic intervention cannot be given without
some appeal to perfectionist considerations. This contention
should reinforce the claim made throughout this book about
the importance of perfectionist considerations.

One of the important problems facing liberalism is to distinguish, in the case of sane adults, justified cases of paternalism
from unjustified cases of paternalism. An extreme libertarian
solution would be to say that paternalism is never justified in
the case of sane adults. But this solution is too extreme because
there are cases where we would consider paternalism quite
harmless and indeed necessary. Thus even Mill, who was against
paternalism in general, agreed that there were exceptions to
the anti-paternalistic principles. The problem then is to provide
some kind of rationale for such exceptions. Mill considers the
case of a person attempting to cross a bridge that he does not
know is unsafe; if there is no time to warn him of the danger,
the public officer is entitled forcibly to turn him back. Mill
believed that in such cases the use of force does not involve
any real infringement of liberty for liberty consists in doing
what one desires and the person in the case he gives does not
desire to fall into the river.

Now Mill has to face the problem that his rationale for paternalistic interventions in such cases may be the thin end of a wedge. Could it not be used by revolutionaries, who want to force people to be free by destroying their present forms of life? Take, for instance, a sane adult person who believes in false gods, wrongly thinking that they will give him health, wealth, and happiness, in this life and in the next. Suppose that this person does not want to die but that he will die unless he gives up his quack religious cures and takes modern medicine; he is ignorant of the means that he needs to take in order to achieve his ends. If such a person does not heed our warnings, why not force modern medicine down his throat rather than let him persevere in his phoney cures? He does not want to die and the use of force in this case would help him to get what he really wants, so the use of force will not involve any real infringement of his liberty. Instances of forcibly liberating sane adults (such as Jehovah's witnesses) from their religious prejudices would be repugnant to liberals. So the problem remains: how to distinguish the justified uses of paternalism from unjustified ones. One suggestion offered by Mill is that in the case of people in the maturity of their faculties coercion is justified only when the danger is certain; when the danger is only probable the person should only be warned of the danger but should not be forcibly prevented from taking the risk.[1] Here his rejection of non-certain knowledge seems similar to Rawls's view that all controversial knowledge, including knowledge of metaphysics and of intrinsic values, should be bypassed. While Mill applies this caution in the case of paternalistic intervention against adults in the maturity of their faculties, Rawls goes much further and wants to exclude such controversial knowledge from all political principles.

It will not do to take the line that only that knowledge is admissible which all adult human beings would agree about. Exceptions would have to be made to this principle in order to deal with lunatics who may not even agree about the existence of chairs and tables in front of us. But even leaving aside such complications, this agreed body of knowledge will not provide a sufficient basis on which to construct an adequate political theory. People agree about the existence of

[1] Mill, *On Liberty*, chapter V, para. 5.

tables and chairs and many other facts, but to construct an adequate political theory one has to appeal to more controversial views as well, such as the view that autonomy is a good. Even when there is considerable agreement about things like pain and death being evil and autonomy being good, there is considerable disagreement about how much weight to attach to all the evils and goods, about the trade-offs between the different values.

Both Mill and Rawls *in fact* appeal to controversial views about human nature and the controversial methods of establishing their views. Rawls does so while insisting that liberal political theory must keep clear of controversial knowledge! But Mills, unlike Rawls, would probably agree that controversial views will have to be appealed to in constructing an adequate political theory. Certain kinds of paternalism would on Mill's view involve an appeal to controversial moral values—thus in the case of children and lunatics, the paternalistic authorities will sometimes have to make major controversial decisions on behalf of the individuals being interferred with. But Mill would claim that in the case of those who have reached the maturity of their faculties, it is necessary that the relevant knowledge, on the basis of which paternalistic interference is justified, must be certain and non-controversial among such adults. Some such claim is implicit in the rationale he offers for using force against the person crossing the dangerous bridge.

Now Mill (and Rawls) have to face the objection that the distinction between certain and non-certain knowledge is itself something problematic. What is (subjectively) certain and non-problematic to one set of people may not be so to another. Indeed, earlier, while arguing against the interference of the public with purely personal conduct, Mill pointed out that 'it is easy for anyone to imagine an ideal public which leaves the freedom and choice in all uncertain matters undisturbed and only requires them to abstain from modes of conduct which universal experience has condemned. But where has there been any public which set any such limits to its censorship?'[2] Mill seems to forget this caution when he offers his rationale for using force against the person crossing

[2] *On Liberty*, chapter IV, section 12.

a dangerous bridge.

Many people are certain that the people who resort to religious prayers instead of modern medicine for their serious physical ailments are doing something as dangerous as the person crossing the dangerous bridge. In the case of many unsafe bridges it is not *certain* that a person who walks over them will fall, let alone hurt himself. So the certainty criterion will not be able to distinguish legitimate from illegitimate cases of paternalistic interference. It is true that in the dangerous bridge case, there is not time to warn, whereas the person who prefers prayers to modern medicine does so despite warnings. But there are cases where we are willing to use force even after warning, for instance if a person is attempting to jump off a cliff even after he has been warned that the cliff is dangerous, we may be justified in using force in order to give him a cooling-off period.

Admittedly, there is an objective use of the term certain; for instance, epistemologists sometimes propose theories of probability which treat it as an objective fact that some things are certain. But this objective sense of certain cannot rescue Mill. For even though some things are objectively certain, a liberal cannot allow such objective certainty to be used as a sufficient guide for paternalistic intervention; if he did, he would not be able to distinguish the paternalism that he permits from the strong kind of paternalism which allows experts to forcibly liberate people who worship false gods.

In order to get clear about the ethics of paternalism we need to stress distinction between the following questions (which was mentioned in chapter 11). First, under what conditions do the authorities have the right to interfere paternalistically with the individual? Secondly, when the authorities do have the right to interfere paternalistically with an individual, what considerations should they bear in mind in order to exercise their right wisely? Utilitarians tend to blur these two questions; for them the answers to both the questions are in terms of utility. But for those who believe in a right-based theory there is a genuine problem about whether the paternalistic authorities have the right to interfere with a person even when such interference is for the good of the individual being interfered with and for the good of society.

In the case of sane adults, for the paternalistic authorities to have the right to interfere with the individual it is normally essential that the individual has consented to such interference. The consent need not be explicit, it may only be presumed or tacit. But it will not do merely to appeal to future consent, consent after the paternalistic intervention has taken place. Admittedly the person whom you forcibly save from walking over the dangerous bridge is likely, when he finds out the facts after the event, to approve of what you did to him, but such future consent can occur in brainwashing also. There is the suggestion[3] that we could add a supplementary test, namely that paternalistic intervention must not be used in the case of adults unless there has been an evident failure of reason or of the will. This supplementary test will rule out brainwashing of sane adults who are in possession of their reason and will. But it seems that this supplementary test is so strong that it may also rule out the use of force against the sane person who is attempting to cross the bridge, without knowing that it is unsafe. To meet this objection, one might interpret the supplementary test less strongly and say that when a person acts in ignorance, then there has been a failure of reason. But now the supplementary test will become too weak. For though it will allow us to interfere with the person attempting to walk over the bridge without knowing that it is unsafe, it may also allow us to interfere paternalistically with and forcibly liberate those adults who worship false gods and pursue illusory cures for their problems.

To avoid such difficulties, it is essential to stress the requirement that the consent must be prior to the paternalistic intervention. Admittedly, people in our society have not explicitly consented to be forcibly saved if they attempt to walk over a bridge without knowing that it is unsafe, but they can be presumed to have consented. Most people in our society would like to be forcibly saved in such situations (assuming that there is no time to be given a warning) and the fact that people do not object to this practice is some evidence that they have given us their tacit consent. I shall

---

[3] Found in Rawls, *A Theory of Justice*, p. 250.

deal later with the complication that not everyone can be taken to consent to such practices. In most cases, however, it seems redundant to ask people, 'Would you like to be forcibly saved if you attempt to cross a bridge, not knowing that it is dangerous?' For we know that the answer would be, 'Yes, of course.' We can presume that they have consented until they tell us otherwise.

The idea of tacit consent has been regarded with suspicion in some quarters because of the way that it has sometimes been used. Thus it has been pointed out that a consequence of Locke's use of tacit consent is that the subjects' decision not to emigrate is evidence of their tacit consent to obey a tyrant. Now I admit that there are things seriously wrong with the use that people sometimes make of the notion of consent (whether explicit or implicit). In particular it is often overlooked that an agreement can be morally invalid even if it was consented to by both parties. For instance, the alleged agreement between the subjects and the tyrant under which the subjects agree to obey the tyrant and the tyrant agrees not to kill them is invalid because it is not a fair one; the subjects agree to obey the sovereign and yet they get nothing in return which is not already theirs by right. Such agreements are invalid, not because the consent was only tacit. They would be just as invalid if the consent had been explicit.

In the case of paternalistic interference, the danger of abuse would be real if we used consent (whether explicit or tacit) as a sufficient condition for justifying such interference. The suggestion that I am making is that in the case of sane adults, their prior consent is (at least normallly) a necessary condition for the justification of paternalistic interference. To fully justify paternalistic interference with sane adults one must be able to show not only that the paternalistic authority was authorized to use paternalistic intervention but also that it exercised this authority wisely, in the interests of the person being interfered with.

The necessary condition just mentioned, of getting the prior consent of the person being interfered with, helps to show why it is quite consistent to make the line that forcible interference is justified in the case of the person attempting to walk over the bridge, not knowing that it is dangerous, but is not justified in the case of the person who is worshipping false gods. For the latter person has not given us his consent, either explicitly or tacitly.

One general principle that might be offered is that the state could use force temporarily against a citizen in order to let him think things over and give him a cooling off period, so that *he* can then decide whether or not he really wants to do what he was prevented by the paternalistic authorities from doing. This does not involve talk of hypothetical choice or choice from some ideal standpoint, but rather it involves an appeal to what the agent actually decides. The bulk of the adult sane population may safely be presumed to have consented to some such principle as the following: The paternalistic authority should be given powers to intervene by force with us for our own good for temporary periods in order to let us think things over. But one must also stress that there are strict limits to what the state should be allowed to do during the temporary periods. With improvements in brainwashing techniques it may become possible for the state to brainwash individuals during a short period. The state should be allowed to use only the minimum of force that is necessary to give the agent time to think things over, and it must not interfere with the autonomy and integrity of the agent.

We need to distinguish interference with a person's autonomy (and/or integrity) from mere interference with a person's liberty of action. If a sane person is forcibly locked up, his liberty of action has been interfered with, but this does not imply that his autonomy has been interfered with in the way that it would be if his beliefs or preferences were altered as a result of drugs, torture, or deprivation of food. In the case of the person attempting to walk over the dangerous bridge, the minimum force that is necessary to let him think things over is nothing like enough to constitute interference with the person's autonomous nature or with his integrity. No doubt the agent's belief has altered after the use of force, for after the use of force he believes that the bridge is dangerous whereas before that he had believed that it was safe. But in such a case the agent's change of belief has occurred without there being any manipulation of the agent's beliefs; he merely changed his beliefs after certain things were pointed out to him. Now sometimes cases of brainwashing succeed in changing the agent's beliefs after the agent has been coerced and exhausted, through deprivation of food, torture, and so forth, and is then in such a vulnerable state that he is ready to 'see the light'. In such cases, too, the final conversion need not involve the use of any force at that late stage; it is just that he is too weak to resist the arguments offered by the authorities, the weakness being due to the force and coercion having been employed against him at an earlier stage. In such cases the final conversions are not cases of the agents being freely converted.

In the dangerous bridge case, it is possible that the force was essential to get the agent to see the evidence, before it is too late, but once he sees the evidence, his change of belief, about whether the bridge is dangerous, is quite natural in the sense that if he had been confronted with the same evidence without the prior use of force or coercion he would have been just as impressed by it. Cases of brainwashing are different. For in such cases the use of coercion and force help to explain not only why the agent came across the arguments and 'evidence' for a particular view, but also help to explain why the agent was so impressed by such arguments and evidence. The difference between brainwashing and non-brainwashing could be illustrated with the help of the following example that does not involve brainwashing. Suppose a Nazi during the Second World War believed that it was false that Jews were being killed in concentration camps but he could not be bothered to go and visit the concentration camps. Now suppose one forcibly kidnapped this Nazi and took him to the concentration camps and showed him the killings of the Jews. Here though there was use of force that in a sense resulted in the Nazi's change of belief about whether Jews were being killed in concentration camps, there need have been no brainwashing. For the evidence that he saw at the concentration camps would have changed his belief, even if no force had been used. It is just that if no force had been used against him he would not have come across the evidence. This particular example is not a case of justified paternalism, but it helps to illustrate a point that is important for the discussion of paternalism towards sane adults, namely the point that not all cases of force and coercion, even when in a sense they lead to a change in belief in the agent, involve manipulation of the agent's beliefs (or preferences) or involve interference with the agent's autonomy (or integrity). Mill's argument that what is important is not just the way of life that we have, but also whether or not we have autonomously chosen that way of life, requires respecting the autonomy of the agent; but it is not clear why it involves placing all that much weight on respecting a person's liberty of action in every particular case. No doubt the interferences with certain liberties of action can virtually have the effect of denying a person the freedom to choose his way of life. Thus if whenever a person tried to go to church, the state prevented him from going to church, he could hardly be said to enjoy the choice of the church-going way of life. But if a person is forcibly prevented from falling over a dangerous bridge, his autonomy can hardly be said to be impaired. Of course if a person wants to live dangerously and the state refuses, even in the long run, to let him do that (for instance, by forbidding mountaineering), then he can complain that he is in effect being denied the choice of certain ways of life. But such objections have much less force if the state confines its paternalistic inter-ferences in accordance with the principles laid down earlier — for instance, that the use of force should be the minimum that is necessary to enable the agent to think things over.

Of course not all cases of justified paternalism are as simple as the case of the person walking over a dangerous bridge. Sometimes a person in a fit of depression may want to commit suicide. Here again we may be justified in using force to enable him to think things over, to give a 'cooling-off period'.[4] But for how long can the use of force be continued? A week, a month, a year? Here one would need to distinguish the case where the depression has resulted in the person ceasing to be sane, where he has lost his powers of judgement from the case where he retains his sanity and his powers of

[4] See G. Dworkin, 'Paternalism', in *Morality and the Law*, ed. R. Wasserstrom (Belmont, 1971), p. 124.

judgement. In the former case the paternalistic authorities would have to try to restore him to his former rational state, whereas in the latter case the authorities should proceed much more cautiously, they should not use any further force, beyond the force that is necessary to give the agent a cooling-off period to think things over.

There is also the problem regarding what forms of treatment the paternalistic authorities should be allowed to impose on adults who are in a coma, or are so depressed that they have lost their powers of judgement. Here one should respect the views of the individual when he was sane. Thus if a Jehovah's witness believes that he should never have a blood transfusion then we must not give him a blood transfusion while he is in a coma. For in such cases we have no authority to give him blood transfusions, even if we believe that a blood transfusion would be good for him.

There are cases where people do not consent, not even tacitly, to some of our paternalistic practices. Some people may not want the state to interfere with their carrying out their projects even for a short period. Thus a person may want to commit suicide in order to make a protest against some unjust practices and it may be that the most effective way of making the protest is to burn oneself at a particular time. It might be suggested that in such cases the agent should give prior notice to the state mentioning that his impending suicide is a considered act and he should not be intefered with. But often such opting out of paternalistic practices is not practicable. Suppose a lot of people want the public officers to save them from ignorantly walking over dangerous bridges, or from committing suicide in a state of delirium, while others do not want to be forcibly saved even in such situations, say, because they are afraid of what the state may do to them with so much power or because a Brahmin might rather risk injury or even death then be touched by an untouchable policeman.

The simplest solution would be to use paternalistic measures against those who, in their sober moments, in their ordinary, everday life, approve of the relevant paternalistic measures, but not against those who have declared that they do not want such help. But the trouble is that often it is not easy to tell which class of people a person belongs to; for instance, if you see someone about to walk over a dangerous bridge, you may not know in time whether or not he belongs to the class of people who approve of the authorities using force in such eventualities. Sometimes a person can opt out of a paternalistic practice; thus he could carry a card saying that he is a member of a sect that does not approve of blood transfusions, and so if you find such a person in a coma you must respect his wishes and not give him blood transfusion. But such opting out is not always easy. In the case of those sane adults who are against all paternalistic measures, one could devise some sort of identification that they would carry. But in the case of most of us, we want certain kinds of paternalistic interference but not others, and it will not do simply to declare oneself for or against paternalism in general. Thus the Jehovah's witness who docs not want blood transfusion even if that is necessary to save him when he is in a coma, may well want to be forcibly saved should he attempt to walk over a dangerous bridge not knowing that it is dangerous. Nor can we satisfactorily operate a system giving *all* the details of our preferences regarding which paternalistic interference we want and which we do not. If you see someone about to jump off a cliff and commit suicide, there simply may not be enough time for you to find out whether or not he has opted out of the paternalistic practice of using force in such cases. So often we are genuinely in the dark about whether or not the agent would approve of the use of certain paternalistic measures. What do we do then in an emergency?

There are also other cases where people may want to submit themselves to paternalistic practices because they want to protect themselves from their own weakness. Some people may want cigarettes and alcohol and drugs heavily taxed so as to make sure that they consume less of such things in the long run. Some people may want laws requiring seat belts to be worn while driving cars and helmets to be worn while driving motor cycles, because they fear that in the absence of such laws they are likely to be lazy and not take these important precautions. Again, some people may want a law against homosexuality even among consenting adults in private, or a law against the worship of what they regard as false gods and of the devil, because they are afraid that in the absence of such laws they may be more tempted to go astray.

Another reason why people may want paternalistic legislation is because they want to reap the advantages that come when people in general act in concert, which action cannot be effective unless it is backed up by legal sanctions. There are plenty of examples of this. Mill gives the following illustrations:

Let us suppose . . . that a general reduction of the hours of factory labour, say from ten to nine, would be for the advantage of the work people, that they would receive as high wages, or nearly as high, for nine hours' labour as they receive for ten. If this would be the result, and if the operatives generally are convinced that it would, the limitation, some may say, will be adopted spontaneously. I answer that it will not be adopted unless the body of operatives bind themselves to one another to abide by it. A workman who refused to work more than nine hours while they were others who worked ten, would either not be employed at all, or if employed must submit to lose one-tenth of his wages. However convinced therefore, he may be that it is the interest of the class to work short time, it is contrary to his own interest to set the example, unless he is well assured that all or most others will follow it.[5]

Now one problem that arises with paternalism is this. Paternalistic legislation can often be in the interest of those who want such legislation, as the above examples show. But for all, or almost all, paternalistic practices, there will be some people who want to opt out of such practices. When we do allow a paternalistic practice because the majority consents to it (either explicitly, or tacitly by not objecting to or by not trying to opt out of the practice), but the minority does not, there is the problem of how such a practice can be justified to the minority that does not consent to it. The legislation must not be justified to the unwilling minority on paternalistic grounds, for the attempt to do so would involve the strong kind of paternalism which liberalism does not permit and which involves forcibly imposing laws on people for their own good against their own considered judgement about what is for their own good. Yet to forbid such

---

[5] *Principles of Political Economy*, Book V, chapter XI.

strong paternalism against the unwilling minority is not always to grant the minority a veto on paternalistic legislation. For first, one can try to have measures allowing the minority to opt out of the paternalistic scheme where that is feasible, as it is in the case of Jehovah's witnesses who do not want blood transfusion under any circumstances. Secondly, when such opting out is not feasible, the minority may in some cases be compelled by the law to conform to the practice for the benefit of the majority rather than be allowed to wreck the whole scheme. In such cases, although the scheme is justified on paternalistic grounds to the majority, who have consented to it and whose consent ensures that they are not being subjected to strong paternalism of the kind that liberals disapprove of, the justification of imposing the scheme on the minority is not a paternalistic justification and *a fortiori* it does not involve strong paternalism. The justification for imposing it on the minority is that sometimes, *when minority rights are not involved*, the minority interests may have to give way to the majority interests. The fact that paternalistic practices involve balancing the interests of some against the interests of others raises the problem of how such balancing is to be done. But such problems are not peculiar to paternalism; they arise in the case of virtually all controversial laws.

A minority should not be allowed to veto a paternalistic practice, unless it is not feasible for the minority to opt out of the practice and unless minority rights are involved. Thus if the majority want to ban certain kinds of religious worship because they want to protect themselves against the temptation to worship what they regard as false gods, and assuming such a ban infringes the rights of the minority to worship the gods of their choice, then such a ban must not be allowed. If the majority wanted to tax cigarettes as a means of reducing their consumption of cigarettes, and if no rights of the minority were violated, then such a tax could be permissible. But how do we decide whether people have the right to freedom of religion but not the right to smoke cigarettes at economical prices? In chapter 13 there is a discussion of why some liberties are ranked higher than than others: it is argued there that perfectionist considerations are one of the considerations used in dealing with such problems.

I have stressed that in order to have the right to impose paternalistic measures upon sane adults the state should get the consent of the individuals. The consent need not be explicit; it may be tacit, as in the case of people who knowingly do not opt out of a paternalistic practice, such as the practice of being given a blood transfusion when they are unconscious or the practice of using force to give people wanting to commit suicide in a depressed state time to think things over. Although the consent could be tacit it will not do to appeal *merely* to future consent (that is to say 'consent' of the agent after the use of paternalistic force has been used) or hypothetical consent.

Future consent can be got even in cases of brainwashing. Now it might be suggested that we could rely on future consent provided it was not obtained by brainwashing. But this suggestion will not do. Suppose we forcibly marry a woman to a nice man. We may well get her future consent without brainwashing her in any technical sense. She may genuinely even get to love him and the children that she bears him. Yet such future consent cannot authorize us to use paternalistic force now. Sometimes, however, people can give tacit consent to the practice of forcibly doing things to them when it is likely that they will give their future consent. For instance, a person may forcibly prevent his wife from giving away, in a fit of generosity, all her savings to an undeserving charity; he may know that she will later thank him for the use of force, whereas if he did not use force, she would bitterly criticize him in the future for not forcibly preventing her from such a foolish course. But here it is necessary to assume that she had in her sober moments tacitly consented to the practice among husbands and wives that the husband may use force against the wife in such situations. So here, if one gives the full story, one does not appeal merely to future consent but also to the tacit consent of the practice of relying on future consent in such situations.

For similar reasons hypothetical consent by itself will not provide the necessary authority to use paternalistic intervention

(See also chapter 11, section 3). People who worship false gods and pursue illusory and non-existent goals would, if they saw things clearly, see the absurdity of their ways of life. It does not follow that the state or anyone else has the necessary authority forcibly to liberate them from their ways of life.

In the last chapter two problems connected with parternalism were distinguished. First, under what conditions do the authorities have the right to interfere paternalistically with the individual? Secondly, when the authorities do have the authority to interfere paternalistically with the individual, what considerations should they bear in mind in order to exercise their right wisely? I have argued that in the case of sane adults the first question has to be answered by appealing to the actual consent, explicit or tacit, of the individuals; hypothetical or future consent, since it is not actual consent, cannot authorize the authorities to use force against them for their own good. But if we turn to the second problem mentioned above, hypothetical consent and future consent may have some role in answering it. Let us now turn to a discussion of this second problem.

Even if an individual consents to become a slave or to have his healthy arm cut off, it does not follow that the authorities should oblige him. Even leaving aside the repercussions of their actions on third parties that the authorities should take into account, the authorities must make sure that they do not seriously harm the individual when they act for him. This can be illustrated by considering some of Mill's ideas. It is sometimes thought that Mill, in refusing to allow the state to recognize and enforce contracts under which a person voluntarily agrees to become a slave, was departing from his liberal doctrine according to which force should not be used against sane adults (in civilized countries) for their own good, moral or physical. I shall argue that Mill was not making any such departure in this case. But first I want to say something about Mill's ideas of what is good for an individual, since it contains some insights and since it is essential for understanding his views on paternalism of sane adults.

Rawls thinks that Mill adhered to the choice criterion of value.[6] In fact I think Mill used people's voluntary choices

---

[6] *A Theory of Justice*, p. 209 n. 7.

only as evidence of value or of what is good for them. The choice criterion that Rawls believes in and which he (perhaps mistakenly) attributes to Mill has a more existentialist flavour. The Good is not anything objective; whatever way of life a free man voluntarily chooses for himself constitutes the good for him, the only proviso being that the contractarian principles should not be violated. According to Rawls, if a person's plan of life is deliberately and rationally chosen, 'and if he succeeds in carrying it out and in doing so finds it worthwhile, there are no grounds outside the contractarian framework for saying that it would have been better if he had done something else'.[7]

For Mill, however, such choices of the individual, even when they are voluntary choices, are at best evidence of what is good for him. Thus, when discussing whether to allow people to voluntarily enter into a contract of slavery, he says 'a person's voluntary choice is evidence that what he so chooses is desirable.'[8] It is clear that he thinks that the presumption provided by such evidence about the person's good can be rebutted if other relevant evidence is forthcoming. While discussing irreversible contracts of marriage, Mill says that even · when a person voluntarily enters such a contract the presumption that what he now chooses is in his long term interest can be defeated.[9] Talk of 'evidence' suggests that Mill regarded a person's good as something objectively there, the job of human beings is to discover the good rather than to create it in the way that some existentialist would have us do. Mill's use of the expert test also suggests this. For he says that where the experts disagree about what form of life is desirable, we should go by the views of the majority of the experts. This view of his makes more sense if we take the experts' majority verdict as providing evidence of the good rather than as the criterion of the good. The view that the good varies with the experts' majority verdict is more difficult to accept than the view that the experts' majority verdict is good evidence of the good, the good being there independently of the majority verdict.

[7] Ibid., p. 564.
[8] On Liberty, chapter V, para. 11.
[9] Principles of Political Economy, Book V, chapter XI, para. 10.

Mill believes that the only evidence of what is desirable for a person is to be found in human desires.[10] Neglecting for the sake of simplicity the distinction between desires and choices, we can say that although Mill allows that in particular cases (such as when a person voluntarily contracts himself into slavery or into irreversible marriage) a *single* voluntary choice of a person may not reflect his good, yet he believes (quite consistently) in something like the choice test of value, for he believes that voluntary human choices over a long period (what the particular individual chooses and is likely to choose in the future under different conditions, and perhaps what the experts choose or would choose) would provide sufficient evidence of what is good for a person.

To be accurate, we should say that Mill was more impressed by people's preferences than by their choices, in deciding what is valuable: 'Men often from infirmity of character, make their election for the nearer good, though they know it to be less valuable.'[11] However he goes on to say that in such cases people do not 'voluntarily choose the lower description of pleasures in preference to the higher'. But there is a case which Mill does not seriously consider. A person may *voluntarily* choose the lesser good, preferring the higher good; he may choose it out of weakness of will. A choice can be both voluntary, and weak-willed; in such cases the person acts against his better judgement or against his real preferences. In such cases what he prefers rather than what he chooses is a better guide to what appears valuable to him. However, for the sake of simplicity, such complexities can be neglected.

It is worth seeing why Mill did not want the state to allow a person to voluntarily enter into a contract of slavery. Mill was suspicious of the view that such a choice would lead to the person's long-term good. Mill believes that often a person's good is best provided for by allowing him to take his own means of pursuing it, but he did not think that in this particular case this was so. Gerald Dworkin complains that the individual may be correct in thinking that his interests are best provided by entering such a contract.[12] But Mill could

[10] *Utilitarianism*, chapter IV, para. 3.
[11] Ibid., chapter III, para. 7.
[12] 'Paternalism', p. 118.

reply that though any particular voluntary choice may provide for the agent's long-term interest, it is also possible that it may not. An indvidual's choice is at best presumptive evidence about his long-term interests; the presumption could be defeated by other choices in the future. He thinks that some choices are based on insufficient experience, where the real experience necessary for making an adequate decision will only come in the future.

The presumption in favour of individual judgment is only legitimate, where the judgment is grounded on actual and especially on present, personal experience, and not suffered to be reversed after experience has condemned it; and any such presumption which can be grounded on their having voluntarily entered into the contract, perhaps at an early age, and without any real knowledge of what they undertook, is commonly next to null. The practical maxim of leaving contracts free is not applicable without great limitation in case of engagements in perpetuity.[13]

He goes on to say that such considerations are 'eminently applicable to marriage, the most important of all cases of engagement for life'; he might have added that such considerations are equally applicable to contracts that allow a person to voluntarily sell himself into slavery.

The view that the sole evidence of what is desirable for a person is to be found in his voluntary choices and desires is quite consistent with the view that in deciding what is desirable for a person we must take into account not only his present desires and choices but also his future ones. Such considerations help to show how Mill can consistently allow the state not to recognize certain irreversible contracts.

Mill's view was that society should not forcibly interfere with an individual (who is in the maturity of his faculties) when the latter is not harming anyone else. Now this principle of liberty of his was *not* based on the view that society *always* knows less about the individual's good than the individual himself does. Mill believes that even when society knows more about the individual's good than the individual himself does, there is a good case for not using compulsion, for instance because it is better to let the individual exercise his own choice and judgement.[14]

[13] Mill, *Principles of Political Economy*, Book V, chapter XI, para. 10.
[14] See *On Liberty*, chapter III, para. 3.

Now we can see that Mill did not make an exception to his doctrine of liberty when he said that the state should refuse to recognize contracts under which a person voluntarily undertakes to become a slave. His position is quite consistent. To see this, we need to appreciate an important distinction: 1. Should the state facilitate an individual or group of individuals to carry out their plans, when such plans do not harm others? 2. Should the state be allowed to use coercion or compulsion (for instance by using threats through the criminal law) in an attempt to prevent such plans from being carried out?

Even if one takes the line that the state should not forcibly (or coercively) interfere with the individual's plans in such cases, it does not follow that one is committed to the view that the state should positively facilitate such plans. It is one thing to let a man die if that is what the man wants to do (not just in the heat of the moment, but even in his sober moments, even after a 'cooling off period'); it is quite another to co-operate with and further such behaviour by allowing him to use the facilities of the civil law. Admittedly, even when the state knows more about what is good for the individual than the individual himself does, the state may not have the authority to impose its views about his good upon the individual. But this is quite consistent with the state's refusal to co-operate with the individual in his pursuit of his illusory good. It does not need any authority to refuse to co-operate with an individual. Compare: if I kill you there is the problem of whether I had the authority to kill you; but if I refuse your request to kill you there is hardly a problem of whether I had the authority to refuse to kill you.

The case of voluntary slavery is similar. Suppose A and B get together and A in return for some favour promises B that he (A) will live like B's slave for the rest of his life. As long as the state does not agree to enforce such agreements, it has not interfered with the individuals concerned; refusal to co-operate is not interference, unless there is a duty to co-operate. But if and when the state agrees to enforce such agreements (by recognizing them in law), it becomes, as it were, a party to the agreement, it co-operates with the parties to the agreement; and so in such cases the state would bear more responsibility than if it simply allowed the individual to live in a slave-like state, without agreeing to enforce such agreements. So before agreeing to recognize and enforce such agreements, the state has some responsibility to find out if such agreements could be seriously harmful to one or both of the parties to the agreement. And so it seems reasonable to take the line that the state could take into account not only the present desire and choices of the relevant individuals, but also the likely future desires of such persons; and hypothetical choices of the individual may also be taken into account to the extent that they are indicative of what is or is not good for the individual.[15]

Mill believed that some forms of life are superior to others. He thought that individuals make mistakes even in their self-regarding actions. But he thought that the errors that an individual commits are 'far outweighed by allowing others to constrain him to do what they deem his good'.[16] Although Mill's doctrine does not allow us to constrain an individual in his self-regarding actions, it allows us to regard his form of life as inferior, it allows us to have contempt and pity for the person who wants to lead a degrading form of life, it allows us to shun his company.[17] So his doctrine does not require that we must positively co-operate with an individual who is leading a degrading life; it only requires that we must not constrain him. Now when the state refuses to recognize and enforce slavery agreements, it is not constraining the individuals concerned, any more than I would be constraining you if I refused your request to flog you. So the state's refusal to recognize and enforce slavery contracts does not form an exception to Mill's doctrine according to which the state must not constrain the actions of adults for their own good.

But now suppose A agrees to become B's slave, and it is also agreed that C, a private agency, will enforce the agreement. Should the state stand by and let such voluntary agreements take place, or should it actually forbid such agreements? Now there is the complication that the state may indeed forbid such arrangements, not for paternalistic reasons, but for other reasons, for instance because it will not be in the interest of

---

[15] See chapter 11.
[16] *On Liberty*, chapter IV, paras. 4 and 5.
[17] Ibid., para. 5.

society to have private agencies that act like the Mafia or like mini-states within the state. If the state bans such agreements for non-paternalistic reasons, the state will not be involved in an exception to the doctrine of liberty; but if it bans such agreements for paternalistic reasons, then it will be involved in an exception to Mill's doctrine of liberty.

Before concluding this chapter, it is worth vindicating the claim made at the beginning of the chapter about the importance of perfectionist considerations even in the case of paternalism towards sane adults. In the case of paternalism towards sane adults (including adults who have become temporarily insane), the appeal to perfectionism is not as great as in the case of paternalism towards children; because in the former case, often the state in deciding what is good for the individual can resort to the sane agent's own value system (while he is or was sane), provided the agent has consented to this practice. But even in the case of sane adults there is need for appealing to perfectionist considerations. For, first, we saw that often in deciding whether or not to adopt a paternalistic practice, we shall have to weigh the interests of the minority who do not want the practice against the interests of the majority who do. We noted that a minority should not be allowed to veto a practice that furthers the majority's interests, unless minority rights are involved. When its rights are not allowed, the liberties of the minority can be curtailed. Now in chapter 13 it is argued that perfectionist considerations are one of the determinants of what rights we have; if this contention is correct, it would follow that perfectionist considerations cannot be bypassed even in the case of paternalism towards sane adults.

The other reason why perfectionism cannot be bypassed even in the case of paternalism with regard to sane adults is this. Sometimes sane adults are not at all certain about what is good for them; they are a bit lost and in need of help, not only about the best means of achieving their goals but even about what goals to have. Thus some people with alleged sexual abnormalities profess to be genuinely in the dark about whether or not it is in their interest to be 'cured' of their way of life. Sometimes they ask for help largely because they have been encouraged to do so by the conventional people they meet every day, and not because they really need it. In some cases it may be the responsibility of the paternalistic authorities to help the agent, even though he is sane, to decide what is really good for him. To carry out this responsibility, the paternalistic authorities, even when the agent asks them for help, may have to appeal to perfectionist considerations, they may have to take a stand on whether or not certain deviant sexual practices are inherently degrading or inferior. The paternalistic authorities cannot appeal to the agent's own value system to the extent that such a value system is itself indeterminate.

13

Preferred Liberties and Perfectionism

This chapter contains a discussion of some of the views of Ronald Dworkin and Nozick and contrasts their views with the approach defended in this book. Dworkin, Nozick, and I all adopt a right-based approach, but unlike me they both take an anti-perfectionist line. Nozick is in favour of a minimum state which acts as a kind of policeman or referee; according to him the state would exceed its legitimate authority if it imposed perfectionist ideals. And Dworkin thinks that the liberal-egalitarian state must be neutral between different conceptions of the good life, so he too is against perfectionism as a political principle.[1] Dworkin is an egalitarian, Nozick is anti-egalitarian, while the view defended in this book is that egalitarianism has to be supplemented by perfectionist considerations.

In section 1 it is argued, as against Dworkin, that perfectionist considerations have to be appealed to, in order to operate a liberal-egalitarian set up and in order to show why we should have a right to some liberties but not to others. In section 2 Nozick's views are discussed, and it is contended that his arguments against egalitarianism become less plausible if egalitarianism is supplemented by perfectionism.

1. Dworkin's theory and preferred liberties

Some liberties are more important than others. We have a right to some specific liberties, such as freedom of speech, whereas there are other less important liberties, such as the

[1] R. Dworkin, *Taking Rights Seriously*, pp. 272-3.

liberty to drive our car uptown on Lexington Avenue (to take an example of Dworkin's) or the liberty to masturbate in public, where we do not have the corresponding rights. We need to rank liberties in some rough order of importance. In this section it will be argued that there are two legitimate ways of ranking liberties: social criteria and perfectionist criteria. And I shall contrast my views with Dworkin's.

Dworkin rightly points out that there is no general right to liberty as such.[2] When for reasons of convenience we have a law preventing us from driving up Lexington Avenue, it is wrong to say that our right has been sacrificed or overridden by social considerations. Such talk of a general right to liberty creates a false sense of necessary conflict between liberty and other values whenever any social regulation is proposed. It suggests that the citizen who has been deprived of his liberty, however trivial the liberty, has been deprived of something that he was entitled to have. Dworkin does not of course deny that it may be in our interest to have liberty in the sense that it is good for us if we have it. But so is it in our interest to have vanilla ice cream. It would not follow that we have a right (in any strong sense) to vanilla ice cream. It may be in my interest to have a million pounds; it does not follow that I have a right to the million pounds. Similarly, it may be in my interest to have liberty; it does not follow that I have a right to liberty. I agree with all this.

Now the problem arises, since there is no general right to liberty, why should citizens in a democracy have the right to some liberties, such as freedom of speech, or freedom of religion, or freedom of political activity, but not to others? Dworkin's answer is that our right to specific liberties is grounded in our more general right to equal respect and consideration. I agree with him in this, but would add that in order to derive our liberties from egalitarian premises we need to supplement egalitarianism with perfectionist considerations.[3]

Does the right to free speech involve a right to use obscene words? Some people would say that it does not. They would say that although you have a right to say things like 'Down with the draft', you do not have the right to say 'Fuck the draft'. Dworkin implies that such views are implausible. He

---

[2] Ibid., chapter XII.   [3] See chapter 10.

thinks that the doctrine of equal respect implies that the dissenters must be allowed to use their rhetoric to match their sense of outrage:

It may be said that the anti-riot law leaves him (the dissenter) free to express these principles (of political morality that he holds most passionately) in a non-provocative way. But that misses the point of the connection between expression and dignity. A man cannot express himself freely when he cannot match his rhetoric to his outrage, or when he must trim his sails to protect values he counts as nothing next to those he is trying to vindicate. It is true that some political dissenters speak in ways that shock the majority, but it is arrogant of the majority to suppose that the orthodox methods of expression are the proper ways to speak, for this is a denial of equal concern and respect. If the point of the right is to protect the dignity of dissenters, then we must make judgments about the appropriate speech with the personalities of the dissenters in mind, not the personality of the 'silent' majority for whom the anti-riot law is no restraint at all.[4]

Now Dworkin's argument is too strong; it needs supplementation. If Dworkin's argument were valid then the following arguments would also be valid. People who eat their excrement may complain that their right to equal respect is being violated if they are not allowed to eat their excrement in public, while people who eat conventional food are allowed to indulge their tastes in public; the fact that they are allowed to eat their excrement in private does not give them equal status with people who have more conventional tastes. Again, nudists may complain that they are not allowed publicly to indulge in their way of life and so they are not being shown equal consideration compared to non-nudists. People who indulge in bestiality may complain that they are not given facilities for their way of life comparable to the facilities given to people with conventional ways of life. Homosexuals may complain that they are not allowed to marry, while heterosexuals are allowed to marry, and so their right to equal respect is being violated. And so forth.

A person who is asked to confine his way of life to a private or semi-private place (such as nudist beaches) may complain that such inferior treatment makes him feel ashamed of his form of life, when he sees people with more conventional forms of life being allowed to indulge their form of life in

[4] *Taking Rights Seriously*, p. 201.

public; and he may complain as Dworkin does on behalf of the Chicago dissenter, that he is being asked to 'trim his sails to protect values [such as public decency] he counts as nothing next to those he is trying to vindicate'.

So, unless one is willing to approve of Dworkin's argument in all such cases, one must reject it in its present form; it is too strong.

How, then, should we justify the fact that some liberties are more important than others? Now one criterion, as was pointed out earlier, is the social one. Some liberties, such as liberty of speech on political matters, freedom of association, liberty to vote, are more important for the working of a system of representative democracy than the liberty to eat one's excrement in public, or the liberty to make love to an animal. Why does Dworkin deny or play down the social criterion for the ranking of liberties? Probably the reason is that he thinks that a right is a right that an individual has against society and the government. It is of the essence of a right, according to Dworkin, that an individual's right must be respected even if it is not in the general interest to do so. Now Dworkin overstates his case. I think it is quite plausible to argue that some fundamental rights are set up for social reasons, though once they are set up an individual acquires such rights under the system, that the government must not take them away.[5] It is quite true that a right in a strong sense cannot be said to exist, if it can be withdrawn by the government at its pleasure. Rights that are at the mercy of the governments are not really any different from mere privileges; a fundamental right must be a right that the citizens have against the government in the sense that the government must respect it. But this is quite consistent with the view that the rationale of their possessing such a right is found by appealing to social good, more specifically by appealing to the values of a system of representative democracy where there are certain things that a government must not be allowed to do, such as taking away the citizen's right to vote.

But such social considerations do not provide the only criterion for ranking some liberties above others. We also

[5] See Haksar, 'The Nature of Rights'.

have to appeal to what is essential for individual dignity, well-being, and self-development.[6]

Do we have a right to choose our marriage partners? Do we have the right to choose schools for our children? Do we have the right to travel abroad? We cannot answer such questions without taking a stance on what constitutes a worthwhile life. Dworkin thinks that busing of school children does not infringe the right to equal respect. He would probably agree that a system of enforced sex designed to benefit the worst off would violate human dignity and rights; and he would probably agree that our treatment of criminals must respect their dignity; we must not, for instance, use them as guinea-pigs for medical experiments in a way which violates their dignity. But how can such views be defended without appealing to perfectionist considerations?

In the next section it is argued that the system of enforced sex designed to benefit the worst off, as well as other undesirable extensions of egalitarianism, can be avoided if we supplement egalitarianism with perfectionism.

I have maintained that there are two sorts of justification we can give for ranking some liberties higher than others, for saying that we have a right to some liberties but not to others: the social justification and the perfectionist justification. Sometimes the two justifications reinforce each other. For instance, freedom of speech may be thought desirable partly because it is necessary for human dignity, human well-being and self-expression, and partly because it is necessary for the prevention of tyranny and despotism and for the working of a system of representative democracy, for citizens have to make up their minds about whom to elect and whom to sack, and without free and open discussion they cannot perform such tasks rationally and wisely.

Of course the social justification may ultimately turn out to be an individual perfectionist justification also, for society's good is made up of the good of its individual members. Thus though some liberties are ranked higher than others, because they are essential for a system of representative democracy, we can raise the further question of what justifies such a

[6] See J. Hyman and W. J. Newhouse, 'Standards for Preferred Freedoms: Beyond the First', *Northwestern University Law Review*, lx (1965), 1–93.

system. To answer this last question adequately, we may have to contend that under a system of representative democracy, human beings flourish more, whereas under alternative systems such as hierarchical and paternalistic societies, individuals are warped and do not develop their potential, even though they may have been conditioned into accepting the system.

However, at a less ultimate level we can distinguish the social justification for ranking some liberties above others from the individual perfectionist justification. The former is less directly a perfectionist justification. Be that as it may, perfectionism provides at least one important criterion for ranking liberties.

There is a non-perfectionist device that Dworkin suggests for deriving a liberal set-up from egalitarian premises and for protecting individual human interests from being sacrificed by crude utilitarian considerations. He distinguishes personal preferences from external preferences and forbids external preferences from being used in our utilitarian calculations. A similar device was suggested by Barry earlier. It is instructive to see why Barry and Dworkin felt it necessary to resort to such a device.

Hare, like Rawls and Dworkin, but unlike me, implies that a liberal set-up can be derived from egalitarian premises, without resort to perfectionism. If my arguments in this book to show the need for appealing to perfectionist considerations are sound, it would follow that Hare and others are wrong on this important issue. Hare distinguishes the liberal from the fanatic.[7] According to Hare it is the fanatic who universalizes his ideals; the liberal is content to be neutral between different ideals, giving equal weight to everyone's ideals and interests. Now Barry pointed out that Hare's liberal-utilitarian position can be extremely illiberal.[8] Suppose homosexuals are in a small minority and suppose that the majority are disgusted by homosexuality and subscribe to the ideal that homosexuals should be behind bars. In that case giving equal weight to everyone's ideals might commit a utilitarian to permitting homosexuals to suffer in prison. In order to deal with such difficulties, Barry distinguishes privately oriented wants which have oneself or one's family as their object, from publicly

[7] *Freedom and Reason* Oxford, 1963), p. 178.
[8] Barry, *Political Argument,* pp. 295-6.

oriented wants, which have a larger group such as the nation or the class of homosexuals as their object. Barry suggests that publicly oriented wants should not count in making calculations about what ought to be done at the political level. The bigot's want that the homosexual should suffer is a publicly oriented want and hence should carry no weight.

More recently, Dworkin has suggested the distinction between personal preferences, which are preferences that a person has for his own enjoyment of some goods or opportunities, and external preferences, which are preferences for the assignment of goods and services to others.[9] Dworkin illustrates this distinction with an example. A white law student might approve of segregation because of a personal preference, for instance because such a policy improves his own chances of success, or because of an external preference, for instance because such a policy would keep blacks out and prevent races from mixing.

Dworkin realizes that in practice personal and external preferences are often inextricably mixed together, but he thinks that utilitarianism can only be made acceptable to an egalitarian if external preferences are excluded from the utilitarian calculations. He thinks that utilitarianism minus external preferences harmonizes with the doctrine of equal right to respect and leads to a liberal set-up.[10] If he is right about this, then there is no need to appeal to perfectionist considerations in order to derive a liberal set-up from egalitarian premises; utilitarianism minus external preferences can suffice. But in fact Dworkin's non-perfectionist device for deriving liberalism from egalitarianism does not work.

A democracy cannot, according to Dworkin, satisfactorily discriminate between personal and external references for the two are in practice inextricably linked. An actual vote in an election or referendum must be taken to represent an overall rather than a personal preference. So Dworkin points out that the concept of an individual political right, in the strong anti-utilitarian sense, is a response to the philosophical defects of a utilitarianism that counts external preferences and the practical impossibility of a utilitarianism that does not.[11] But

[9] R. Dworkin, *Taking Rights Seriously,* pp. 234 ff.
[10] Ibid., p. 236.   [11] Ibid., p. 277.

now Dworkin has to face the problem we mentioned earlier, that since there is no general right to liberty, why do we have the right to some liberties but not to others? Dworkin does not adopt the perfectionist solution that I advocate. His response to this problem is to appeal to the distinction between personal preferences and external preferences. We have according to Dworkin a right to certain liberties such as liberty of free expression and the liberty of choice in personal and sexual matters because the utilitarian argument to restrict such liberties is corrupted by the presence of external preferences, whereas there are other liberties, such as liberty of contract, where we do not have rights because the utilitarian argument for restricting these liberties is not corrupted by the presence of external preferences, for the utilitarian argument would be strong even without the presence of any external preferences.

But Dworkin appears to be involved in an inconsistency, for he says that we need the concept of a right (in the strong anti-utilitarian sense) because utilitarianism uncorrupted by external preferences cannot work in practice. Yet when he has to explain why we have a right to some liberties but not to others, he resorts to the very utilitarianism that elsewhere[12] he finds unworkable! Perhaps his point is that a satisfactory utilitarianism cannot operate via the system of popular democracy (via the system of voting at elections and in the legislatures), but that it can operate at another level; those who have to make judgements about the citizens' rights, such as judges and moral critics like Dworkin, have the time and discrimination to judge in particular cases whether or not the corresponding utilitarian arguments are sufficiently corrupted by the presence of external preferences. Thus, as we saw, Dworkin seems to claim that he can tell that the utilitarian argument for restricting liberty of contract is not sufficiently corrupted by the presence of external preferences, whereas the utilitarian argument against freedom of speech and against freedom of choice in sexual and personal relations is corrupted by the presence of external preferences. Again Dworkin thinks that the utilitarian argument in favour of segregation is corrupted by the presence of external preferences; therefore people

[12] Ibid.

have a right to non-segregated education

> The preference that might support any such argument are distinctly external, like the preference of the community at large for racial separation, or are inextricably combined with and dependent upon external preferences, like the associational preferences of white students for white classmates and white lawyers, for white colleagues[13]

Utilitarian arguments that justify a disadvantage to a group are always unfair according to Dworkin, unless it can be shown that they would justify the disadvantage in the absence of the prejudice against the group.

Dworkin rejects perfectionism as a political principle[14] and this explains why he insists that a group must not be put at a disadvantage because the group's way of life is considered inferior by others. Such preferences against a group's way of life constitute external preferences and they corrupt the utilitarian argument that tries to restrict the liberties of the despised group. The liberties must only be limited when the utilitarian argument for limiting them would be sufficient even without the external preferences.

But in fact perfectionism cannot be bypassed so easily. Utilitarian arguments in favour of a policy are not the only arguments to be taken into account. Even if Dworkin is correct in thinking that the utilitarian argument for a particular policy is corrupted by the presence of external preferences, it does not follow that the right-based argument for that view is rendered invalid. Thus even if the utilitarian argument for the existence of separate but equal education is corrupt because of the presence of external preference, may there not be a right-based argument for such segregation based on the right of free association? It may of course be that such a right to free association is less important than the right that people have for non-segregated education. But can such a hierarchy of rights be justified without appealing to perfectionist considerations?

Utilitarian arguments for limiting liberties or for not limiting liberties are not the only arguments to be taken into account. Indeed it is arguable that if a person has a right to x in a strong sense, then ordinary utilitarian considerations (even if they are purified by subtracting all external preferences)

---

[13] Ibid., p. 237.   [14] Ibid., p. 273, lines 1-5.

must not be allowed to deny the existence of such a right. If a woman has a right in a strong sense to choose her sexual partner, then no amount of utilitarian pleasures that others (including the worst off) get if they are allowed to have sex with her, must be allowed to deny her the choice of her sexual partner. The fact that the pleasures would be personal preferences, not corrupted by external preferences, would not make any difference. Utilitarianism, even minus external preferences, needs to be constrained by a doctrine of rights. In chapter 8 we saw that utilitarianism, unconstrained by a doctrine of rights, could sanction replacement policies. Not all such horrific consequences of utilitarianism can be avoided if we purify it by not counting external preferences. Again punishment of the innocent could be sanctioned by utilitarianism even if external preferences were not counted.

We have seen that Dworkin uses the following form of argument to establish the existence of a right: if the utilitarian argument for restricting a liberty such as freedom of speech or freedom in personal and sexual matters is corrupted by the presence of external preferences, then we have a right to such a liberty. But this form of argument is too strong. The utilitarian arguments for restricting the individual's liberties to make love to animals in public, or to eat his excrement in public, or to masturbate in public, are also corrupted by the presence of external preferences; people have contempt for such forms of life or at least for their public manifestations, which is why they want to ban them, at least in public. Yet it would be quite wrong to argue that individuals have a right to indulge in such practices in public because the utilitarian arguments for restricting such liberties are corrupted by the presence of external preferences. And it will not do to take the line that we have a right to eat our excrement in public or to masturbate in public but that such a right is overridden by considerations of decency and by utilitarian considerations such as the distress that would be caused to the prim spectators. For a right in the strong sense cannot, as Dworkin would rightly admit,[15] be overridden by considerations of mere decency or by ordinary utilitarian considerations.

So if we are to defend people's right to free speech or their

[15] Ibid., chapter VII.

right to the choice of their sexual partner, but deny them the right to make love to children (even in private) or the right to masturbate in public or the right to eat their excrement in public, will we not have to appeal to perfectionist considerations? Do we not have to take the line that a woman's liberty to choose her sexual partner is more essential to her well-being and dignity than her liberty to masturbate in public, which is why she has the right to the former liberty but not to the latter?

Dworkin allows the black man's right to non-segregated education to trump the white man's right to freedom of association. Presumably, Dworkin would not allow the right to equal treatment of the worst off among the sex starved to trump the women's right to choose their sexual partners. Can such views be justified without appealing to perfectionist considerations? His method of excluding external preferences from our utilitarian calculations may appear to explain why we should trump the white man's liberty of association, for the white man who does not want to associate with blacks is full of prejudice against black men and so his preference not to associate with black men is an external preference. But this argument is too strong. For the decision of women not to sleep with the worst off may also reflect their prejudice and contempt for the worst off. Yet it would be quite wrong to argue that the right of the worst off to equal treatment trumps the woman's right to choose her sexual partner. Do we not have to appeal to the idea that a woman's liberty to choose her sexual partner is essential for her well-being and dignity and so it constitutes a right in the strong sense?

Dworkin grants that when there are competing rights, such as right to free speech and right to security, then the relevant authorities may have to balance the competing rights.[16] But can such balancing always be done without appealing to perfectionist considerations? Dworkin, when discussing the Chicago demonstrations, argues that citizens have a right to use obscene words when that is necessary to match their rhetoric to their outrage, when they need to express their indignation. But he does not think that the timid old lady in Chicago whose peace and quiet is disturbed by the demon-

[16] Ibid.

strators is entitled to the degree of peace and quiet that would imply that her right to peace and quiet was disturbed by the Chicago demonstrators. But how can such alleged judgements of rights be fully justified without appealing to perfectionist considerations? The view that the demonstrators express their personality when they use obscene words whereas the old lady's need for peace and quiet is of a lower order of importance, seems to express a perfectionist judgement. Of couse free speech can often be justified by appealing to the argument that it is essential for the working of representative democracy. But the alleged right to use obscene language is not essential for the working of representative government.

2. Nozick's theory and perfectionism

There are some philosophers, such as Nozick, who have argued that we must not use the coercive apparatus of the state to enforce perfectionist ideals or to enforce paternalistic measures or to redistribute income and wealth from the rich to the poor. Thus, Nozick believes that the state should be confined to the narrow functions of enforcement of contracts, and protection against force, theft, and fraud. Anything more than such a minimal state is ruled out by Nozick on the grounds that it would violate individual rights. I shall in this section contrast my views with Nozick's.

Now Nozick derives his minimal state from his doctrine of rights and it is worth seeing briefly what his views on rights are. He believes, like I do, that rights set moral constraints, within which our policies must operate. But he and I differ about what specific rights we have and also about how absolute these rights are. In particular he stresses our right to property, and some 'negative' rights such as our right not to be killed and assaulted. But he seems to deny 'positive' rights, or social and economic rights (such as the right to food and medicine) that many people, including myself, believe human beings have in virtue of their humanity. Of course, a sceptic may well ask people like myself what reason do we have to believe that human beings have such social and economic rights. But similar sceptical doubts would be raised about the rights that Nozick believes in. What reason do we have to think that we have a right not to be killed and assaulted?

There is a problem regarding why our dealings with each other are limited by moral constraints. Nozick is rightly sympathetic to the approach according to which these constraints are based upon the fact that human beings can lead a meaningful or significant life.[17] But now it seems to me arbitrary to stress certain 'negative' rights, such as the right not to be assaulted and killed, and neglect more 'positive' rights, such as the right to food and medicine. For the latter are as essential for our leading a significant life as the former are.

Cranston gives greater prominence to what I have called 'negative' rights (such as the right not to be killed or assaulted, not to be interfered with) than to what I have called 'positive' rights (such as social and economic rights), on the grounds that the former, unlike the latter, are universal and practicable.[18] As for universality, Cranston is right in thinking that some of our negative rights are universal in the sense that they involve correlative duties for all human beings. My right not to be assaulted implies that all human beings should refrain from assaulting me, and this is unlike my right to food which does not imply that all human beings should provide me with food. A person's right to food may only impose a duty on some people such as his family or on the state to which he belongs. But Cranston is wrong in implying that rights that are universal, in the sense of being held against all human beings, should get more importance than rights that are only held against some individuals. Positive rights, such as right to food, can be universal in the sense that they are held by all human beings, even though it is the case that they are not universal in the sense that we referred to earlier. Cranston's second reason for giving greater prominence to 'negative' rights is that unlike the 'positive' (or social and economic) rights, they satisfy the test of being practicable. We can have laws forbidding murder, assault, and so forth but we may not have the resources to provide all human beings with food, health, and other necessities (but then do we have the

<hr/>

[17] See Nozick, *Anarchy, State and Utopia*, p. 50.
[18] M. Cranston, *Human Rights Today* (London, 1962).

resources to enforce all the laws against murder and assault?). It seems to me that even if it is true, as it is in poor countries, that the state cannot provide all of its citizens with the basic economic and social needs, the citizens can still have a right that the state should strive towards providing them with such essentials. Sometimes it may not be desirable to make such rights justiciable, that is to say enforceable through the courts, for the courts may not be experts in economic matters, they may not have the competence to decide whether the state is doing enough to secure such rights for its citizens. But it does not follow that such non-justiciable rights are less important than rights (such as right to free speech) which are enforceable through the courts.

The Irish constitution distinguishes between justiciable rights and non-justiciable rights. On the other hand the Indian Constitution distinguishes between justiciable rights and Directive Principles (which are non-justiciable). But it would be quite wrong to argue that the Directive Principles are less important than the justiciable rights. The reason why the Directive Principles were made non-justiciable was not that they were considered less important but that it was thought that the courts were not experts in deciding whether the state was doing enough to further the Directive Principles; such judgements were left to others such as the legislatures and the electorate, who could change the rulers at election time if they thought that the rulers were not doing enough to further the Directive Principles.

To come back to Nozick. In order to understand his views on rights, on why we have some rights and not others, we have to examine his views on ownership and entitlement. Nozick, like John Locke, attaches great importance to the right to property. Theft is wrong because it violates the owner's right to property. Like Locke, he even seems to derive the right to liberty from the right to property—we must not forcibly kill or interfere with a person because the person owns himself, including his body. Nozick thinks that we own our bodies, as well as the things that we acquired justly. We did not acquire our bodies, but perhaps first possession gives us ownership over our bodies, on Nozick's views. (But what of the parents who possess their child and its body from its birth? Do they own the child's body?)

Now as for the alleged positive rights, which are just as essential to lead a significant, meaningful life as the negative rights are, Nozick does not acknowledge them. Nozick does not think that our basic human needs automatically give us rights, for we must respect the rights and entitlements of other human beings, and if they justly own the food that we need, the state must not forcibly redistribute such food from those who have justly acquired it to those who need it. Forcible redistribution from the rich to the needy is ruled out by Nozick. Why, he asks, should the man who does extra work in order to go to a movie have his extra earnings taxed in order to provide for the needy, while the person who prefers to look at the sunset (and hence does not bother to earn extra money) is not taxed? One wonders what Nozick would say about the obligations of a father to pay for the medical expenses of his sick child from his extra earnings, assuming that there is no welfare state, as there would not be if Nozick had his way. Suppose the child falls ill after the father has earned the money to go to the movie but before he has spent it by going to the movie. Does the child have no claim on the father's extra earnings? Could the father deny such a claim by arguing that if he had chosen to enjoy the sunset instead of earning money to go to the movie he would have had no money to spend on the child's health and so he has a right not to spend money on his child's health even though he has the extra money?

If one admits that a child has a right to food, medicines, and so forth which its father must respect, it is difficult not to extend such family arguments to cover society as a whole, for our society too constitutes a kind of family. No doubt our family ties with other members of our society are weaker than our ties with our own children. This may be an argument for denying that I have an obligation to provide as much for a sick child in our society as I have for providing for my own child, other things being equal. But it is not a reason for denying that I have an obligation, that should be enforced through taxation, for providing for poor children in our society. Suppose there are a million poor families and a thousand rich ones. Even though a rich man has much greater obligation towards his own child than to any other single child in the society, it may well be that the total amount that he should be compelled to spend on the children of the poor is more than the total amount that he should be compelled to spend on his own child.

But I expect Nozick would be unmoved by such arguments, for he may not grant that a rich man should be compelled to provide even for his own child. For if the rich man allows his child to starve to death, he is not violating any property rights of his child.

If one believes as I do that our right not to be killed, assaulted, interfered with, and so forth derives from our right to life and the right to lead a significant life, then it is odd to deny that we have the right to things like food and medicine that are also needed in order to live properly. Perhaps Nozick's point is that our right not to be killed and assaulted is derived not from our right to lead a significant life but from the fact that we own our bodies and ourselves. If this is our reason, then such a reason does not automatically provide us with claim over the food that we need but which others own. For by not giving us food no one is denying the fact that we own ourselves or our bodies, and so such cases are very different from cases of assault or killing where our right to ownership of our body is being violated. So on Nozick's views if a child or an unemployed man starves to death in an affluent society no right of his need have been violated. But if the rich man, who acquired his riches justly, is taxed in order to save people from starving to death, then such taxation involves a violation of the rich man's property rights.

One of the things that Nozick neglects is that our right to property is not absolute but defeasible in the sense that it can sometimes be defeated by a stronger claim.[19] Earlier, in chapter 8, it was pointed our that perhaps some rights are absolute, but to admit this is not to admit that all rights are absolute. Our property rights to the money we have earned or inherited is a defeasible one, even though we have acquired the money justly. If this is so, there would be nothing strange if our right to property were to be defeated by someone's claim for the food that he needs; To say this does not commit me

[19] Feinberg, *Social Philosophy*, chapter V, section 3.

to the view that the poor man has a right to steal from the rich man. The view that there should be compulsory redistribution from the rich to the poor does not commit one to the view that the poor can take the law into their own hands.[20]

Some philosophers would prefer to use the term 'privileges' rather than 'rights' to cover what I have called defeasible rights; they may like to reserve the term 'rights' for more absolute rights. Such terminological points do not affect the substantial point that our alleged right to the property that we own is not an absolute one, even when the property has been justly acquired.

There is no need to accept Nozick's views about ownership and about the primary importance of property rights. His views are made to look more plausible because the alternative views, such as egalitarianism, unrestrained by considerations of ownership, appear to give strange results. Thus Nozick complains that an application of the principle of maximization of the interests of the worst off would lead to the compulsory redistribution of bodily parts. And there are other apparent difficulties facing an egalitarian position that a Nozickian could revel in. Consider the following suggestion. Why not have a system of making it obligatory for women to sleep with the worst off men who cannot 'get' women in the 'free market'? Is it because the men who would be provided with women under such a system are being treated passively, as objects rather than as agents who go and win the favour of women? Surely this reason is not decisive. Compare the case of those who are starving in our society for lack of food. Are we not willing to redistribute food to the needy? How much better for their morale if the starving could earn their living for themselves; but if they cannot, is it not better to give them food rather than let them starve? Similarly, if a person is sex starved, is it not better for him to be 'given' a woman rather than let him remain sex starved, assuming that he cannot make it in the 'free market' of love! To see what if anything is really wrong with such a system, we should have to look at things from the point of view of the women who are being used to make the worst off men better. Nozick would say that women own their bodies and so any such compulsory scheme would violate their property rights. Later in this chapter it will be argued that we can reject such practices without appealing to Nozick's views about ownership. If this is so, one motive for believing in Nozick's views will disappear. Take another example which provides a problem for egalitarianism. If we are willing to use compulsory measures in schools, such as busing of school children and abolition of privileged schools, out of deference to the doctrine of equal right to respect and consideration, why not abolish or drastically alter the family, if and when it is a source of considerable inequalities in our society? Why not have a system of communes where there is a greater equality of opportunity? Or why not have a system where children of rich families are forced to spend some part of their childhood with less well off families? Is it that we own our children and therefore they cannot forcibly be taken away from us, or that the children own themselves and therefore they must decide with which family they want to live? We must be able to deal with such cases without appealing to such weird ideas of ownership.

In order to see what, if anything, is wrong with extending egalitarianism into such areas we shall have to appeal to certain perfectionist ideas of what constitutes human well-being and human dignity. We shall have to take a stand on whether human beings flourish more in a system of the family as we know it now, or under some alternative system. Rawls defends our family system by appealing to the advantages to the worst off; he appeals to the difference principle and claims that the advantages of the family stystem trickle down to the worst off.[21] But here once again he is using an argument from general facts, which elsewhere he rightly centures utilitarians for using.[22] It seems to me that we are still left with the problem of why we should not abolish the family if the worst off are better off in terms of primary goods under some alternative system. A system of arranged marriages may increase the national income, for instance because the people, under such a system, lead more stable lives and do not waste their time in pursuit of girl friends. If they have been suitably conditioned

[21] *A Theory of Justice*, pp. 301 and 511–12.
[22] Ibid., p. 120.

since birth, they may not rebel against such a system and they may not resent the use of compulsion. And the economic advantages of such a form of life may trickle down to the worst off. One may still want to reject such a form of life on perfectionist grounds because we think that such a form of life is degrading.

Again, in order to decide whether we should have communal living and abolish the individual family, we should not go merely by the effects of income and other primary goods; we may also have to take a stand on whether human beings flourish more under a communal family set-up or under an individualistic set-up.

Rawls may appeal to the value of autonomy or integrity in order to show what is wrong with some of the suggested extensions of egalitarianism, that I have just discussed. But for reasons given earlier in chapters 10 and 11, the view that an autonomous life is a constituent of human well-being cannot be defended without appealing to perfectionist considerations. Why should making a woman sleep with a man against her will, even for a couple of hours, destroy her integrity, while pulling down her house in order to make room for a hospital or a school (which Rawls would allow) does not? Can this be shown without appealing to perfectionist ideas? Some people would object to undesirable extensions of egalitarianism by appealing to the value of liberty, but such objections would have to be supplemented by perfectionist considerations. We do often constrain a person's liberty, when the exercise of that liberty conflicts with other people's rights or basic needs. So there still remains the problem that if we are willing to do this, why should we not, in order to satisfy a man's need for sex, trump a woman's liberty to choose her sexual partner? As was suggested in the last section such conflicts cannot be resolved without appealing to perfectionist considerations. We could construct a system of rotation where a woman had to spend only a small part of her life, say a couple of days, with the sex starved. If the law applied to all women of the relevant age group, no woman need spend a large part of her life against her will with a man. We could also have a law making it compulsory for men to be available for the sex starved women, so as to avoid the charge of being biased towards the male population. We could also minimize the risk of psychological damage, including damage to the self-respect of the participants, by suitable upbringing, and by the use of tranquillizers and pills that minimize such damage. In any case in some cases we are willing to approve of compulsion even if there is risk of pyschological damage. We sometimes pull down an old woman's house in order to build a hospital or a school for the needy, we sometimes, by taxation, take away a rich man's luxuries to which he may be attached, we allow people to drive cars even though in some cases pedestrians, some of whom never consented to the system of driving cars, get hurt. Sometimes such practices too can cause psychological damage. Old women sometimes go mad when they are forcibly moved out of their old houses, the rich sometimes suffer enormously when their luxuries are taken away, and the pedestrian who gets hurt by a car can suffer psychological damage. So the mere risk of psychological damage cannot tell us what is particularly adhorrent about the practice of making women sleep with the worst off. To rule out such a practice we shall have to appeal to the view that such a practice is inherently degrading.

What the foregoing discussion is supposed to show is that egalitarianism, when supplemented by considerations of perfectionism, can deal with certain problems that would arise for a non-perfectionist egalitarianism. Since perfectionism can come to the aid of egalitarianism, there is no need to abandon egalitarianism and embrace Nozick's positive views.

Let us now come back to the example of compulsory redistribution of bodily parts, from the well endowed to the worst off. Nozick would rule out such forcible redistribution because he would argue that people own their bodily parts. Even our surplus blood must not forcibly be taken away from us, however much others need it and however little we need it. Now it seems to me that even if we do own our bodily parts, it is arguable that our right to ownership is defeasible, in the sense that it can be defeated by a stronger claim.

It is true that in the case of bodily parts such as kidneys and eyes many people will think there is something terrible about a system of compulsory redistribution. But even if this intuition is a sound one, it does not necessarily point to the truth of Nozick's theory of ownership. One could argue instead that our body is very intimately connected with ourselves, it is, as it were, the embodiment of our mind and soul. This view does not necessarily imply that we own our body; yet some such view could perhaps be used as a partial check against an extension of egalitarianism into redistribution of bodily parts. As Hegel observed,

it is therefore only abstract sophistical reasoning which can so distinguish body and soul as to hold that the 'thing in itself', the soul, as not touched or attacked if the body is maltreated . . . To be free from the point of view of others is identical with being free in my determinate existence. If another does violence to my body, he does violence to me . . . This creates the distinction between personal injury and damage to my external property, for in such property my will is not actually present in this direct fashion.[23]

When my house is taken away, I may feel hurt, but the connection in general between myself and my body is much more intimate than between myself and my property, even though in particular cases I may be more distressed if my property is taken away, than if, say, my blood is taken away. Some such considerations may be used as a basis for arguing that normally it is not arbitrary to apply egalitarianism with much more vigour in the case of property redistribution than in the case of bodily parts.

One of the standard objections made against egalitarianism is that it conflicts with freedom or liberty. Indeed it has been argued by Nozick that any theory that involves our distributing income and wealth in accordance with some abstract principle, such as 'To each according to his need', is incompatible with liberty. For liberty upsets patterns of distribution. For suppose we start from a pattern of distribution that is just according to some abstract principle, such as 'To each according to his need.' Now if we introduce liberty, then this distribution is liable to get upset by gifts, inheritance, exchanges, and so forth. People with talents may make contracts with their admirers, displaying their talents in exchange for money. A person may give a gift to another. As a result of such free activities the initial pattern of distribution may get upset. Are we then to forbid such free dealings and gifts between people? The children of clever parents have an advantage over

[23] Hegel, *Philosophy of Right*, transl. T. H. Knox, section 48.

the children of the stupid, so should the family be abolished? The friends of the talented get advantages that are denied to the friends of dull people, so should the institution of friendship be abolished whenever the advantages of the institution do not trickle down to the worst off? One can ask hundreds of such questions.

Now egalitarianism when supplemented with perfectionist considerations can defend itself against such objections. Thus one might think that if the family as we know it now is essential for the well-being and flourishing of members of our society, then it may be worthwhile to put up with inequalities that are inherent in the family system. But one need not put up with more inequalities than are necessary. For instance, even if the family is essential for human flourishing, the freedom to bequeath all of one's inheritance may not be essential to the survival of the family. The family system (including many of its desirable features) could survive heavy taxes on transfer of wealth from one member of the family to another. Hayek thinks that a family's function of passing on standards and traditions and culture to its offspring is closely tied with the possibility of transmitting material goods.[24] I admit that some cultures (such as those that involve living in castles) can only be transmitted if one is allowed to transmit the bulk of one's wealth to one's offspring. But there are plenty of other cultures, which can be transmitted more economically, and we could allow some traditions to die out if the social cost of maintaining them is too great. Moreover, while in the case of many traditions it is true that if one's offspring do not have similar amounts of wealth they cannot carry on the old traditions in the old fashion, yet some of these traditions could survive in a modified form. Transmission of culture and tradition from one generation to another is a good thing, but there is no obvious harm if such traditions are gradually modified and adapted to changing conditions.

In fact the family system and its desirable features could survive heavy taxes on transfers of wealth between parents and their offspring. But I admit that there are some inequalities that are inherent in the family system, and they could only be got rid of if we abolished the family system, a price that

[24] *Constitution of Liberty* (Chicago, 1960), chapter 6, section 4.

would not be worth paying. The same applies to the institution of friendship. There are some advantages that friends confer on one another (such as the advantages of intelligent conversation and of loyalty) that could only be abolished if we abolished the whole institution of friendship, but there are other contingent inequalities that could be minimized by a system of taxation—thus bequests to friends could be taxed.

As for freedom to make agreements and contracts, this too is an institution that contributes to human well-being. You and I may both be better off as a result of exchanges, contracts, and so forth. And it certainly would be a great loss to abolish such an institution. But it does not follow that the desirable features of such an institution would be lost if we taxed those who gained through such exchanges. If taxes were raised beyond a certain point, it might well happen that we would not find it worthwhile to display our talents to our admirers for money, and as a result all the parties concerned might be worse off than they would have been if there were no taxes. But this is no argument for not taxing such activities at all. Again the system of gifts is a desirable institution. What a wonderful thing giving is, it enriches (at least spiritually!) even the giver. But this institution would not necessarily be destroyed if the recipients were taxed to some extent.

So it is true that in order to allow people to flourish through institutions such as the family, friendship, contract, and gifts, we must allow egalitarian patterns of distribution to be upset to some extent. It does not follow that we should embrace Nozick's view and abandon egalitarian redistribution altogether.

We need to remind ourselves that there is no right (in the strong sense) to liberty as such, but only the right to specific liberties that are essential for our well-being and our dignity and self-respect, or that are essential for the working of representative democracy. If we forget this we are likely to be more impressed by the conflict between equality and liberty than we need to be.

There is, however, a danger that an overzealous implementation of egalitarian ideals can lead to state tyranny, for the state that is responsible for redistribution may become too powerful and abuse its power. But here the conflict is not between the doctrine of equal respect and some other values such as liberty. The doctrine of equal respect itself would imply that where there is a danger of such tyrany, we must proceed cautiously. For such tyrany would go against the doctrine that urges us to respect persons.

The doctrine of equality of respect consists of two parts. Firstly, it urges us to respect persons and secondly it tells us that each person is in virtue of his nature equally worthy of respect. In chapter 9 we saw that 'equality' was not otiose in the phrase 'equality of respect'. It is equally important to stress that 'respect' is not otiose. Critics who claim that egalitarianism would sanction beauracratic tyranny or the torture of all the citizens provided everyone suffers equally, forget that such inhuman practices would violate the principle of respect for persons. Compare: Your hating all your children equally would violate the principle 'Love all your children equally'.

14

Perfectionism and Toleration

In the first section of this concluding chapter, the perfectionist approach (which has been adopted in this book) is defended against possible misunderstandings and criticisms. In the second section the view that there should be toleration without equal liberties for all forms of life is defended and shown to be in harmony with the liberal-egalitarian doctrine.

1. Some misunderstandings of perfectionism

In this book an attempt has been made to combine a perfectionist approach with a right-based one. Now it might be objected that this attempt is bound to fail for the perfectionist approach is inherently a consequentialist or utilitarian one. Thus if your grounds for respecting a person's rights are found in certain wonderful qualities or wonderful potential that he possesses, then how can you show that his rights should never be trumped by the rights of another person who also possesses an equally wonderful potential? And if you do allow such balancing between one person's rights and another person's rights, then does this balancing not commit you to a consequentialist position?

This objection can be answered by pointing out that the answer to the last question is No. Not all balancing is utilitarian or consequentialist balancing. There are thinkers such as Ross, Hart, and Ronald Dworkin who allow balancing even though they adopt a non-consequentialist approach. And they are quite consistent. The view that an individual's rights can be trumped by another person's rights does not commit one to the utilitarian view which allows mere social utility to trump individual rights. One could illustrate the difference between the right-based approach and the utilitarian approach by pointing out that the latter approach, unlike the former, allows the production of greater utility through the adoption of replacement policies (which destroy some existing individuals, especially of some of the young ones (see chapter 8).

But if you value individual persons because of their wonderful potential then why not replace some existing persons by the creation of new persons who also have the wonderful potential and who are more likely to realize their potential than the ones we destroy? Such objections against the attempt to combine perfectionism with the right-based approach appear more powerful than they are because of an ambiguity. The perfectionist view that a person is valuable because of his wonderful potential can be interpreted in two different ways. First, it may be used in the sense which implies that a person is only valued as a means to the realization of the wonderful potential. Or secondly, it may be taken to imply that a person's wonderful potential (which he can develop without destroying his identity) is evidence of his being sacred and inherently valuable, of his being an end and not a mere means. The right-based approach uses the perfectionist view in this second sense. Compare: suppose you regard persons as sacred because they are children of God; this will not excuse your killing your child and replacing him by the production of new children, even though the new ones will also be children of God. The view that a human being is sacred because he is a child of God does not imply that he is a mere means to the maximizing of the population of the children of God.

If a person on my account were valued merely as a means to the realization of his potential, then I would not have stressed (see chapter 5) that what is essential to his being sacred is that the person should be able to realize his potential without destroying his identity.

Now it might be objected that even if one can succeed in combining perfectionism with a right-based approach, yet surely one cannot successfully combine perfectionism with the special version of the right-based doctrine that I have constructed, namely, the egalitarian version. For does the doctrine of perfectionism not go naturally with a non-egalitarian approach, such as that of Nietzsche? What are we to make of such objections?

Now it is true that perfectionism even in its moderate version (that is to say, version 2 mentioned on p. 1 of the Introduction) is sometimes thought to be inconsistent with the doctrine of equal respect and concern. Thus Dworkin believes that the liberal conception of equality is incompatible with the government treating some forms of life as inherently more valuable than others.[1] I disagree with Dworkin. Although the view that some human beings have greater intrinsic worth than others is incompatible with the doctrine of equal respect and consideration, the view that some forms of life (such as the pursuit of truth and beauty) are intrinsically superior to other forms of life (such as a life devoted to the eating of one's excrement), and that the government should take such differences of worth into account, is compatible with the doctrine of equal respect and consideration. Those who believe in the first view normally believe in the second view, but the converse is not true. One can quite consistently believe that some forms of human life are inherently superior to other forms of human life, without believing that the person who practises the latter form of life has inferior worth or deserves less (intrinsic) consideration than the former.

But does not the liberal doctrine of equality commit the state to seeing things from the point of view of the individuals concerned, and how can the state do this, if it treats some forms of life as inherently more worthy than others? Will not such perfectionism commit the state when dealing with an individual to using its own conception of the good instead of the agent's conception of the good, thus undermining the whole basis of liberalism? I think such objections are based on a confusion. The view that some forms of life are inherently superior to others, and that political principles should take this into account, does not commit one to a policy of paternalism with regard to those who practise the inferior forms of life. We can give inferior status to the way of life of the person who goes in for bestiality or smoking or for eating his excrement, not because we think that by doing so we shall force

[1] R. Dworkin, *Taking Rights Seriously*, pp. 272–3.

him to be better but, for instance, in order to provide a decent and morally healthy environment for the coming generation or even for the adult members of society who want to protect themselves from the temptations of the inferior forms of life (see chapter 12). Of course if and when the state's rationale for regarding some forms of life as inferior is that it regards as inferior those who practice such forms of life, then such a state would be violating the egalitarian doctrine.

Now in a sense the person who is practising the inferior form of life will get a worse deal under the scheme that I am suggesting than the person who practises better forms of life. But this does not go against the fundamental equality of respect owed to all human beings, any more than does the view that a kidney machine should be given to a young man rather than to a senile old man (see chapter 9). Later on in this chapter it is argued that the doctine of toleration and unequal liberties is in harmony with the egalitarian approach.

Of course there may be considerable disagreement over perfectionist judgements, about whether for instance human beings flourish more under a system of individual families or communal families, whether enforced sex to benefit the worst off is degrading. But this does not undermine the point that egalitarianism needs to be supplemented by perfectionist considerations, which include considerations about human well-being, human dignity, etc. The existence of disagreement among human beings over perfectionist values does, however, seem to create a problem about whose judgement regarding such values should carry the day.

But such problems are not peculiar to perfectionist theories. Even if one takes a purely want-regarding line, there is the problem about who has the authority to impose the recommended policy, and about whose views should carry the day on what the want-regarding approach implies in practice. Even if one takes a non-perfectionist approach like that of B. F. Skinner, who wants to jettison all ideas of autonomy and dignity and concentrate on scientific means of making human beings conform to desirable goals, there is still the problem about whose views about what ought to be done should carry the day. Skinner is sometimes accused of being dictatorial, of trying to impose his own solution of behaviour conditioning on an unwilling population. He can reply to such accusations by making a distinction between recommending a policy that should be adopted by legislators and dictatorially imposing a policy. He could admit that he has no right, no authority, to impose his views by dictatorial means, but this does not prevent his views from being correct and from being deserving of implementation by the state through democratic channels.

Similarly, the person who believes in perfectionism as a political principle is not committed to being a dictator. The view that bestiality is degrading and should be given an inferior status compared to conventional sexual practices, does not commit one to abolishing liberal democracy and becoming a dictator. One could, as a good democrat, try to convince the democratically elected legislators of the correctness of one's views. Elsewhere I have argued that the failure to appreciate such points has led to the spurious paradox of democracy.[2]

Some philosophers are so obsessed with avoiding disagreement that they urge us to adopt some kind of negative utilitarianism as our main political principle. On this view the state should not try to promote positive goals such as happiness about which people disagree, for even among people who pursue happiness, individuals pursue different things under the name of happiness, and doctrines such as that of the greatest happiness of the greatest number give an illusory and spurious unity to people's diverse goals; instead the state should concentrate on reducing evils that are generally regarded as evils. Thus negative utilitarians stress that there is general agreement that suffering is an evil and so the state should be encouraged to reduce suffering among its citizens.

But even negative utilitarianism gives only the illusion of getting general agreement. Even in the case of reduction of suffering there is enormous disagreement about what compulsory methods of reducing suffering are legitimate (is it for instance legitimate to kill some innocent people if there is a net reduction of suffering?) and how much weight to attach to the reduction of suffering compared to other legitimate goals. Moreover, as R. N. Smart has pointed out, negative utilitarianism would imply that we should approve of a tyrannical and benevolent person who blows up the world as a means

2 See Haksar, 'The Alleged Paradox of Democracy'.

to preventing infinite future misery. Bernard Gert believes that his own negative approach can avoid such pitfalls. He suggests that there are other evils besides suffering; for instance, he stresses, death is generally regarded as an evil. But I do not see how this helps. By blowing up the world we could abolish death! Admittedly, if we take a contractarian approach, then we could argue that the contractarian parties would not like to be killed themselves in order to abolish deaths in the future. But then we have seen in chapter 2 the limitation of the contractarian approach; for instance, we saw that it cannot deal with the problem of people in weak bargaining positions, such as future generations, children, and weak foreigners.

It might be thought that both perfectionism and non-perfectionist utilitarianism of the kind that Skinner recommends get us involved in controversial judgements about what values the state should promote and about the most effective means of promoting them. For people disagree a lot about the good. And it might be suggested that the way to keep the state neutral and above controversies is to adopt something like Nozick's minimal state. But it seems to me that even then there will be much controversy regarding what all the state is entitled to do. Nozick points out that the state must not violate the individual's rights. But it seems to me that there can be much disagreement about what rights individuals have. For instance, there can be much disagreement about whether or not your property was legitimately acquired and consequently there will be disagreement about whether you have rights over your property. Even with regard to your bodily parts, there can be dispute about whether you have an absolute right. Thus it may be objected that you have fattened as a result of exploiting poor people in the past, and so the healthy blood, kidneys, and so forth that you have are not wholly owned by you. And, as we saw earlier, there can be dispute about whether property rights are absolute or defeasible and whether human beings have a right to food, medicine, and so forth that can sometimes trump other people's property rights. Again, there can be dispute about whether or not the minimal state should respect animal 'rights', the 'rights' of foetuses, of infants, and so forth. So how can we keep clear of controversies and disagreement?

So the argument that perfectionism should be ruled out as a political principle because it involves the use of controversial, non-neutral principles is too strong.

Often we do make judgements to the effect that some forms of life (such as bestiality) are inherently less desirable than other forms of life. Even Rawls admits that comparisons of intrinsic value can be made and that the ends of some people have more intrinsic value than the ends of others.[3] But he complains that people disagree so much about the application of the perfectionist standard.[4] But how does he get from this to the conclusion that perfectionism should not be allowed as a political principle[5] or to the conclusion that it should never be allowed to override any of the contractarian considerations? There can also be much disagreement about what is required by the contractarian model.[6] Whether they ought to or not, many people will disagree with Rawls, as I do, about how to construct the model, about what principles follow from it, about their priorities and about their application. Rawls himself admits that the infractions of his difference principle are difficult to ascertain.[7] Why then should the perfectionist principle be rejected as a political principle, while the difference principle is accepted? In any case, it is important to realize that the extent to which a principle commands general acceptance is only one of the determinants of how good and important the principle is as a moral and political principle.

2. Toleration without equal liberties

Rawls thinks that the contractarian parties would rule out perfectionism as a political principle, for since they have disparate goals and aims they cannot be expected to agree on which of these goals should be ranked higher and which lower. Their concern for their integrity would not allow any of them to consent to anything less than equal liberties. Rawls believes that it would be wrong for the parties to take a gamble and opt for unequal liberties in the hope that their own religions and moral views come out on top. To take such gambles may show an irresponsibility towards one's religious and moral

[3] *A Theory of Justice*, p. 328.   [4] Ibid., p. 331.
[5] Ibid., p. 329.   [6] Cf. ibid., p. 147.   [7] Ibid., p. 372.

interests, for if we lose the gamble, such views will not fare too well. Moreover, how would one justify such gambles to ones's descendants? Suppose our descendants belong to the religion that has been given inferior status, will not our decision to gamble in the original position appear grossly irresponsible to them? Even if they can break the law, they may have to put up with the humiliation of being given inferior status, unless they have been suitably conditioned and reconciled to their inferior status.

Such Rawlsian arguments at best show that it is irrational for the parties in the original position to gamble with religious and moral liberties; but suppose the parties opt for unequal liberties, not because of a gamble but for better reasons. For instance, because they believe that some forms of life are better than others, that the worship of false gods needs to be discouraged because it impoverishes and alienates the individual. If that is their reason for opting for unequal liberties, there is nothing for them to be ashamed of, and they could attempt to justify their decision to their descendants. Compare: a person in the original position may opt for a system that permits life imprisonment for murderers, even though there is a chance that he or his descendants may turn out to be a murderer; or again he may opt for a system that bans the use of LSD even though it may turn out that when the veil of ignorance is removed, he or his descendant may long for LSD.

It has been argued in this book that perfectionism is presupposed by egalitarianism, and also that perfectionist judgements are required if we are to derive a liberal society from egalitarian premises. If this argument is sound, it is absurd for an egalitarian liberal to ban the admission of perfectionist considerations into his theory of justice. And once one admits perfectionist considerations it is difficult to see what is wrong with giving some forms of life (such as a life devoted to bestiality and the eating of one's excrement) lower status than other forms of life.

It is true that the doctrine of equal respect and consideration gives equal intrinsic weight to every human being's interests. But a person's interest has to be understood dynamically by seeing what is in his interest taking his life as a whole and not just by seeing what is in his interest at a particular stage in his life. And the doctrine of equal respect commits us to balancing his rights against the rights of other individuals, such as children who need a morally healthy environment and adults who want to protect themselves from their own weaknesses (see chapter 12); an acceptance of a right-based account is consistent with the view that rights have to be balanced against other rights, though it is not consistent with the view that rights can be sacrificed for ordinary utilitarian reasons.[8]

Admittedly, an individual, especially an autonomous individual, might find that at some stage in his life he wants to embrace a form of life that under a system of unequal liberties gets only inferior status. An autonomous individual may be a Christian this year, but next year he may want to become a Zen Buddhist and the year after he may want to become, say, an atheist. So it might be suggested that an autonomous individual would need to keep his options open and would prefer to live in a system of equal liberties rather than in a system of unequal liberties where he may find himself practising a form of life that is given only inferior status. Some such argument for equal liberties is found in the writings of Rawls and T. Scanlon. What are we to make of this argument?

Now such considerations have to be balanced against other considerations. When we are looking at an individual's interests we must, as I have stressed, go by what is in his interest taking his life as a whole, and not just by concentrating only on some stage of his life, such as his life after he has become an adult. Now if we take an individual who is just born and if we admit that some forms of life are inherently superior to others, then it seems that it could be in the interest of this person to be brought up in a society where inferior forms of life such as bestiality and smoking cigarettes are given inferior status and are discouraged, but tolerated in private, rather than to be brought up in a society where there is a greater chance of his getting 'hooked' on such inferior forms of life. For the better forms of life are like a tender plant that need cultivation.

What I would suggest is a system of toleration but not of equal liberties for different forms of life. This suggestion tries to get, as far as possible, the best of both worlds. Admittedly,

[8] See Dworkin, *Taking Rights Seriously,* chapter VII.

an individual taken at random may get 'hooked' on an inferior form of life, such as bestiality, and so if we have his interests in mind, we must tolerate his way of life. Yet we must also help individuals to try to avoid the inferior forms of life and encourage them to go in for one of the non-inferior forms of life, and this may be better done in a system of unequal liberties where the inferior forms of life are given lower status than in a system of equal liberties. So under the compromise I am suggesting, the state, by giving lower status to inferior forms of life, should discourage people from embracing such forms of life, but also it should tolerate those who have embraced such forms of life.

My suggestion of unequal liberties with toleration is quite compatible with respect for an individual's autonomy. An individual in order to exercise his autonomy does not have to live in a society where all major options are equally encouraged or discouraged. An individual does not lose his autonomy because the legal system forbids murder and theft. And there is no reason why he should lose his autonomy if, say, bestiality is given lower status than conventional sexual practices. Moreover, the fact that some forms of life are to be given inferior status is consistent with having equal liberties between the non-inferior forms of life; so there can be plenty of scope for people to exercise their autonomy in choosing their way of life.

I have commended unequal liberties only in the sense which would imply that some forms of life would get lower status than others. This view does not imply that human beings who practise such forms of life should be regarded as inferior; it does not imply that such people should have any less of the worthwhile liberties such as the liberty to vote or freedom of discussion. It is important to stress that a system which gives some forms of life lower status than others is quite consistent with people being allowed full liberty to discuss and criticize and try to change the ranking between different forms of life. In extreme situations they may even be justified in using disobedience as a means of getting greater recognition for their form of life and altering the majority's moral perceptions.[9] So there is plenty of scope for exercising one's autonomy

---

[9] See Haksar, 'Rawls and Gandhi on Civil Disobedience', *Inquiry*, xix (1976), 151-92.

under such a system. People are engaged in a constant debate about not only the correct application of political principles but even about their very foundations. The debate is not just at the theoretical level; discussion, debates, protests, disobedience, are all parts of the process by which people sometimes cajole and haggle with each other, and sometimes even convert others to their point of view, or themselves get converted to another point of view.

One of the fears that some liberals such as Rawls have in admitting perfectionist considerations into political arguments is that they fear that this will lead to the banning of degrading forms of life, even in private, 'if only for the sake of the individuals in question irrespective of their wishes'.[10] But my view is that if perfectionism is combined with egalitarianism it will not imply that people who practise degrading forms of life in private should be punished. The doctrine of transitivity of ends in themselves ensures that people are not expelled from the egalitarian club merely because they happen to practise inferior forms of life. Earlier in chapter 9, it was pointed out that even murderers are not expelled from the egalitarian club. Now if individuals who practise inferior, degrading forms of life are not expelled from the egalitarian club, then their interests must be given equal intrinsic weight to the interests of other people. So an individual's well-being must not be sacrificed lightly, even though he is practising degrading forms of life. Of course, sometimes, as in the case of paedophiles, we may prevent them practising their form of life even in private; for their form of life involves violating the rights of children—the example of paedophilia again shows the importance of perfectionist considerations, for we have to appeal to such considerations when we maintain that an adult person who makes love to a child violates the child's right or his dignity. But when a person is indulging in his degrading form of life in private, without violating anyone else's rights, then it seems we should tolerate him rather than punish him.

It might be objected that a perfectionist approach would tend to encourage the state to be intolerant towards those who practise degrading forms of life, because on the perfectionist view a person's good and his well-being is understood in terms

[10] Rawls, *A Theory of Justice*, p. 331.

of some objective Good rather than in terms of the form of life that the agent may have got 'hooked' on. So should the perfectionist state not try to forcibly liberate him, for his own good, from his inferior form of life? One way of answering this objection would be to contend that there is value in the free choice of a way of life. As Mill said, a person's 'own mode of laying out his existence is the best, not because it is the best in itself, but because it is his own mode'.[11] The great value that Mill places on an adult autonomously choosing his own form of life could be quite consistent with some forms of life being intrinsically superior to others. It is quite consistent to say that, other things being equal, a form of life A is superior to a form of life B, but if other things are not the same, if for instance a person has autonomously chosen form of life B, then this situation is preferable to the situation where the form of life A is imposed on him. There is the complication that Mill at times implied that people would not autonomously choose the lower form of life. Indeed, part of his criterion for saying that some forms of life are superior to others was that if people had a free or autonomous choice between the superior and the inferior form of life, they would choose the former. If this is so, then the choice of inferior forms of life must be a non-autonomous choice. So might the state not be justified in liberating such people (for their own good) by force?

There are several reasons for saying that the answer to the above question is No. First, as we have seen, forms of life are like a tender plant that needs cultivation in the early stages. If the better forms of life have not been properly cultivated in the early stages of a person's life, then it is likely that the person's potential for such forms of life is destroyed. If Mill is right in this, it would follow that it is dangerous to try to forcibly alter an adult person's form of life in the hope that he may after all still be able to pursue the higher forms of life. Why forcibly destroy his inferior form of life, if he is no longer capable of leading the higher form of life? True, had he been brought up in a proper environment, perhaps he would never have got addicted to the inferior form of life; but once an adult person has embraced an inferior form of

[11] *On Liberty*, chapter III, para. 14.

life he is likely to be miserable if he is forcibly prevented, for instance by threats of punishment, from indulging in his form of life. As for brainwashing him, it is *possible* that, as techniques of brainwashing improve, the person brainwashed may be less miserable at the end of the brainwashing than when he was indulging in his own mode of existence. But brainwashing of adults for their own good without their consent raises several dangers and problems.

Secondly, one can point out that even if the adult person who leads an inferior form of life did not autonomously choose his way of life, but has followed it, for instance, because it was the only real option in the social circles where he was brought up, it does not follow that his present judgement about his own good is worse than the judgement of the state about his good. The man who, through getting addicted to an inferior form of life, has lost his wonderful potential, does not necessarily lose his ability to judge what is now good for him. It is true that in some cases of addiction, such as addiction to hard drugs, a person's powers of judgement about his good is seriously impaired, but in the case of many other inferior forms of life, such as bestiality, it is not obvious why this should be so. In general, as Mill pointed out, the state has less interest in an adult individual's welfare than he does himself and is likely in general to make less competent judgements about which form of life is suited to him. And there is the danger that the state could abuse its powers if it was allowed to liberate people for their own good.

Finally, even when more good than harm were to come from the state trying to forcibly liberate its citizens, there is the problem (at any rate for non-utilitarians) that the state may not have the right to interfere with the adult individual for his own good.

There are also utilitarian arguments for toleration, such as those found in Mill, *On Liberty*. Thus Mill points out how society could gain by tolerating and sometimes even encouraging unconventional experiments in living. Some, though not most, of the experiments in living way well get adopted by others and be an improvement on customary practices. Moreover, even the people who continue to hold to established practices will be better off if they can choose their form of life in preference to the alternative experiments in living, rather than if they just followed the customary practices mechanically without any *new* challenges from alternative life styles.

It might be suggested that on a right-based account such utilitarian advantages are a desirable and important by-product of toleration, but they are not the main justification for toleration. The main reason for tolerating such forms of life is to be found by appealing to the right to respect and consideration of individuals who practise such forms of life.

However, there is the point that the good utilitarian effects of toleration can help to show that such toleration does not harm the rights of the coming generation. And this can be important on a right-based view; for on such a view an individual's right can be trumped by a competing stronger right of another individual And so some people might argue against tolerating inferior forms of life even in private on the grounds that such toleration could lead to the violation of the right of the young to grow up in a morally healthy environment. A society that bans such forms of life even in private might, by deterring individuals from practising such forms of life, reduce their incidence, and this could (so the argument runs) lead to a morally healthier environment for the young to grow up in. For one cannot in practice wholly isolate what children are tempted to do from what adults in their society do, and are allowed to do.

Now it seems to me that such arguments have some *prima facie* force but one could reject them by pointing out the good effects of toleration. If such good effects are real, then the overall effect of toleration may well be to produce a morally healthy environment in which children grow up. For instance, if there is intolerance they may grow up in a smug, dogmatic, and bigoted atmosphere, which is not good for them. Such considerations show that there is a case for tolerating inferior forms of life, even from the point of view of the coming generation, but they do not show that such forms of life should be given equal status to the ordinary ways of life. To give equal status to all forms of life is to refuse to learn from experience that some forms of life are *prima facie* more suited to human beings, including children. In chapter

11, section 4 we saw that Mill is also committed to some such view.

Against tolerating inferior forms of life even in private, it is sometimes argued that if a majority feels disgust at a practice then it has a right to ban its practice even in private. But it seems to me that on a right-based approach the majority is not entitled to tyrannize the minority in this way. The interests of people who practise degrading forms of life must on a right-based egalitarian approach carry equal weight to the interests of people who lead more conventional lives. If we use the test that an individual's right to his well-being can only be trumped by a competing right of at least comparable strength that another individual has, then it can be seen that we should not punish people for practising their forms of life in private merely because of the feelings of disgust that many conventional people feel at the thought of such practices taking place in private. To be deprived of being able to indulge in one's form of life even in private poses too severe a psychological hardship on such people, whereas the disgust that many conventional men feel at the thought that degrading forms of of life are taking place in private does not or need not upset their well-being and it must not be allowed to trump the right of the minority to choose their form of life in private, any more than the hurt feelings that rejected suitors have provides a ground for trumping a woman's right to choose her sexual partner.

Of course, there may be unusual cases where a person may have a neurotic and excessive reaction to the thought of people being allowed to practise degrading forms of life in private. Now such abnormal people should try to get cured rather than impose their way of life on others. However, in order to show why such reactions are abnormal we may need to appeal to perfectionist considerations and argue that it is better for a person not to be bigoted and intolerant of what other people do in private. Another way of tackling the problem would be to appeal to the idea that external preferences of people must not be allowed to trump an individual's rights— though this would still leave us with the problem of what rights an individual has, which cannot be solved without appealing to perfectionist considerations.

We can now appreciate the difference between the view that some forms of life are superior to other forms of life (and that political principles should take this into account) and the view that some human beings are intrinsically superior to others (and that political principles should take this into account). The latter view, but not the former, is incompatible with egalitarianism, and would lead to intolerance and sacrifice of the interests of the inferior for the sake of the superior.

My view that some forms of life should get lower status than others is not quite as outrageous and eccentric as it may appear at first. It harmonizes with what happens in liberal democracies. For instance, even when there is equality between all religions, the equality does not automatically extend to all groups that claim to be religious. Thus, in the United States there are groups that go in for drugs such as LSD as a means of attaining spiritual salvation, yet such groups are not automatically given all the legal privileges and rights that are extended to all recognized religious groups. Again, there are forms of life, such as bestiality, nudism, eating one's own excrement, and so forth, which get only an inferior status in our society compared to the conventional forms of life.

It is quite plausible to assert that some of the unconventional forms of life that are given inferior status in our society should have equal status with the conventional forms of life. But in the case of any particular form of life that has an inferior status the case for upgrading it is not an automatic one but has to be made by appealing to perfectionist considerations. For instance, whether homosexuality ought to be given equal status to heterosexuality would depend (at least partly) upon whether homosexuality is as fulfilling and worthwhile as heterosexuality. One must not bypass such perfectionist considerations and simply argue that all forms of life (that are not obviously anti-social) should get equal status.

Bibliography

BARRY, B. *Political Argument*. London, 1965.
— *The Liberal Theory of Justice*. Oxford, 1973.
— 'Justice Between Generations', *Law, Morality and Society*, ed. P. Hacker and J. Raz. Oxford, 1977, pp. 268–84.
BENN, S. 'Egalitarianism and Equal Consideration of Interests', *Equality: Nomos*, ix, ed. J. R. Chapman and J. R. Pennock. New York, 1967, pp. 61–78.
— 'Abortion, Infanticide, and Respect for Persons', *The Problem of Abortion*, ed. J. Feinberg. Belmont, 1973, pp. 92–104.
BENTHAM, J. *The Principles of Morals and Legislation*. London, 1789.
BRODY, B. *Abortion and the Sanctity of Human Life*. Boston, 1975.
CALLAHAN, D. *Abortion: Law, Choice, and Morality*. New York, 1970.
COLLINS, L. and Lapierre, D. *Freedom at Midnight*. Glasgow, 1975.
CRANSTON, M. *Human Rights Today*. London, 1962.
DEVLIN, P. *The Enforcement of Morals*. London, 1965.
DWORKIN, G. 'Paternalism', *Morality and the Law*, ed. R. Wasserstrom. Belmont, 1971, pp. 107–26.
— 'Non-Neutral Principles', *Reading Rawls*, ed. N. Daniels. Oxford, 1975, pp. 124–40.
DWORKIN, R. *Taking Rights Seriously*. London, 1977.
FEINBERG, J. *Doing and Deserving*. Princeton, 1970.
— 'Legal Paternalism', *Canadian Journal of Philosophy* (1971), pp. 105–24.
— *Social Philosophy*. Englewood Cliffs, 1973.
— Introduction to *The Problem of Abortion*, ed. J. Feinberg. Belmont, 1973, pp. 1–9.
— 'The Rights of Animals and Future Generations', *Philosophy and Environmental Crisis*, ed. W. Blackstone. Georgia, 1974, pp.43–68.
FOOT, P. 'Abortion', *Morals and Medicine*. London, 1970, pp. 29–47.
GERT, B. *The Moral Rules*. New York, 1966.
GEWIRTH, A. 'The Justification of Egalitarian Justice,' *American Philosophical Quarterly*, viii (1971), s331–41.
GLOVER, J. *Responsibility*. London, 1970
— *Causing Deaths and Saving Lives*. London, 1977.
HAKSAR, V. 'Autonomy, Justice and Contractarianism', *BritishJournal of Political Science*, iii (1973), 487–509.
— 'Coercive Proposals', *Political Theory*, iv (1976), 65–79.

— 'Rawls and Gandhi on Civil Disobedience', *Inquiry*, xix (1976), 151-92.

— 'The Alleged Paradox of Democracy', *Analysis*, xxxvi (1976), 10-14.

— 'The Nature of Rights', *Archiv für Rechts- und Sozialphilosophie*, lxiv (1978), 183-204.

HAMPSHIRE, S. *Morality and Pessimism.* Cambridge, 1972.

HARE, R. *Freedom and Reason.* Oxford, 1963.

— 'Abortion and the Golden Rule', *Philosophy and Public Affairs*, iv (1975), 201-22.

HART, H. L. A. 'Are there any Natural Rights?', *Philosophical Review* lxiv (1965), 175-91.

— *Law, Liberty and Morality.* London, 1963.

— *Punishment and Responsibility.* Oxford, 1968.

— 'Bentham on Legal Rights', *Oxford Essays in Jurisprudence*, ed. A. Simpson. Oxford, 1973, pp. 171-201.

— 'Rawls on Liberty and its Priority', *Reading Rawls*, ed. N. Daniels. Oxford, 1975, pp. 230-52.

HAYEK, F. A. *Constitution of Liberty.* Chicago, 1960.

HEGEL, G. *Philosophy of Right*, translated by T. H. Knox. Oxford, 1967.

HUME, D. *Treatise of Human Nature*, ed. L. A. Selby-Bigge. Oxford, 1888.

— *Enquiry concerning the Principles of Morals*, reprinted in *Hume's Enquiries*, ed. L. A. Selby-Bigge. Oxford, 1902, pp. 169-323.

HYMAN, J. and NEWHOUSE, W. J. 'Standards for Preferred Freedoms: Beyond the First', *Northwestern University Law Review* lx (1965), 1-93.

JAMES, WILLIAM. *Talks to Teachers on Psychology and to Students on Some of Life's Ideals.* New York, 1899.

KANT, I. *The Philosophy of Law*, stranslated by W. Hastie. Edinburgh, 1887.

LOCKE, J. *Second Treatise of Civil Government*, ed J. Gough, Oxford, 1948.

LUCAS, J. 'Against Equality', *Philosophy*, xl (1965), 296-305.

MACKIE, J. *Ethics.* London, 1977.

MARCUSE, H. *Eros and Civilization.* London, 1969.

MILL, J. S. *Principles of Political Economy.* London, 1848.

— *On Liberty.* London, 1859.

— *Utilitarianism.* London, 1863.

MOORE, G. E. *Principia Ethica.* Cambridge, 1903.

MURPHY, J. *Kant: The Philosophy of Right.* London, 1970.

— 'Moral Death: A Kantian Essay on Psychopaths', *Ethics*, lxxxii (1972), 284-98.

NARVESON, Jan. *Morality and Utility.* Baltimore, 1967.

NOZICK, R. *Anarchy, State, and Utopia.* Oxford, 1974.

PARFIT, D. 'On the "Importance of Self-Identity"', *Journal of Philosophy*, xxi (1971), 683-90.

— 'Later Selves and Moral Principles', *Philosophy and Personal Relations*, ed. A. Montefiore. London, 1973, pp. 137-69.

PARFIT, D. (cont.).

— 'Personal Identity', *Philosophy of Mind,* ed. J. Glover. Oxford, 1976, pp. 142–62.

PLUHAR, W. 'Abortion and Simple Consciousness', *Journal of Philosophy,* lxxiv (1977), 159–72.

RAMSAY, P. 'Points in Deciding about Abortion', *The Morality of Abortion,* ed. J. Noonan. Boston, 1970, pp. 60–100.

RASHDALL, Hastings. *The Theory of Good and Evil,* vol. i. London, 1907.

RAWLS, J. 'The Sense of Justice', *Moral Concepts,* ed. J. Feinberg. Oxford, 1969, pp. 120–40.

— *A Theory of Justice.* Oxford, 1971.

— 'Fairness to Goodness', *Philosophical Review,* lxxxiv (1975), 536–54.

ROSS, D. *Foundations of Ethics.* Oxford, 1939.

ROUSSEAU, J. J. *The Social Contract and Discourses,* translated by G. D. H. Cole, revised by J. Brumfitt and J. Hall. London, 1973.

SCANLON, T. 'Rawls' Theory of Justice', *Reading Rawls,* ed. N. Daniels. Oxford, 1975, pp. 169–205.

SIDGWICK, H. *Methods of Ethics.* London, 1874.

SKINNER, B. F. *Beyond Freedom and Dignity.* London, 1972.

SMART, J. J. C. 'An Outline of a System of Utilitarian Ethics', *Utilitarianism For and Against,* by J. J. C. Smart and B. Williams. Cambridge, 1973, pp. 3–74.   s

SMART, R. N. 'Negative Utilitarianism', *Mind,* lxvii (1958), 542–3.

TOOLEY, M. 'A Defense of Abortion and Infanticide', *The Problem of Abortion,* ed. J. Feinberg. Belmont, 1973, pp. 51–9.

VLASTOS, G. 'Justice and Equality', *Social Justice,* ed. R. Brandt. Englewood Cliffs, 1962.

YOUNG, M. *The Rise of the Meritocracy.* London, 1958.

WARNOCK, G. *Object of Morality.* London, 1971.

WIGGINS, D. *Identity and Spatio-Temporal Continuity.* Oxford, 1967.

WILLIAMS, B. 'A Critique of Utilitarianism', *Utilitarianism For and Against,* by J. J. C. Smart and B. Williams. Cambridge, 1973, pp. 77–150.

— 'Persons, Character and Morality', *Identities of Persons,* ed. A. Rorty. London, 1976, pp. 197–216.

Index

abortion, 47, 90, 92, 156-7, 218, *see also* foetus

animals, 1-6, 18-80 *passim,* 100-112 *passim,* 124, 141, 144-7, 150-5 *passim,* 197, 218-19, 221, 226, 231, 267

Aristotelian principle, 6, 11, 128, 193-205, 232

babies, *see* children

Barry, B., 149, 166-7, 200, 220, 263-4

Benn, S., 29, 62, 71, 103-5, 107-8

Bentham, J., 32, 52, 54, 66, 79, 103, 135

Brahmin, 12-13, 149, 245

Brave New World, 3-4, 11, 115, 168, 172-184, 188, 194-5, 198-9

Brody, B., 87-8

Buddhist theory of personal identity, 10

Burke, E., 214

Callahan, D., 87

children (babies, infants), 10, 12-13, 17-18, 26-62 *passim,* 66, 71, 76-134 *passim,* 144-5, 150, 152, 162, 173, 175-6, 178, 184-192, 217-224 *passim,* 233-6, 256, 268, 278-9, 283, 285, 287, 290, 292, 295

choice criterion of value, 3, 11, 193-235

Collins L. and Lapierre D., 200

complex view, *see* simple versus complex view

contingent rights, 36, 61, 85, 101, 105, 131, 137

Cranston, M., 270

Devlin, P., 217

difference principle, 165, 275, 288

Dworkin, G., 244, 252

Dworkin, R., 7-8, 10-11, 17, 53, 161, 258-69, 282, 284, 290

dynamic versus static view, 9, 13, 95-129 *passim*

education, 17, 97, 176, 188-92, 218-24 *passim,* 233-4

family argument, 8-10, 36, 38-45, 50, 70-9, 106, 120-1, 123-4, 150-6, 272

Feinberg, J., 36, 60-2, 81, 85, 96, 100-5 *passim,* 108, 115, 117, 139, 217, 273

foetus, 10, 12-13, 27-8, 61-2, 81, 85-109 *passim,* 126, 156-7, 287 *see also* abortion

Foot, P., 91-3

fraternity, 8-9 *see also* family argument

future generations, 10, 31, 34-7, 120, 124, 130-48, 287

Gert, B., 287

Gewirth, A., 67

Glover, J., 131-9, 142-4, 209

Haksar, V., 26, 29, 58, 199, 203, 261, 286, 291

Hampshire, S., !21-3

Hare, R., 86, 263

Hart, H., 54-5, 62, 103-5, 113, 115, 130, 195, 214-7, 282

Hayek, F., 279

Hegel, G., 22, 59-60, 97-8, 101-3, 278

Hitler, A., 40, 182

Hobbes, T., 31

Hume, D., 10, 26, 46-7, 49, 51, 202

Hyman, J. and Newhouse, W. J., 262

idiots, 1, 10, 18, 23, 33, 38-9, 46, 54, 66-7, 71-9, 109, 128

infants, *see* children

James, William, 18, 67-8, 70, 84, 124

Kant, I., 2, 6, 22-3, 32, 53, 55, 60, 155, 167, 169, 179

Karma, law of, 140-1